essential guide

TO DANCE

Second Edition

Linda Ashley

ACKNOWLEDGEMENTS

To all my friends and loved ones who have tolerated my irritations/absences, supported me, cooked for me and put up with my endless delegation of duties, I would like to say a deep-felt thank you. This book is for you, and for my parents who have had a lifetime of the above-mentioned.

Copyright holders of photographs reproduced in this book:

Catherine Ashmore 112, 114; The British Museum 94, 109; Anthony Crickmay 72, 177, 244, 246; Photographs by Anthony Crickmay and Houston Rogers, Theatre Museum, Victoria and Albert Museum 41, 214, 88; Zoe Dominic 96; James Klosty pp104; Hugo Glendinning 239; Royal Opera House 175a; Chris Nash 67, 90, 175b, 63, 10, 98, 23, 165, 6, 45, 233, Gabrielle Crawford 199; Bill Cooper 75

To all dance students, young dancers and older dancers whom I have worked with, many thanks to you also for your inspiration:

Come and trip it as you go
On the light fantastic toe

(*John Milton*, Pastoral Ode)

Orders: please contact Bookpoint Ltd, 130 Milton Park, Abingdon, Oxon OX14 4SB. Telephone: (44) 01235 827720, Fax: (44) 01235 400454. Lines are open from 9.00-6.00, Monday to Saturday, with a 24 hour message answering service. Email address: orders@bookpoint.co.uk

British Library Cataloguing in Publication Data
A catalogue record for this title is available from The British Library

ISBN 0 340 803207

First edition published 1996; reprinted 2004

Typeset by Fakenham Photosetting Ltd
Printed in Great Britain for Hodder & Stoughton Educational, a division of Hodder Headline, 338 Euston Road, London NW1 3BH by Martins The Printers, Berwick Upon Tweed

CONTENTS

FOREWORD

I have been involved in the teaching of dance in education for many years and have spent hours trying to unravel the mysteries of the various syllabi. It was with enormous relief, and much excitement, that I received a copy of the first edition of *The Essential Guide to Dance*. Finally, I had not only a text book for my students, but also a user-friendly manual for myself which has proved invaluable throughout my teaching career. At last we had a guide which demystified the syllabus rubric!

Over the years I have found the first edition incredibly useful as a resource for students studying A and AS level Dance, and BTEC and GNVQ in Performing Arts. This new updated and improved version is particularly current and relevant to the present day. It relates clearly to Key Skills and is a vital resource for all teachers involved in the delivery of dance in education.

Used alongside practical studio work this book is particularly useful for students as they grapple with terminology and as they discover the potentially problematic process of making and rehearsing dance. In class or studying individually, students can access the required information quickly and easily. They will also enjoy this text because it has been specially written for them in language which is easy to understand.

This book is packed with information and ideas, alongside which we find illustrations and selected quotations to back up everyday practical work. The student is led through a well-planned, most comprehensive manual which includes aspects of dance training, performance, choreography, dance appreciation and notation. The numerous practical tasks inspire and provide areas of exploration for all students, making the theory come alive off the page.

In my current role as Dancer and Education Officer for the Newbury Contemporary Dance Company, I would have no hesitation in recommending this second edition to all dance students and their teachers. It is full of information and inspiration for all.

Ros Pryor
(Education and Outreach Officer, Newbury Contemporary Dance Company)

INTRODUCTION

Essential Guide to Dance is for A2, AS Level, AVCE and GNVQ Dance and Performing Arts students. This book is a practical working text *for students*. It is intended to be used as a text to be read with guidance during practical daily classes. As part of daily learning, it integrates practice with theory.

Facts, practical tasks, context and appreciation are all woven together. The sections emphasise *applied* knowledge, so rather than following the linear logic of, say, anatomy, specific parts of the body appear within a training context – for example, when addressing the issue of flexibility, the hip joint in particular is examined because the mobility of this joint is of great importance to dancers.

The book is not intended to be read from cover to cover – although of course individuals may choose to do so. It would be more effective for teachers to guide the reading of it as part of a structured course. Some of the text may, for example, be used as homework or for distance learning. And it most certainly would also be well used to animate daily practical classes.

Much of the slog of teaching specification work involves making the different layers of knowledge explicit for the learner. This I have tried to do, and wherever possible I have used language which is not only user-friendly but also 'specification-friendly'.

In this second edition I have addressed in greater detail the problems students encounter during the process of making dances. Some tasks are now signposted with Key Skills to help students and teachers integrate them with their dance studies. Similarly there are some new tasks which are designed to offer students, and their teachers, easier strategies to track and monitor progress in a variety of areas.

It has been suggested to me that the book may be of interest to theatregoers who may sometimes feel baffled when they see dance performance. Knowing more about how dances are made may enhance their viewing experiences. To fulfil this aim I am grateful to Michael for suggesting the alternative title of *The Essential Guide to Dance for Couch-Potatoes*.

Icons

Throughout this book, the set tasks are given suggested timings. The icons used to indicate these timings are as follows:

10 to 20 minutes: 

20 to 30 minutes: 

45 minutes to 1 hour: 

Several hours:   

Key skills: 

ONE

THE DANCER IN TRAINING

In your study of dance training, you may be presented with names of bones, joints, muscles and so on. These and the basic physiology of *how* the body works are important, but it is an *applied* working knowledge which is most useful and meaningful to you. For a dancer or a choreographer, an active awareness of safe practice can serve to explain both how to execute a certain movement and why a particular phrase is giving difficulty. It is with this in mind that this chapter is written. Individual parts of the body are dealt with in the context of how they may arise in class or in performance. Similarly, unsafe practice and the potential for, and how to deal with, injury are also examined.

> Don't say, 'Oh well, we did that, and I kicked my leg five inches higher than she did.' Who cares? Did you understand the movement? That is what matters.
>
> (*Hanya Holm in* The Vision of Modern Dance, *1980*)

The body of a dancer is like the piano of a musician: it is a *working tool*, and so must be finely tuned. This needs an intelligent, aware, sensitive and disciplined approach to dance training. Dance training pursues the improvement of capabilities which the body already has naturally. As with an athlete, these capabilities need to be developed in order for their potential to be maximised. Safety and efficiency of movement need to be ensured so that injury is more likely to be avoided.

Dance training pursues the improvement of the following main areas of basic body fitness:

- alignment
- flexibility
- strength and stamina
- co-ordination
- general body maintenance.

Different technique classes vary in how much emphasis is placed on these areas. Often, because of the stop-go nature of these classes, there is not enough time for effective all-round conditioning of the body. This is a problem because these basic areas of fitness are all vital in ensuring safe practice and injury prevention.

Let us now consider each of these five main areas in turn.

Alignment

> Discipline is, or should be, a voluntary course of regulated and regular actions where effort brings about the desired results. Too often it becomes something else. I am not interested in how high a person can extend his leg or how high he jumps into the air, but rather what he looks like while he is doing these things.
>
> (*Judith Dunn in* Dance from Magic to Art, *1976*)

During movement, the body should remain aligned, whether in a fall or jump or turn. In the well-aligned body, there is a feeling of freedom, easy movement, effortless carriage of the head and awareness of all parts of the body. It is a more expressive body that 'looks good' whatever it is doing, at any given moment.

Good alignment is not static, it is a dynamic position of readiness to move. There is an ever-present 'plumb line' (the straight line from the head to toes) which should be maintained during movement. Without this, movement will be inefficient and possibly unsafe, as energy is wasted pulling certain segments of the body into line. This line runs through the ear lobe, through the centre of the shoulder and hip, in front of the ankle and down through the foot (see Figure 1.1). The shoulders, hips and knees should be level. Rolling in on the arches of the feet or out to the border should be avoided. Generally, a triangular distribution of weight on each foot is best (see Figure 1.2): the weight is spread evenly here between points 1, 2 and 3, under the 1st and 5th metatarsals and under the heel bone (calcaneus).

Of course this plumb line is imaginary. Similarly your centre of gravity is an imagined point lying slightly below your navel (around the middle of the sacral vertebrae). It will vary depending on the shape and weight distribution of the dancer. A dancer with a deeper plié can lower the centre of gravity when moving and have a greater range of control. We hear this from a dancer when she is doing class:

> ... doing Jeremy's (Nelson) combinations ... is challenging ... but exciting. We're doing a lot of work connecting from the tail bone to the floor – the sit bones to the heels and trying to find ways to lower our centre of gravity. I must say that it looks amazingly clear and easy when Jeremy does it, but they are his moves and his centre of gravity is already lower than most of ours!
>
> (*Dancer Catherine Quinn in* Dancer's Work log, *1999*)

Good posture is vital for control, safety and expression: poor posture or alignment of one part ricochets throughout the rest of the body. For effective movement, each segment of the body must therefore be in proper relationship to its adjacent sections. The anti-gravity postural muscles (see Figure 1.5) are responsible for maintaining upright posture, so that the weight-bearing points on the skeleton will be balanced and the muscles will be able to release energy for action safely and economically. Alignment thus relies on there being *reciprocal relationships* between all body parts. This means that different segments of the body give and take (are extended and contracted in muscles) in equal measure in order to maintain skeletal balance.

Figure 1.1 *To show points that the line of gravity will pass through in correct alignment*

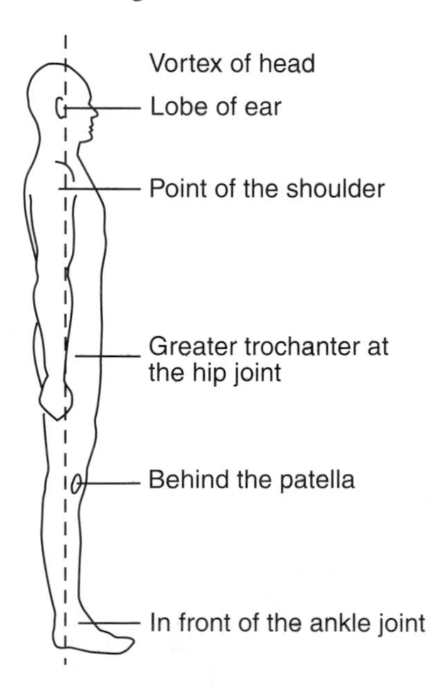

Figure 1.2 *Correct distribution of weight on the sole of the foot*

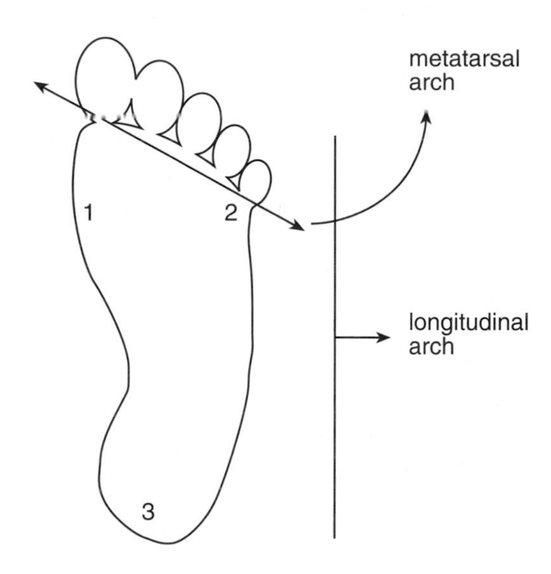

At this point, it would be helpful to examine three specific areas of the body which are crucial for good alignment:

- the skeleton
- the spine
- the foot.

THE SKELETON

The main functions of the skeleton are:

- support;
- protection of organs, e.g. brain, heart, lungs, spinal cord;
- to allow accurate movement when muscles contract by giving rigidity;
- some bones contain red marrow which is a part of the blood-forming tissue.

Bones make up the skeleton, and the size of these depends on their function. Bones bearing larger body weights are bigger and denser, whereas those bearing lesser body weights are smaller and lighter. For example:

- The *femur* of the thigh supports more weight than the *humerus* of the upper arm, and so it is larger and heavier.
- The *vertebrae* of the spine are larger near the bottom to support the increased mass from above.

In addition, the *shape* of a bone similarly depends on its function. For example:

- The *vertebrae* are like rounded building blocks stacked to form the spinal column which surrounds and protects the spinal cord.
- The *ribs* are slender and curved to protect the lungs and heart.
- Bones like those in the lower arm – i.e. the *radius* and *ulna* – are long and slender to allow the system of levers to operate efficiently.

Table 1.1 *Injuries to bones*

Injury	Symptoms/causes	Treatment
Stress fracture (including 'shin splints')	Localised cracks in bones due to repeated stress on one area of bone. Causes: Use of unsuitable (unsprung) floors. Poor alignment in any of following: *fibula* – sickle foot/inversion; *tibia bow* – weight back; *lumbar vertebrae* – weak abdominal muscles	Rest. Remedial correction of weaknesses, including specific exercise for weak musculature. Heat. Stretch front of lower leg for shin splints (see Task 1).
Fractures	Uncommon as a dance injury. Most common is of 5th metatarsal and of ankle, when twisted – i.e. if inverted and rotated in the fall.	Plaster cast. Immobilise for 6 weeks or many months. May be treated with strapping if a minor fracture. Dancer may not dance, but should exercise areas not in plaster to stay strong/mobile. Once out of cast: ice and ultrasound, plus exercise of inactive muscle.

The skeleton is divided into two parts:

1 the axial (head, chest, pelvis): the *skull*, *vertebrae*, *clavicle*, *scapula*, *sternum*, *ribs*, *ischium*, *ilium*;

2 the *appendicular* (legs and arms): the *humerus*, *radius*, *ulna*, *carpal bones*, *metacarpals*, *tarsals*, *metatarsals*, *phalanges*, *femur*, *tibia*, *fibula*.

THE SPINE

> The spine is a long limb . . . Allow the rest of the body to balance around the curving river of the spine.
>
> (*Miranda Tufnell in* Body Space Image, *1990*)

In the well-aligned dancer, the healthy spine is the power centre for moving. The way you sit, lie, stand, travel or fall is affected by the spine. Its elasticity absorbs the shock waves.

The main functions of the spine are to:

- protect the spinal nerve chord;
- support the head, ribs and hips;
- maintain upright posture;
- absorb shock of movement.

The spine has four curves (see Figure 1.3) which correspond to the four groups of vertebrae:

1 the *cervical curve*: seven *cervical* vertebrae (neck);

2 the *thoracic curve*: 12 *thoracic* vertebrae (chest/rib area);

3 the *lumbar curve*: five *lumbar* vertebrae (lower back);

4 the *sacral curve*: *sacrum and coccyx* (fused at bottom).

Figure 1.3 *The curves of the spine*

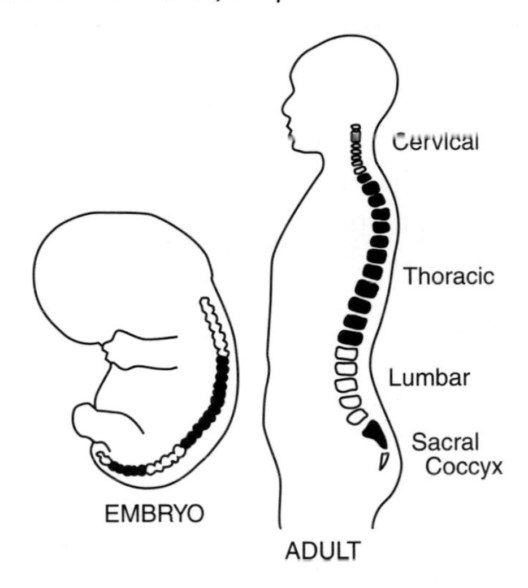

These curves help to take some of the stress involved in weight-bearing, as do the cartilage discs in between the vertebrae which act as shock absorbers. The spongy discs are essential, for example, when landing from jumps and in allowing the spine to flex, extend and rotate.

Postural problems/injuries of the spine

Generally speaking, if a particular form of dance training encourages bad habits and unsafe practice – for example, if movements are attempted that are beyond a dancer's ability – alignment and muscular balance will break down. Serious postural problems or

Table 1.2 *Postural problems of the spine*

Problem	Symptom(s)	Causes	Treatment
Scoliosis – lateral deviation of the spine	From the back, appears as 'S' or 'C' curve.	Numerous misalignments.	If diagnosed from childhood, dance training can help ease the condition by emphasis on symmetry of movement.
Lumbar lordosis – swayback	From side view, the normal *lumbar curve* is exaggerated.	Weak abdominal muscle/tight lumbar spine and hamstrings.	Stretch lower back, hamstrings and hip flexors/ strengthen abdominals.
Flat back	Flat lower back (opposite of lordosis), posterior tilt of pelvis/ elongated thoracic.	Weak lower back muscles/tight hamstrings.	Strengthen lower back and hip flexors/stretch hamstrings.
Kyphosis – round back	Abdominal round upper back (thoracic curve) as seen from side.	Tight chest muscles and weak upper back.	Stretch chest muscles of upper trunk and strengthen upper back.

injury, or both, may then result. There are also various *anatomical* defects – e.g. curvature of the spine – which require medical diagnosis and cannot be changed by exercise. In training, dancers with these defects need expert advice on how to accommodate the problem whilst maintaining correct posture. Some postural problems are listed in Table 1.2.

The neck (the *cervical curve*) is also vulnerable to strain because it is so mobile, and because it bears the weight of the head. The neck muscles must therefore be in good condition. In the event that the neck *extensor* muscles are weak and the *flexors* are too tight, the dancer's chin may jut up and the ear will be in front of the plumb line. This is known as *cervical lordosis/forward head.*

- Extensor muscles are those which stretch the body.
- Flexor muscles are those which curl or bend the body.

Many surveys report that the lower back is the most common site of injury for dancers.

The *sacroiliac joint* (where the lumbar curve meets the sacrum) is vulnerable. This is the point where the mobile spine meets the immobile *pelvis.* If the lower abdominal muscles are weak and combined with tight lower back muscles, then there will be weakness in this joint.

A general word abut injury would be helpful here. The '*Fit to Dance?*' (1996) survey found a link between poor fitness and number of injuries to dancers. It also gave examples of dance companies like V-Tol who planned swimming and fitness training into the dancers' contracts.

The use of the spine in different dance genres

There are interesting contrasting uses of the spine in the various genres of dance. The classical ballet genre has maintained the vertical spine as one of its characteristics from the fifteenth century. This relates back to its noble beginnings when correct deportment, how to walk, sit, stand and bow were taught and denoted status and power. The nobility would perform dances in this manner, and later this tradition was taken on by professionals to become ballet as we know it today. The style of the vertical torso gives ballet its distinctive ethereal lightness, and facilitates the execution of characteristic multiple pirouettes and soaring jumps with greater ease.

The characteristic deep back bends and high arabesques require strong abdominal muscles to resist gravity, making a stable platform for the thoracic spine to arch away from. A safety tip is to stretch the lumbar spine upwards before bending. The épaulement of the shoulders starts in the thoracic vertebrae. This is where the 'wind-up' preparation for pirouettes begins.

Even this defiance of natural forces was not enough, however, for the pioneers of *modern dance*, and at the start of the twentieth century individuals like Isadora Duncan emerged in rebellion. For her, the *solar plexus* was the creator of all movement, and the name of the game was freedom. Along with this went a mobile, *tilting, twisting, curving* spine. This allowed a wider range of expressivity for the choreographer, and dance has never looked the same since. The spiral twists of the torso typical of many modern styles start in the thoracic vertebrae. The so-called '*contraction*' of the Martha Graham Technique is in fact an extension of the spine not a bend. The corset of abdominal muscles contract as the *erector spinae* extends downward resulting in the characteristic curving torso.

THE FOOT

Another crucial part of the body for dancers' correct alignment is the foot. Isadora Duncan, with her defiant rebellious bare-footed look, named dance 'the religion of the foot'. It is surprising, really, that such a small device is yet strong enough to support the whole of the rest of the body.

There are 26 bones and many small *intrinsic muscles* in the foot which are layered. These intrinsic muscles are vital because they allow the foot to point strongly with straight toes. Weak intrinsics will cause the toes to claw, because the flexor muscles will be over-powerful.

Good practice in dance training aims to increase strength and suppleness of feet. In ballet, exercises such as *battement tendu, dégagé, frappé* and *rélevé* strengthen the intrinsic muscles of the feet.

The other muscles which move the foot start below the knee and connect to the bones of the foot. The movements produced by these muscles are:

- plantar flexion – pointing downward, ankle extends
- dorsiflexion – top of the foot points upward, ankle flexes
- inversion – inner border of foot lifts
- eversion – outer border of foot lifts
- adduction – turns foot inward
- abduction – turns foot outward
- supination – combines adduction and inversion (sickle)
- pronation – combines abduction and eversion (looks like a flat, duck-footed walk).

The foot is divided into three sections – *tarsus, metatarsus* and *phalanges* (toes). We notice these sections as we walk, run or jump. When doing exercises like foot pushes and prances the 'going through the foot' is felt particularly clearly as springy and strong. Strong, flexible feet are one of a dancer's most valuable assets. These two relatively small body parts are true 'feats' of engineering!

Figure 1.4 *The bones of the foot*

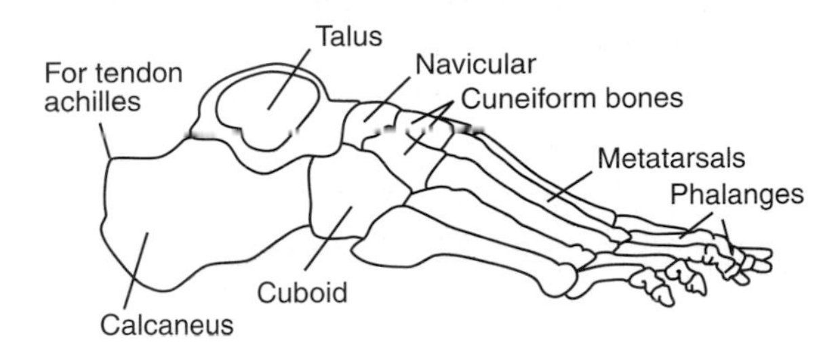

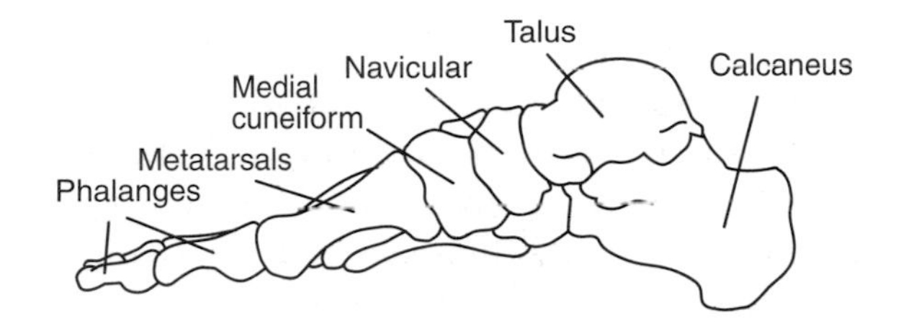

The tarsus section of the foot is made up of seven bones; *talus* (ankle), *calcaneus* (heel bone), *cuboid, navicular* and three small *cuneiform* bones, (see Figure 1.4). In correct alignment the lower leg (*tibia/ fibula*) rests on the *tarsus* on the same medial line as the ball of the foot (*metatarsus*). This means that when you plié the knee should align over an imaginary line extending out from the middle toes. Look down as you plié in turn out and you should be able to see your big toe and the one next to it. This is crucial for safe landing from jumps. The *metatarsus* consists of five long metatarsals and leads to the toes (*phalanges*) (see Figure 1.4).

The foot has several arches for normal function (support and stepping) and protection:

- the inside *medial arch*: from heel to heads of metatarsals;
- the outside *lateral arch*: from heel to head of the 5th metatarsal;

- the *transverse* arch runs across the foot and at its most forward becomes the *metatarsal arch*: dome-shaped, and running across the front heads of the metatarsal bones.

The metatarsal arch is supported by ligaments and lumbrical muscles. The two most important ligaments of the foot are:

- the spring ligament (between *calcaneus* and *navicular*).
- the plantar ligament (between *calcaneus* to *cuboid* and the three middle *metatarsals*).

The arches give the foot its strength and flexibility and allow it to withstand the shocks involved during weight transference (stepping and jumping). If arches collapse serious misalignments occur not only in the foot but also in the rest of the body. If the body weight is placed on the outside of the foot ('sickling' or inversion) it not only looks bad but can lead to sprained ankles from incorrect landings by damage to the lateral ligament.

A collapsed medial arch leaves a pronated foot and the foot rolls in on the inner border (eversion). When this happens you can see the *navicular* is misaligned nearer to the floor. Check your feet when standing to find the position of the *navicular*. It is the little knobbly bone sticking out on the inside of the foot just under and forward of the ankle.

Postural problems/injuries of the foot

- *Stress fracture of metatarsals*: 'March Fracture' appears as a pain under the foot when pushing through the foot in jumps, on a rise or when stepping. Soldiers marching on hard surfaces are prone, hence the name. *Causes*: Poorly aligned body weight/barefoot work where extra pressure has been put on the metatarsal

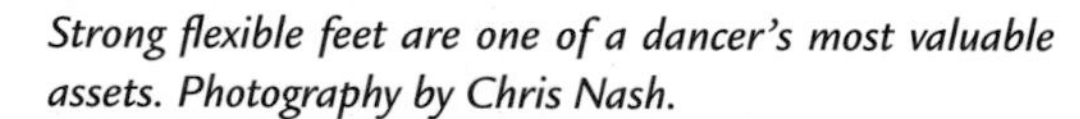

Strong flexible feet are one of a dancer's most valuable assets. Photography by Chris Nash.

arch/increase in work. *Treatment*: rest recovery over approximately 6–8 weeks; physiotherapy which encourages the intrinsic muscles of the foot to support properly.

- *Morton's Foot. Appearance*: abnormally short and hypermobile first metatarsal which can destabilise the foot and cause pain in the metatarsal area. *Treatment*: a foot pad to correct faulty weight placement.
- *Hallux Valgus and Tailor's Bunion. Appearance*: an enlargement on metatarsophalangeal joint of either the 1st or 5th toe. Inflammation appears on the bursa where extra mineral deposits accumulate. Pain occurs when the ankle is rolling inwards. The big toe distorts away from the midline and the little toe towards the midline. *Causes*: Hallux Valgus from foot pronation combined with walking with outwardly rotated hips. Tailor's Bunion foot supination combined with inwardly rotated hips. Incorrect weight placement results. *Treatment*: by chiropodist placing a pad. Physiotherapy may use ice/ultrasound/corrective exercise. Check weight distribution on feet. Avoid tight shoes and barefoot work.
- *Hammer toes. Appearance*: crooked toes, big toe points upward and phalanges 2 and 3 are flexed downward, and the ends are often callused. This can lead to corns. *Causes*: too narrow or short shoes. *Treatment*: keep toes in extended position in jumping and travelling. If pain becomes too great, special footwear/surgery may be necessary.
- *Plantar fascial strain. Appearance*: aching on the sole of the foot. *Causes*: incorrect landing from jumps. *Treatment*: ice/strapping/reduce workload/ultrasound/support pads in shoe. Can be stubborn and recurring.
- *Flat feet (pes planus). Appearance*: lowering of the medial arch. Aching under big toe and along to heel. *Causes*: unsuitable footwear/rolling in on ankles. Often related to poor turn-out and knee problems/bunion. *Treatment*: ultrasound/arch support/corrective exercises for the intrinsic muscles of the foot.
- *Rolling and sickling*: if there is a bow in the tibia bone, a misalignment in the angle of the ankle joint will result. The knee will be out of line with the ankle and foot. Rolling and sickling will occur.

TASK ONE

A corrective exercise for feet to strengthen the *dorsi flexors* and to help the prevention of, or to heal, shin splints of the lower leg:

- Sit on a mat on the floor, legs straight out in front.
- Extend one foot. Place the other foot on top.
- The top foot puts downward pressure on the bottom foot. Flex the bottom foot against the pressure for 10 seconds, then pull back the foot through the whole range of flexion.
- Repeat two or three times.

The sole of the foot also provides the brain with information. It receives sensations from nerves which directly relate to a dancer's knowledge of orientation, alignment and support. For example, when jumping, the feet would tell you that there was no ground support.

It is common for athletes to have analysis of stress loads on the feet by monitoring and filming them on a treadmill. If poor alignment is diagnosed corrective inserts in shoes can help with treatment.

> Dancers should do as many exercises for their feet as for other parts of the body, since it is so important that the feet should be strong enough for the work demanded.
>
> (*Dr. P Brinson and F. Dick in* Fit to Dance?, *1996*)

The use of the foot in different dance genres

In classical ballet the foot is normally *plantar flexed* (pointed), whereas in the modern genre it is often *dorsi flexed* - this is particularly noticeable in the Martha Graham technique. Some post-modern styles prefer a more neutral, relaxed position of the non-weight-bearing foot. Obviously, these all have very different expressive qualities - the light endless line of the ballet in contrast to the harsher, broken and more natural throw-away feel of the post-modern dancer. An even length in the metatarsals and toes will assist support in *demi-pointe* (weight distributed evenly on heads of metatarsals and phalanges) and *full-pointe* (weight on phalanges only) work. The feet on the ground gives a further contrast between the genres - the floating ethereal look of the ballerina on pointe as contrasted with the earthy gravity-bound flat look of the modern dancer. Needless to say, the rigours of pointe work may cause alignment problems. Shoes must fit correctly, with, if necessary, high *vamps* (support pads) to protect high arches (*pes cavus*). Pointe work should never begin until over the age of 12 when the bones have ossified sufficiently to cope with the weight. Continual pointe work may result in a thickening of the metatarsals, and this is why the feet may seem to widen. When pointe work is stopped completely, however, the feet will return to their original size.

> South Asian dance has long emphasised the importance of the strengthening and caring for the feet, with the result that some of the dancers have the most mobile, expressive and strong feet.
>
> (*Dr P. Brinson and F. Dick in* Fit to Dance?, *1996*)

As well as the spine and feet, other parts and functions of the body are also crucial in maintaining correct alignment:

- the *lateral flexor* muscles of the trunk help to hold the trunk in place, for example during multiple pirouettes.
- *Visual cues*: the eyes send information to the brain on the body's position in space.
- *Semi-circular canals in the inner ear* send information on the body's orientation in space.
- *Receptors in joints, tendons and muscles* provide continual information to the brain on the body's relative position in space.

ALIGNMENT – SUMMARY

It is clear that this fundamental skill of alignment is crucial to the prevention of injury for any dancer. Becoming aware of and correcting poor posture can improve alignment. The stretching and strengthening of appropriate muscle groups is required (see Figure 1.5) when misalignments/injuries are encountered.

Other examples of faulty alignment in training are:

- weight too far back;
- failing to turn out from the hips;
- twisted hips;
- feet overturning/rolling;
- misuse of muscle groups during *plié* (knees flex) and *relevé* (rise on toes either demi-pointe or full pointe).

Many dance programmes nowadays stress the importance of body awareness, as taught in such techniques as Alexander and Pilates, which emphasise a balancing of the body. Regular attendance to good technique classes in the presence of an observant teacher will help to maintain alignment and keep the chance of injury to a minimum.

> Learning to dance is an extremely vulnerable activity ... Dancers must learn to treat themselves with respect.
>
> (*Julia Buckroyd in* Dying Swans, *New Scientist, 25 December 1993/1 January 1994*)

To help you check some of the information in this section, there now follows a further task.

Figure 1.5 *The main muscles controlling alignment*

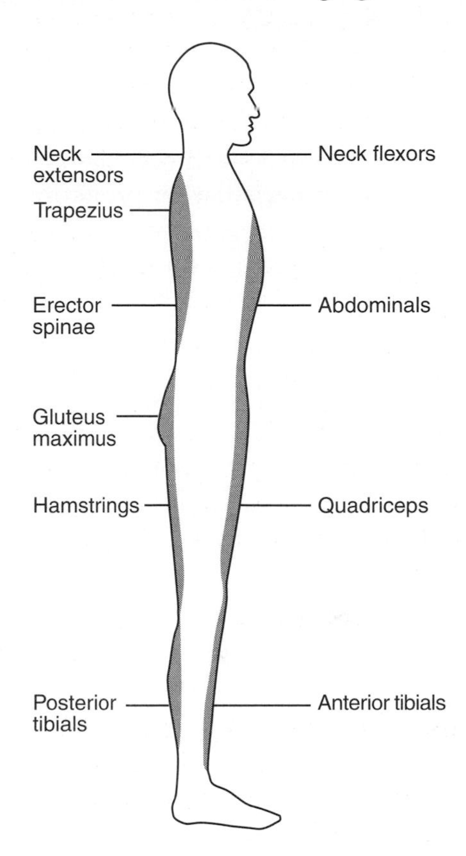

TASK TWO

In pairs, let one read instructions and the other adjust posture. Check list for standing in parallel first position:

- Weight evenly spread over the metatarsal arch. *Check*: long toes; lift inner medial arch, position of navicular for pronation.
- The *tibia* and *fibula* (lower leg) balance on top of the *talus* (ankle).
- The pelvis balances on the *femur* (thigh bone), so that the muscles of the lower back, abdomen and thighs are in equal contraction. *Check*: the thighs lift to support the hips; to check for level hips; place forefingers on the iliac crest. At the back place thumbs on the sacroiliac joint (where the two dimples are); drop the tail bone (*sacrum*)/flatten the abdomen so that the pelvis is in reciprocal relationship with the *lumbar* spine.
- Knees relaxed; soft patella; facing straight ahead.
- Upper back supported by *thoracic vertebrae. Check*: proper amount of anterior-posterior curvature; shoulder girdle rests easily on thorax. Shoulders relaxed/*scapulae* dropped and level.
- Weight of head even on top of cervical spine. *Check*: jaw at right angle to the floor; long neck lifted lightly from ears.
- Chest lifted, and *sternum* above balls of feet. *Do not*: lift shoulders/tighten neck/hold breath/lift chin/tuck seat under.

Now read this to your partner:

- Now hold this position and try to rise easily. (Check your partner does not: shift their weight forward or back when rising; flex at the hip or knee.)
- Move your arms and head easily without loss of balance.
- Use your bones for support – think X-ray!
- Feel control coming from the centre outwards.
- Let your arms connect to the centre of your back.

Flexibility

Increasing flexibility involves increasing muscular elasticity so that the range of mobility from a joint will increase. It does *not* involve stretching the ligaments that provide the joints with stability: the elongation of the ligaments increases the possibility of injury. The limit to flexibility is either the ligaments themselves or bony restriction. Individual structural differences like the shape of the bone will affect the range of motion/flexibility. Tight ligaments will reduce mobility, as will tight musculature.

> **Myth: a dancer can never be too flexible:**
>
> **Natural flexibility is not necessarily a bonus for a dancer. Flexible joints which are not protected by adequate muscle strength are more susceptible to injury.**
>
> **(*Rachel Harris in* Dance Dates, *Birmingham National Dance Agency, 1994*)**

The assumption that all dancers should be able to achieve the same range of motion is thus false. Other factors which will influence flexibility are: gender; age; body temperature; training. When flexibility is increased through warm-up the range of motion in the joints increases. A more flexible body helps to avoid malalignment, muscle tears and injury generally.

The main concerns surrounding flexibility are:

- the joints – particularly the hip, knee and ankle;
- stretching.

THE JOINTS

Where two bones meet, there will be a *joint* which allows movement to occur. There are several types of joint which allow different degrees of mobility – from fully mobile to very restricted. In dance, we clearly need a wider range of movement in the hip/leg joint (the 'break' of the leg) than in, say, the knee which needs greater stability for its protection in actions like landing from a jump.

There are three types of joint:

- cartilaginous
- fibrous
- synovial.

Cartilaginous joints

These allow little movement but give great strength. The joints between the vertebrae where the *intervertebral cartilage* is placed are such joints. The limitation of movement here is crucial in absorbing both the shock from, say, jumps and jarring to the skull and brain. These joints are characterised by the presence of *cartilage* between the bones.

Fibrous joints

These allow little or no movement; for example, the flat bones of the skull.

Synovial joints

These are the most mobile, so in dance these are the ones that are of greatest concern – e.g. the hip joint (ball and socket – see Figure 1.6), fingers, toes, knees and ankles (hinge joints) which all allow a range of free movement.

Of all the joints, the synovial ones are the most complex in structure, having the following structural characteristics:

- a joint cavity, (a space inside the joint).
- *articular cartilage* covers the bone reducing friction and allowing smooth movement.

Figure 1.6 *The hip, showing features of a synovial joint*

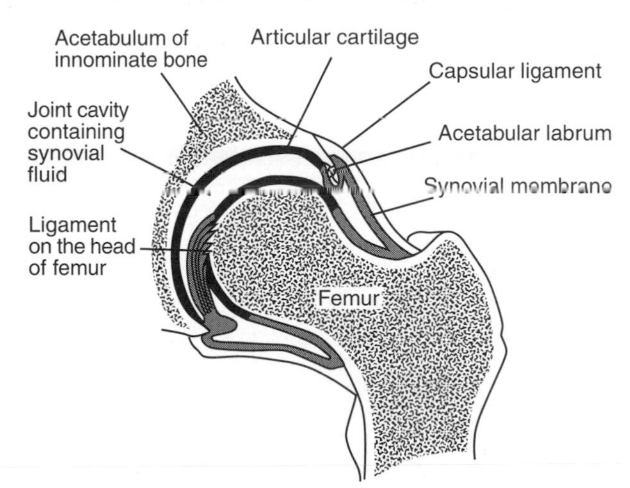

- a *capsule* surrounds the joint holding together the bones and enclosing the cavity. Ligaments also strengthen the joint and protect from strain or dislocation.
- *synovial membrane* lines the joint.
- *synovial fluid* fills the joint cavity and lubricates the joint.

As we can see, these different joints either *allow* or *restrict* movement, according to their structure. The point here is to know which movements are suitable for which joints, and to be able to move *within the body's potential*, thus avoiding injury. It is important to recognise your own limitations. Forcing or twisting a joint in directions for which it is not structured will cause injury. Therefore, it is helpful to know not only the joints' *structures* but also their correct movement range - see Figure 1.7.

Generally, joint movements include a range from the following:

- *flexing:* bending a joint;
- *extending:* straightening a joint;

Figure 1.7 *Movements possible in the joints*

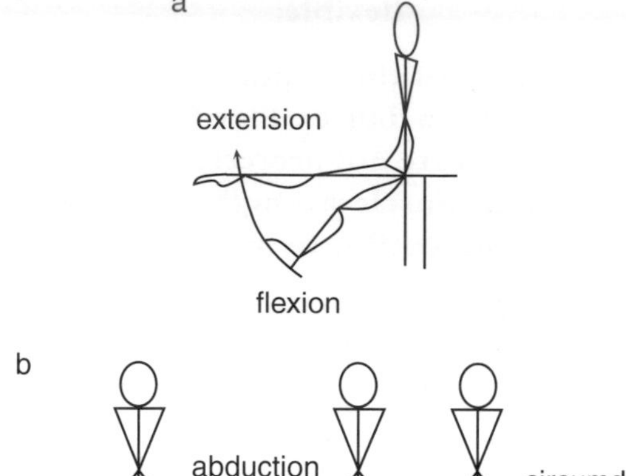

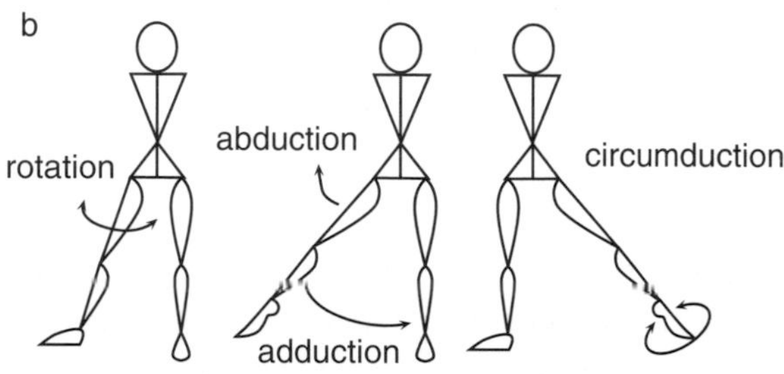

- *abducting:* motion away from the centre line;
- *adducting:* motion towards the centre line;
- *rotating;* motion around the joint axis line;
- *circumducting:* a combination of the above involving motion in a circle.

TASK THREE

In groups of three or four, use sitting, standing and lying positions.

1 Experiment with bending and stretching all the joints in varying degrees - 45°, 90°, 180° - noticing which joints are more or less mobile.

- Work on circling, rotational movement in the joints.
- To music of your choice, put a phrase together to be performed in unison which contrasts rotations with bends and stretches, and uses different joints.

2 It may be fun to use chance procedures to make the phrase by writing down on separate pieces of paper the names of different joints and turning them face down. Select at random the joints, and perform the phrase in the order that you chose them.

Reflecting on the task, consider now that different joints can be classified by their correct movement range, as follows:

- *nonaxial:* linear movement only;
- *uniaxial:* movement in a single plane around a fixed axis;
- *biaxial:* motion in two planes around two axes;
- *triaxial:* motion in all three planes (front to back – *frontal* plane; the *horizontal* plane divides top from bottom of body; the *sagittal* plane divides right from left) around three axes. This joint is sometimes also called a *ball and socket joint.*

Table 1.3 classifies the main joints in this way. Joints have sacs of fluid between the tendons and bones called *bursa*. These allow the smooth movement of tendon over bone. If overused, joints may become inflamed, and this is known as *bursitis*.

The hip/pelvis

A useful image for dancers is to see the pelvis as a bowl. The rim of the bowl tilts during movement. Visualising it like this may help to feel correct vertical placement.

The hip/pelvis (see Figure 1.8) is the strongest joint in the body due to its heavy net of ligaments and strong musculature. The ball and socket are also deeply set to give greater stability. At the same time, the top of the head of the femur stands out from the pelvis, giving a greater range of movement in all directions. Consider this the next time you are performing *ronds de jambe en l'air,* an exercise which increases hip flexibility. The turn-out associated closely with classical ballet depends on the 'Y'-shaped *ilio-femoral ligament* and the angle at which the femur is set in the bowl of the *acetabulum* of the hip socket. The powerful ligament holds the femur, and if gently stretched at an early age, it can become more elastic and so increase the range of motion in the hip. The gluteal muscle group (buttocks) with the abdominals hold the pelvis in place. *Gluteus maximus* is the largest muscle of the group and it extends the hips, for example in jumps when you extend legs in the air or in landing recovering after the plié.

Table 1.3 *Classification of joints by type and movement range*

Joint	Joint type	Movement range
Shoulder Hip	Ball and socket, synovial, triaxial	Adduction, abduction, flexion, rotation, extension and circumduction
Wrist	Biaxial, synovial	Adduction, abduction, flexion, extension
Atlas on axis	Pivot, uniaxial	Rotation
Knee Elbow Ankle	Hinge, uniaxial, synovial	Flex, extend. Some rotation when not weight bearing
Foot	Nonaxial	Linear only

To show a dance class in the style of Martha Graham, as taught by Robert Cohan at I.M. Marsh College 1974

Figure 1.8 *Bones of the right side of the pelvis*

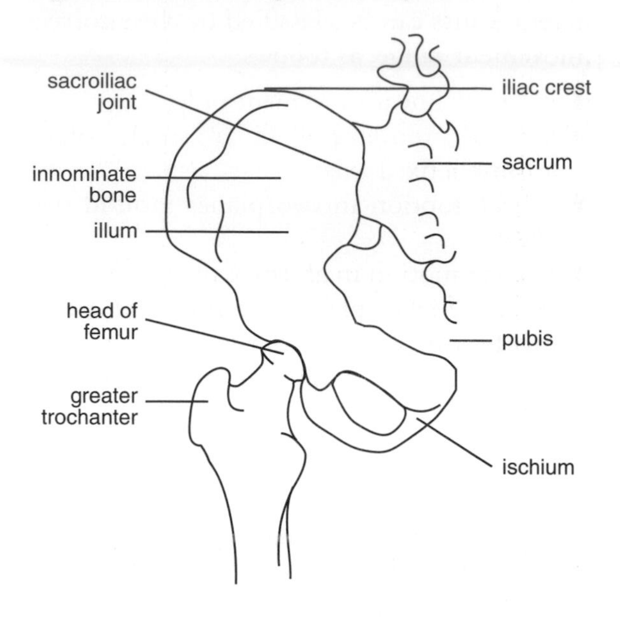

Postural problems/injuries – the pelvis
Tight musculature and ligaments around the hip can affect the back and create misalignments around the body. Forcing turn-out, insufficient warm-up and misalignment are all possible causes of injuries such as strains to the *rectus femoris* or *iliopsoas*. The correct tilt of the pelvis is essential in order to support the normal curve of the spine. 'Sticking the tailbone out' will increase the hollow of the back, and must be avoided.

Some dancers with too-loose ligaments may feel their hip go out of joint. Over time, this may lead to deterioration in the joint. The musculature must be strengthened in order to avoid this condition which, in time, can develop into *osteoarthrosis of the hip* where the joint narrows and the bone surface wears away - this is very painful. Many dancers trained in Graham technique in the early days forced the opening of the hips and have suffered such deterioration as a consequence.

Men who begin training later than most women usually develop less hip flexibility.

The use of the hip in different dance genres
One of the best-known characteristics of classical ballet is the turned out position of the hips, legs and feet, which is like Indian and Eastern genres in this respect. Turn-out starts with rotation of the femur in the hip socket, then involves the whole leg, ankle and foot. It needs a balance of strength and flexibility. It increases the range of motion freeing the hip socket by moving the head of the greater trochanter back and out of the way. Therefore the following are made easier:

- leg extensions
- changing direction
- balance.

The *deep inward rotators* are the muscles which hold turn-out.

Forcing turn-out at an early age by twisting the hips will over-stretch the musculature of the spine and lead to injury of the lower back, groin and knees. In tendu the pelvis stays mainly square but in high leg raises it will tilt slightly in response to the rising leg. The spine too will shift to compensate for a 90 degree or greater leg lift. There should be no collapse in the waist or ribs. Thoracic and lumbar spine should stay long and extended. Similarly in arabesque the pelvis tilts forward slightly, supported by strong abdominals.

In the modern genre, a more 'natural' parallel hold of the hips is preferred. This originated in the work of Isadora Duncan as a rebellion against what she regarded as the artificiality of ballet. Later, Martha Graham used it with greater emphasis to give her choreography a hard-edged look in combination with flexed hands and feet.

The knee

'Knees over toes!' How many times have you heard this? To be accurate it means, for example in plié, that the knee should align directly with the middle toes. Any inward rotation of or excess weight into the knee (for example sitting into a grand plié), will strain ligaments.

The knee joint (see Figure 1.9) is potentially unstable, but the *cruciate ligaments* hold the femur on the tibia making it strong and robust. Also, two *semi-lunar cartilages* help to deepen the joint and circulate the synovial fluid, assisting shock absorption. These do not take weight, but if the knee is twisted whilst weight-bearing, they can be trapped between the femur and tibia and will tear.

The kneecap (*patella*) protects this joint and acts to increase the action of the big thigh muscles (*quadriceps*) by serving as a point of attachment of the tendon and thereby increasing leverage for the movement of the joint.

The *quadriceps* extend the knee. The *hamstrings* flex the knee with help from *gracilis*, *sartorius* and *gastrocnemius* (calf). When the knee first starts to flex it uses its very own muscle, the small *popliteus* on the back of the knee.

Postural problems/injuries – the knee

Most knee injuries occur when bearing weight in flexion, because this is when the joint has least stability. Many such injuries result from repeated twisted misalignment which will loosen ligaments. Such often arises during pliés, when there is a failure to maintain the line of the patella directly over the midline of the feet (which extends out from the middle toe). If the knee is allowed to 'screw' because of inadequate hip flexibility, the *medial ligament* will take undue stress, and there will also be excess strain on the inside of the knee. Foot-rolling may also be a factor.

> On Tuesday afternoon I felt my knee getting tender ... It always comes about once we start doing runs of the piece in the build-up to performances. The physiotherapist has told me that the floor is really taking its toll on my knees as I do a lot of jumping and the floor at Mary Ward Hall is very hard ... it would be better to move to a sprung studio for the three-week rehearsal build-up to our London season.
>
> (*Catherine Quinn in* Dancer's Work log, *1999*)

The maintenance of a straight, secure knee joint with minimal rotation during movement is the main way to protect it. After a knee injury, attention should be given to the quadriceps muscle group in order to compensate for the loss of strength due to lack of use. This muscle group wastes quickly (*atrophy*) and so needs exercise, as do the hamstrings (the pair muscle group to the quadriceps) which provide the necessary eccentric contraction as the quads contract concentrically. This give-and-take relationship of muscle pairs is called *reciprocal*.

Figure 1.9 *The knee joint (a) from the front (b) from the side*

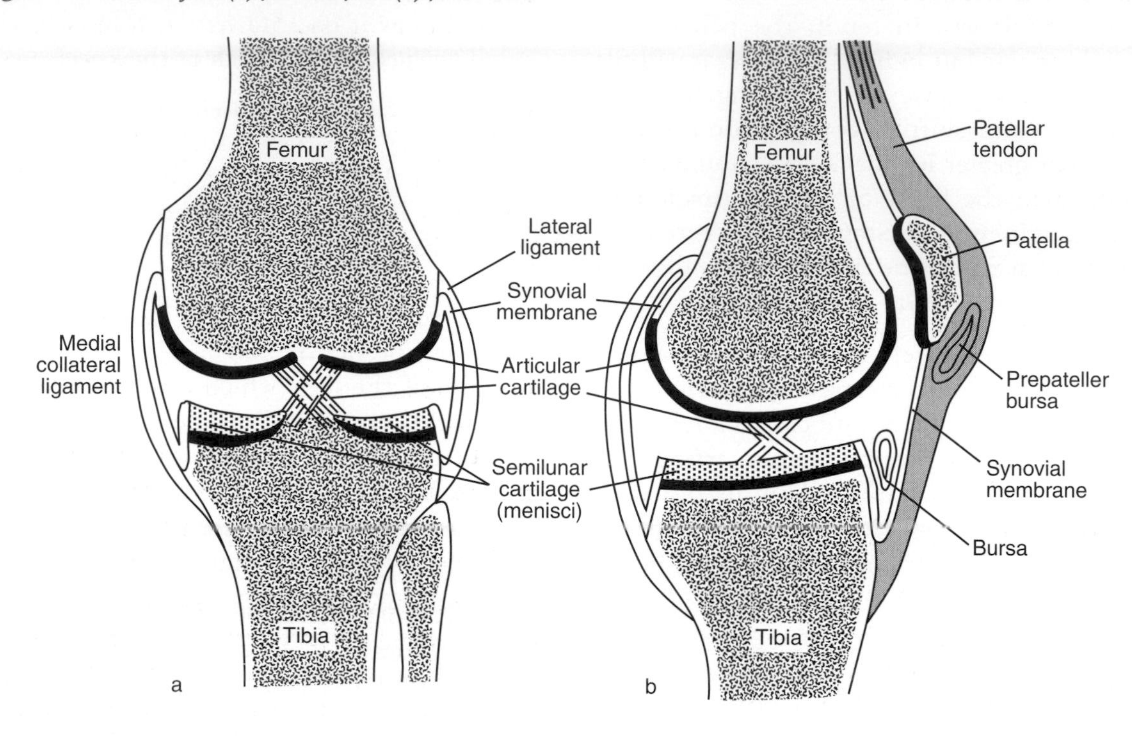

Table 1.4 *Injuries/problems of the knee*

Injury	Symptoms	Causes	Treatment
Torn cartilage	Pain on bent leg, when weight bearing, on inside of knee. Knee locks if bent.	Incorrect pliés alignment – knee drops inward. Poor turn-out in hip.	Rest/operate if badly torn. Exercise quads/hamstrings.
Bursitis (Housemaid's Knee)	Pain on either side of patella – swelling.	Excessive bending – bursa inflame.	Rest/ice/ultrasound.
Jumper's Knee	Pain in plié and jumps, tender on patella under tibia when pressed.	Overuse during jumping.	Massage/ultrasound/ stretch/strengthen quads.

Postural defects of the knee – hyperextension

'Swayback' knees, although useful in classical ballet because they give a long, aesthetically pleasing look, are a sign of weak quadriceps. Overstretching of the hamstrings and locking of the knees should be avoided. Knock knees, bow legs and tibial torsion also impair alignment and safe movement.

Figure 1.10 *The ankle joint*

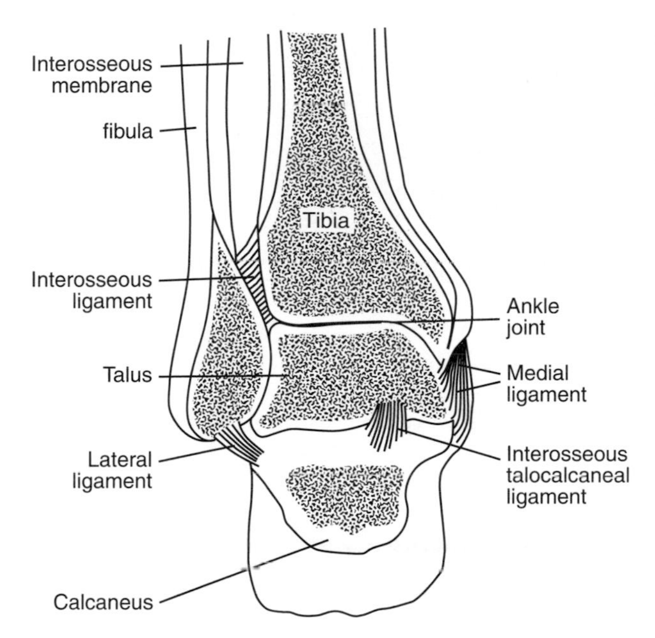

The ankle

The ankle joint (see Figure 1.10) lies between the *tibia*, the *fibula* and the *talus*. The ligaments on the outside and inside are the main means of support. The ankle joint is very stable, but is also the site of large stresses, therefore ankles need to be strong but also have enough flexibility in the ligaments to allow:

- safe turn-out in plié (eases stepping and landing)
- sufficient extension for take-off in jumps.

FASCINATING FACT: on landing from jumps, the ankle can absorb up to eight times the body weight.

Postural problems/injuries – the ankle

- *Sprained ankle:* the most commonly injured part of the ankle is the outside lateral ligament. It can happen from faulty landings causing the foot to sickle inwards as it rolls over on its outside edge. The ligament is then twisted and may tear. *Treatment:* ice, rest, elevation and – if severe – a plaster or strapping. Recovery can take up to six weeks.

TASK FOUR

Look at the photographs on page 23 and answer the following questions.

In the dancer on your left:

1 Choose from rotation/flexion/extension.

(a) What two anatomical actions are *her* right hip performing? (2)
(b) How are the actions in the knees of supporting legs of the two dancers different? (2)

2 (a) Which muscle group is mainly responsible for extending the knee? (1)
(b) Which muscle group is mainly responsible for flexing the knee? (1)

3 (a) What type of joint is the hip? (1)
(b) How many axes can it move on? (1)
(c) What name describes this range of its movements? (1)

4 Choose from plantar flexion/dorsi flexion.

(a) What action is *her* support foot performing? (1)
(b) What action is *her* foot in the air performing? (1)

5 (a) Which anatomical action is *her* neck performing? Choose from extension/flexion. (1)
(b) What is the name for this part of the spine? (1)
(c) How many vertebrae are in this part of the spine? (1)
(d) Why is this area of the spine vulnerable to injury? (1)

6 (a) The dancer's spine is rotated or twisted. Which curve of the spine does this action start in? (1)
(b) How many vertebrae are there in this curve? (1)

7 The flexible spine is possible because of the intervertebral discs.

(a) Where are these discs? (1)
(b) What are they made of? (1)
(c) What is the other function of these discs? (1)

The answers are on page 24.

'And Nothing but the truth' by V-TOL Dance Company, 1998. Dancers Chris Devaney, James Hewison.

STRETCHING

Flexibility is improved by *stretching*. This action lengthens the muscle along the direction of the fibres. When stretching there should be a pleasant sensation inside the muscle. There are a number of ways to stretch correctly which may overcome the blocking effect of the *stretch reflex*. This is a protective reflex which makes the muscle contract immediately after a stretch, so that in case of a sudden fall or twist, the muscle is prevented from overstretching to the point of injury.

- *The long sustained stretch*. During a slow action, the brain can override the stretch reflex. With conscious control, this stretch can be sustained, and *gravity* can be used to increase the extension for at least 30 seconds. Letting the muscle 'hang off the bone' and 'nudging around', combined with relaxation and constant breathing, can reach spots that other stretches do not. This relaxed type of stretching is featured greatly in post-modern anatomical release work.
- *Reciprocal inhibition*. Trying to stretch a muscle while it is in any state of *contraction* will reduce the effectiveness of the stretch and may tear the muscle fibres. For this reason, *ballistic bouncing stretches* are ineffective, unsafe, and may cause soreness. The maximum contraction of one muscle will temporarily inhibit the stretch reflex in its opposite muscle. So, if you wanted to stretch, say, the hamstrings, a consciously held contraction of the quadriceps for 20 to 30 seconds first would then allow greater stretch in the back of the thigh. After the contraction, the hamstring stretch should then be held for a further 30 seconds to one minute. For this principle to work, both muscles have to be of similar mass. A bonus of the reciprocal method is the strength gained due to maximal contraction.

Both of the above reflexes are activated at a spinal level by a release of chemicals.

- *The Golgi tendon reflex*. This is another protective reflex, but one which acts as a reaction to pressure. The Golgi tendon organs are sited at the point where the tendon meets the muscle, and they are sensitive to pressure. They totally relax the muscle when the tendon is about to pull off the bone, and they block the stretch reflex for a longer time. A word of warning though to dancers who think 'Ah! I'll use this to stretch more', because the severity of the pull required to activate the Golgi reflex makes it a dangerous way to increase mobility. During intense stretching, if it is experienced, there is a feeling of warm, total release. The muscle goes to jelly, and the range of motion is increased noticeably. The safest way to reach this point is *very* slowly and carefully, and after an adequate warm-up.

Generally speaking, the following guidelines should be used to sequence an exercise programme effectively:

1. Start gently, and gradually build up to a more vigorous level. Do an all-over warm-up first.
2. After the exercise of one muscle group, take time to undo the bad effects or to notice the good. For example, after a maximum contraction for strength, stretch out in the opposite direction. Or vice versa.
3. Before doing a major stretch, do a maximum contraction of the opposite muscle group.
4. Pinpoint the exact muscle or group that needs stretching/strengthening.
5. Listen to your body!

FLEXIBILITY – A SUMMARY

Improving mobility in the joints is crucial if the dancer is to maintain muscular balance in the body. This of course will also help alignment, safe working methods and avoidance of injury. You should learn what proper stretching techniques feel like when you do them, and so avoid unsafe methods.

ANSWERS TO TASK FOUR

(Possible total of 20 marks)

1 (a) Flexion and rotation (2 marks)

(b) The dancer on the left is extended and the dancer on the right is flexed. (2 marks)

2 (a) Quadriceps (1 mark)

(b) Hamstrings (1 mark)

3 (a) Synovial or ball and socket (1 mark)

(b) Three (1 mark)

(c) Triaxial (1 mark)

4 (a) Dorsi flexion (1 mark)

(b) Plantar flexion (1 mark)

5 (a) Extension (1 mark)

(b) Cervical (1 mark)

(c) Seven (1 mark)

(d) Because it has to bear the weight of the head (1 mark)

6 (a) Thoracic curve (1 mark)

(b) Twelve (1 mark)

7 (a) Between the vertebrae (1 mark)

(b) Cartilage (1 mark)

(c) To absorb shock (1 mark)

TASK FIVE

Check a partner's flexibility:

1 For tightness in the back: one dancer kneels down with feet flat and curls forward. Look for: flat places on the spine – these are points of tightness. Swap over.

2 For tightness in the front of the shoulder: raise an arm in abduction until it is parallel to the floor, then take the arm behind. Look for difficulty in this movement – this indicates tightness.

3 For tight hamstrings: lie on your back and raise your legs, keeping the hips on the floor. The leg should be able to reach at least 90° or more. Look out, therefore, for a leg raise of less than 90°.

If any tightness has been found, now do the appropriate corrective stretch from below:

1 For the lumbar area: kneel as before, but stretch out the arms, breathe out and hold for 30 seconds. Apply the long sustained stretch.

2 For the whole back: standing, drop from the head and curve down, lifting the abdominals; keep the legs soft and bent. Curl up again, and repeat three times.

3 For the pectorals (the front of the shoulder area): make one arm reach directly behind you. Repeat with the other arm.

4 For the hamstrings: lie on your back, bend both legs in, then softly place them on the torso. Breathe out and gently hug; hold for 20 seconds.

Any muscular tightness you may have can be lessened by stretching, but any structural limitations of bone and ligament will not be affected by stretching, and so all dancers should learn to work within their own personal range.

The next section is concerned with strength, and it is important to note that only when the muscles which control a joint are strong can a full range of mobility be achieved through gradual stretching. Weak muscles should not be stretched. When flexibility and strength are balanced the dancer can more easily reach and hold a position, for example, high leg extensions.

Strength and stamina

STRENGTH

When combined, increasing levels of flexibility, strength and stamina form a policy of preventative training (prevent injury).

Strength is the capacity to exert a muscle contraction against resistance. Contraction is the opposite muscle action to that of stretching. A strong body moves freely, efficiently and above all safely. The aim is all-round strength, not the overdevelopment of certain muscle groups.

MYTHS:

- **Building strength = bulk.**
- **Building strength = loss of flexibility.**
- **Dancers should not use weights.**

The main concerns are:

- types of muscle contraction
- muscles.

Types of muscle contraction

During exercise, there are two types of contraction: *isotonic* and *isometric*.

Isotonic contraction

This involves a dynamic resistance during which the muscle *changes in length*. Isotonic work may be either:

- *concentric* – muscle shortens, e.g. hip abductors (*gluteus medius*) of the gesturing leg as it is raised to the side.
- *eccentric* – muscle lengthens, e.g. hip abductors of the gesturing leg to control lowering it to the ground.

Exercises may be performed, in the full range of motion of a joint, in sets of 10 to 15. Repetitions slowly build to two or three sets. By adding weights, self-resistance (like another body part), pulleys or elastic bands, overloading may be increased gradually and strength increases.

Isometric contraction

This involves a static resistance during which the muscle tone increases but does not change length.

For example, when a leg is raised to the side, holding it there means that the hip abductors have to work in *static* or isometric contraction to resist gravity.

TASK SIX

Perform the following isotonic exercise to strengthen hip abductors (*gluteus medius*). If a dancer has weak hip abductors and tight external rotators, *grand battement* and *battement tendu* will be performed with hip flexed and externally rotated, rather than in abduction.

1. Lie on your side, with legs straight and feet together.
2. Internally rotate the top leg, and abduct the hip through the full range of motion.
3. Repeat 10 times.
4. Build gradually to a maximum of three sets of 10. Allow two to five minutes' rest between sets.
5. When three sets are possible, perform the exercise standing with an ankle weight starting at 1 kg.

TASK SEVEN

Perform the following isometric exercise to strengthen the lateral trunk flexors and correct scoliosis and an uneven hip tilt.

1. Lie on your side on a mat, with legs straight and feet together.
2. Rest on one forearm, and extend the other arm to shoulder height.
3. Raise the hips sideways off the mat as far as possible, and *hold* for 10 seconds.
4. Repeat, then change to the other side.

A weight-training programme for male dancers of the Birmingham Royal Ballet was devised by Yiannis Koutedakis at the University of Wolverhampton. The dancers used free weights and machines set at high resistance for a low number of repetitions. After the programme, the dancers felt that their physical appearance had improved.

> Some choreographers initially expressed doubts about the outcome ... This meant that the project was restricted to male dancers. But the results have convinced choreographers that their sugar plum fairies are not going to turn into Ms Universe overnight, so Koutedakis is planning to extend the programme to include women.
>
> (*Helen Saul in* New Scientist, *25 December 1993/1 January 1994*)

With the above in mind, the principle of *progressive overload* to build strength can be identified. This involves increasing:

- *frequency:* increasing the number of repetitions or the speed of a movement;
- *intensity:* adding more and more resistance, as with weights;
- *duration:* increasing the length of time a movement takes.

To increase muscle strength isometric (static) work as seen in Task Seven is useful, but the muscles will tire easily so frequent rests are needed. Isotonic (concentric) contraction, as seen in Task Six, is the most effective work to increase strength. Eccentric work should be included if muscles are weak or injured, or to increase flexibility.

Muscles

> I have a big feeling about muscle – to have a muscle, to feel a muscle, to have a muscle warmed up and toned and ready to do something, it's a marvellous, sensual feeling.
>
> (*Edward Villella in* Dance from Magic to Art, *1976*)

Muscles are the meaty part of the body. In dance, it is the *striated* or *skeletal* muscle which is of concern. This is controlled by the nervous system which sends electrochemical energy impulses which cause the muscle fibres to contract and the joints to move. Muscles are attached by tendons to the bone at each end: (a) the end of the *origin* – this stays still; (b) the *insertion* – the end which pulls and moves.

Myth: muscles change to fat if exercise stops. This is not true at all. The strength of the muscle will reduce, and it will feel softer, if exercise stops, but muscle and fat are *completely different tissues*.

Muscles can only *pull* (i.e. contract), and movement is brought about by pulling on the bones so as to turn these bones into *levers*. The structure of each such lever has three main parts:

1 the *load* or *weight*;
2 the *fulcrum* (balance point) of the joint;
3 the muscle action producing the *effort* at the point of the muscle insertion.

There are three types of lever: *first order*, *second order* and *third order* – depending on the position of the fulcrum.

In Figure 1.11, F = fulcrum, E = effort and W = weight. An example of a second-order lever is shown in Figure 1.12.

Most common levers are third-order, where the 'effort' moves a shorter distance than the 'load'. This has the advantage of allowing a large movement to be made with only a slight contraction/shortening of the muscle (see Figure 1.13), thus making it a more efficient movement.

Figure 1.11 *First order lever*

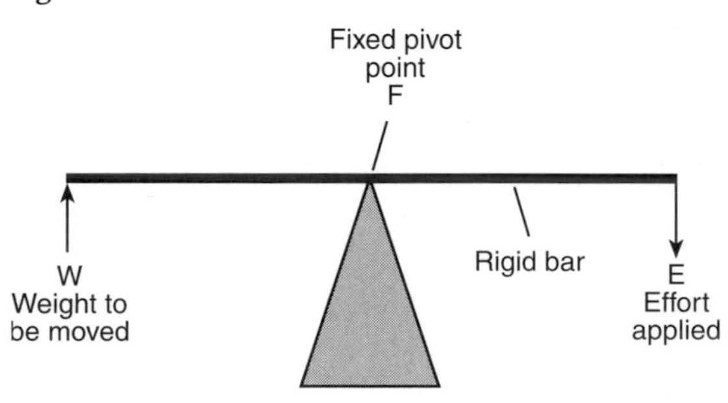

Figure 1.12 *Second order lever in rising onto one toe*

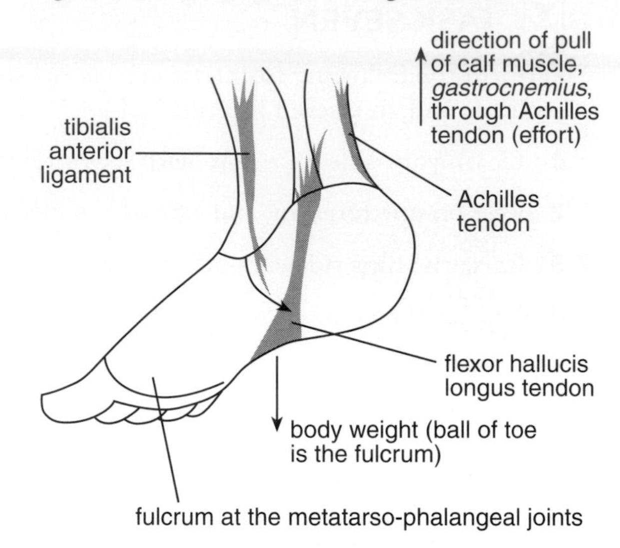

Figure 1.13 *Third order lever action of the arm*

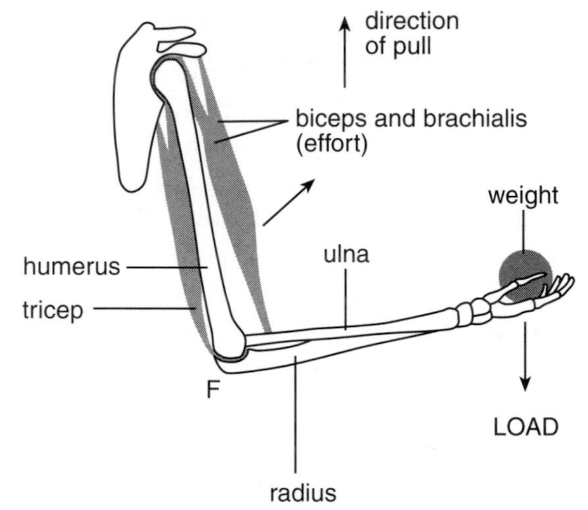

To dance without injury, a muscle needs a high level of efficiency in the *antagonistic* action of its pair muscle. This means that while a muscle is contracting, its opposite muscle must extend smoothly. Poorly trained or tired muscles do not tend to act antagonistically, and they strain easily.

So, for example, in raising a leg forward the quadriceps are the *agonists*, i.e. they concentrically contract to produce the raising movement. The hamstrings are the *antagonists*, on the opposite side of the joint. They relax and lengthen in eccentric contraction to allow smooth control. Similarly in plié, the quadriceps eccentrically contract then in raising the body back to standing they contract concentrically to resist the force of gravity.

Muscle pairs include:

- *biceps* (front upper arm) and *triceps* (back upper arm);
- *rectus abdominis* (front torso) and the long muscles of the back;
- *tibialis anterior* (front lower leg) and *gastrocnemius, soleus* (back lower leg);
- thigh adductors (inside thigh) and *gluteus medius* and others (outside thigh);
- quadriceps and hamstrings.

Injuries – muscles and tendons

The stronger the dancer the less the risk of injury, e.g. stronger hamstrings may reduce the risk of lower back injuries.

Muscles are attached to bones by the much stronger tendons. Both muscles and tendons are liable to injury. If a tendon is irritated by overuse, tendonitis may occur. Rest is then essential. The *achilles* tendon is particularly prone to tendonitis. The symptoms are tenderness and crunching, particularly when plantarflexing the ankle. Careful stretching of the *soleus* and *gastrocnemius* (lower leg) when cooling down reduces the likelihood of tendonitis.

Muscles and tendons are usually injured by too sudden a movement, or by a recurring strain on weak muscles from poor technique or overuse. Vulnerable muscles include: the groin (*iliopsoas, rectus femoris, adductors*), the hamstring group, and the calf (*gastrocnemius*). A thorough warm-up will help to reduce muscle and tendon strains, as it will for joint sprains. However, if you do injure yourself, the following is a good guide, and easy to remember:

Figure 1.14 *Figure showing different muscle sets*

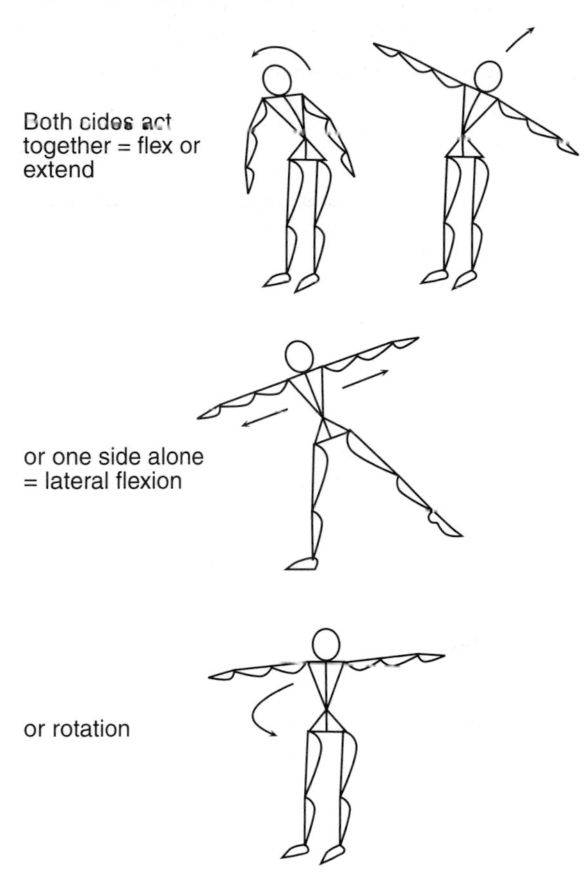

R = rest
I = ice
C = compress (bandage/support)
E = elevate (raise)

Cold therapy will decrease the blood flow and bruising which damages soft tissue. It limits swelling by decreasing the muscle's need for oxygen, and thus relieves pain. Apply ice for no more than 10 to 15 minutes, and repeat if necessary every few hours until the swelling, local heat or bruising stops. After two days, alternate between cold and hot in order to stimulate blood flow to the injury and encourage healing. The ice should not have direct contact with the skin – a bag of frozen peas works! (Or of course you could have rice and peas!)

Table 1.5 *Muscular functions and problems*

Location	Muscle names	Function	Problems/injuries
Feet	Intrinsic muscles	Strengthen arches and keep toes long when foot is plantar flexed.	If toes keep curled, increases stress on Achilles tendon.
	Hallucis longus tibialis anterior	Dorsi flex foot (flexed).	
	Plantaris	Plantar flex foot (point).	
Leg Lower	Gastrocnemius	Plantar flex foot – a 'white' fast-mover muscle for travelling, jumps etc.	Stretch out after use, with ankle flexed, knee straight. Reduces risk of tendonitis in Achilles tendon.
	Soleus	Maintains plantar flexion, in relevé, pointe work – red holding muscle.	After a class with lots of adagio or balances, stretch it, with ankle flexed. Knee should be flexed and legs parallel.
Knee	Quadriceps group	Extend the knee by increasing leverage.	In any knee injury, the quads waste/weaken during recovery.
	Hamstring group	Strengthen alignment of knee over centre of tarsus. Flex knee and extend hip.	Pronation (knees over-rotate) injure patella.
Hip	Small rotators	Externally rotate femur and stabilise hip.	Imbalance between rotators tightens buttocks and pinches sciatic nerve.
	Iliopsoas	Medially rotate femur and flex hip.	Can appear 'duckfooted'. Cause of lumbar lordosis, lumbar back pain.
	Adductors	Laterally rotate femur (inner thighs pull together), stabilise pelvis when acting against the abductors when standing on one leg.	
	Abductors	Stabilise hip by supporting contraction on weight-bearing side.	If too weak or tense, will affect hips or knees.
	Gluteus maximus	Extends hip. Feel it contract when lifting from being flexed at hip.	Low back pain if excess lordosis (sway-back). May 'buck' during jumping.
Torso	Sacrospinalis, quadratus lumborum, rectus abdominis obliques, transversalis	Extend spine. Flex spine.	Strong abdominals help to protect lumbar spine.

Heat sources could be in spray form, an infra-red lamp or heat packs. Only a qualified physiotherapist should apply ultrasound. An appropriate exercise routine should be followed to maintain uninjured and injured parts alike.

STAMINA

> Dancing should look easy; like an optical illusion. It should seem effortless. When you do a difficult variation, the audience is aware that it is demanding, and that you have the power and strength to do it. But in the end, when you take your bow, you should look as if you were saying 'Oh it was nothing. I could do it again.'
>
> (*Helgi Tomasson in* Dance from Magic to Art, *1976*)

This describes stamina. Stamina is staying power, endurance of either the muscles or the heart and breathing. As described in the quote above, it would be easy to think that stamina has to do with how you look. It is more than that, however, because it is crucial for the prevention of injury. In order to maintain quality performance over long periods, the heart and lungs need to deliver oxygen to the blood and muscles as efficiently as possible. Once fatigue sets in, mistakes in judgement or undue stresses on muscles and joints make continued dancing unsafe.

Stamina can be divided into two parts:

1 *Muscular endurance* is the ability of a muscle to continue to contract over a period of time. It is inseparable from muscular strength and size; both these are developed by the above mentioned principle of progressive overload. This type of conditioning needs many repetitions with light resistance, and of course this can be boring! So how many is enough? Listen to your body, and when a burning sensation is felt, the general rule is five more repetitions for increasing muscular endurance. Well-trained muscles are able to contract over longer periods before tiring, and so in class the dancer aims to achieve increased strength and endurance in exercises. Speed will increase if movements are practised at an increasing pace.

2 *Cardiorespiratory endurance* is the ability to continue aerobic activity (activity which uses oxygen or air) over a period of time. The cardiorespiratory system includes the heart and lungs (and associated organs). It would be helpful to take a closer look at these vital systems.

The cardiovascular system

This consists of the heart, the blood and the blood vessels. Together these enable the transport of necessary nutrients and gases to and from the muscles and organs. The blood also carries heat to the skin for removal by sweating and radiation and takes away waste products.

During exercise, changes occur in the cardiovascular system. There is:

- an improvement in the condition of the overall system;
- an increase in the size/strength of the heart muscle and the volume of the heart chambers;
- an increase in aerobic capacity;
- a lowering of the resting heart rate;
- a better venous return of waste products;
- an increase in the volume of blood;
- an increase in the red-blood-cell count (i.e. *haemoglobin* cells which carry oxygen);
- an increase in chemical buffers (potassium

and sodium) in the blood (these lower acidity and help to maintain a lower cardiovascular rate);

- an increase in *stroke volume* (i.e. the amount of blood pumped at each heart beat).

The heart

A muscular pump about the size of your fist, the heart sends fresh oxygen (O_2) through the arteries to the rest of the body. The *veins* then carry waste products and carbon dioxide (CO_2) back, to be expelled from the body.

> **FASCINATING FACTS: the heart**
>
> - **beats at about 70 times per minute (resting rate).**
> - **pumps blood at a rate of about five litres per minute – i.e. about 180 million gallons in a lifetime.**

The heart rate

During exercise, the heart rate (your *pulse*) increases from its usual resting rate to a maximum rate which is related to your age. When the exercise stops, it then decreases in order to maintain circulatory balance. The deceleration here is controlled by the *vagus nerve* which stops the heart from constantly speeding up. This nerve is stimulated by increased blood pressure. In a healthy young adult, normal blood pressure is around 120/80. The higher figure refers to the blood pressure during each heart beat, and the lower figure to your blood pressure *between* beats. The more strenuous the activity and the better the person's physical condition, the more sensitive the vagus nerve is. This is thought to explain why fitter individuals have a lower resting heart rate than untrained individuals.

Other factors affecting the heart rate are:

- The *pacemaker* stimulates a steady heart rate.
- *Chemical regulation* operates when there is an increase in the levels of CO_2 in the blood. The heart rate and blood pressure increase as *adrenalin* is released into the bloodstream.

The target heart rate

Most dance classes do not focus on cardiorespiratory conditioning. In order now to stress this type of conditioning, a medium-to-high 'target' heart rate must be maintained continuously for 15 to 20 minutes. In dance class, it is usual to cross the floor once, then rest and wait for others to do so. This means that aerobic activity is not continued over a long enough time.

The respiratory system

During exercise, both the heart and the breathing rate speed up to increase the supply of O_2 *to* and of CO_2 *away from* the muscle. When we are huffing and puffing, CO_2 is being expelled more forcefully from the *alveoli* in the lungs out of the body. This removes the CO_2 away from the muscles, making an exchange for O_2 possible in the capillaries; and in this way, exercise may continue (see Figure 1.15).

Figure 1.15 *Elements of the respiratory system and gaseous exchange*

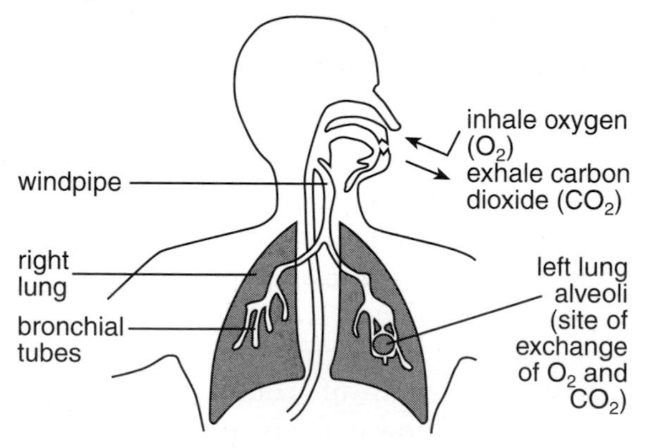

The rate of breathing is controlled by nerve cells in the brain. These detect the levels of O_2, CO_2 and acidity in the blood and stimulate an appropriate increase or decrease in respiration.

Carbon dioxide is a relatively harmless waste gas because it is displaced easily by oxygen in the haemoglobin. However, carbon monoxide, as produced by smoking cigarettes, is extremely poisonous because it combines with haemoglobin to exclude oxygen. It therefore deprives the body of a basic requirement, and so smokers are less able to provide muscle with the necessary increased oxygen as demanded in dancing. Dancers who smoke will have less ability to maintain high-quality performance over long periods, and may be more prone to injury.

The *ribcage* protects the lungs. Attached to it are the muscles which control the expansion and contraction of the *thorax cavity*. These are: the *intercostals*; the *serratus group*; and the *diaphragm*. The lungs have no muscular power of their own.

The overall level of fitness for any sport or dance is something specific to that activity. However, the cardiorespiratory system does need a basic level of aerobic fitness, whatever the activity. An increase in the delivery of oxygen to the muscles by the heart, blood vessels and lungs is improved by slow and steady exercises, such as cycling or swimming, which gradually increase in intensity – in other words, through aerobic exercise where muscles work using oxygen.

The American College of Sports Medicine defines aerobic activity as follows:

> Aerobic activity is that requiring continuous, rhythmic use of large muscle groups at 60–90 per cent of the maximum heart rate and 50–85 per cent of maximum oxygen uptake for 20–60 minutes.

The main effects of aerobic exercise are:

- an increase in muscular endurance/stamina;
- an increase in cardiorespiratory endurance/stamina;
- a reduction of fat deposits (weight loss);
- a maintenance of bone mass.

Muscles can continue to work *without* oxygen, and this is called *anaerobic* activity. Anaerobic exercise begins when oxygen consumption by the muscle stops increasing, despite an increased performance. At this point, an oxygen debt is accumulated, and waste *lactic acid*, which the muscle produces, can only be tolerated to a certain level before exhaustion – i.e. before a point is reached where the muscle can no longer contract.

Aerobic exercise improves long-term endurance while anaerobic exercise improves short-term endurance. Dance tends to use mostly anaerobic activity – during technique class, performing repetitive movements will improve muscular endurance. However, some choreographers may also place vigorous demands on the dancers' aerobic endurance. This will result in progressive overload on the muscles and cardiorespiratory system. Preconditioning/preventative training for building up the stamina of the cardiovascular system is therefore advisable. In the event that the dance class is not providing sufficient training in this respect, the dancer should once again invest in some supplementary training. This supplementary type of work was noted earlier in this chapter in the Birmingham Royal Ballet's programme for male dancers which aimed to increase upper-body strength and power. The programme focused on developing muscle fibres quickly by encouraging anaerobic activity through the use of free weights and machines set at high resistance for a low number of repetitions. But there were also exercises for slow muscle-fibre development in the form of aerobic sports such as cycling or running.

Recovery periods are needed after anaerobic exercise so that the oxygen debt is paid back and a normal chemical balance is resumed. Often, after such exercise, the muscles may feel sore or stiff. This may be caused by mild inflammation in the muscle fibres, which often occurs after new exercises or when adapting to new techniques. This condition reduces flexibility and causes general discomfort when dancing. Warming-up before and cool-down after class is advisable in order to reduce the risk of injury.

Dancers do not always warm up adequately *before* class. Do you? It is generally accepted that class is where dancers learn and improve technique skills for performance. Traditionally South Asian dance has a lengthy mind-body focus in preparation for class or performance but no physical warm-up. Now that work, such as that of Shobana Jeyasingh, is placing greater physical demands on dancers warm-up may be more ncessary. Similarly Western dancers may find the traditional South Asian practices beneficial.

Warm-up is a gradual physical and mental preparation for greater exertion which increases:

- the heart rate;
- the deep temperatures of the muscles – thereby improving their contractibility and flexibility;
- the flexibility of tendons and ligaments – so reducing the chance of injury;
- reaction speed;
- blood sugar and adrenalin levels.

The warm-up should include exercises which: raise the pulse rate; mobilise the joints; stretch the muscles (simple stretches).

TASK EIGHT

Improving Own Learning and Performance

Prepare a suitable warm-up pattern of 15 to 20 minutes along the following lines:

- 5 to 10 minutes' easy prancing in place;
- a light easy moving of joints building to swings;
- gradual stretches;
- some 'technical' exercises, or a rehearsal of the dance about to be performed – this is important for mental readiness and the avoidance of injury;
- a gentle stretch to cool down.

Cool-down is the gradual slowing down of the circulation in order to return to a resting heart rate. Stopping exercise too suddenly can cause the pooling of blood in previously active areas such as the lower limbs, and this can cause soreness, fainting and dizziness. Gentle stretching or breathing for about five minutes is advised. The wearing of warmer clothing will help to avoid pulls and aches.

During exercise, the blood supply to inactive areas – like the digestive system – will reduce so that the muscles in turn can receive *more* blood. Eating too soon before class or a performance will cause increased blood flow to the digestive system and so deprive the muscles of an essential supply.

Strength and Stamina – A Summary

A healthy, well-conditioned cardiovascular system will provide the dancer with sufficient endurance to maintain safe, expressive and efficient movement throughout technique classes, rehearsals and performances. This system, however, works only in tandem with an equally well-conditioned respiratory system.

Strength and muscular endurance are related in a number of ways. If the muscle is strong, it can continue activity for longer. In progressive overload, which conditions for muscular endurance, the fatigue level rises, and the last few repetitions can be 'maximal'. Such overload can thus serve to build strength and stamina.

Generally speaking, prevention is better than cure when it comes to injury. Technique classes and rehearsals are not always considered adequate conditioning to build a body which is 'dancefit'. The level of conditioning in any training programme must take into account the *individual* physical system.

Rest periods, although beneficial and necessary, can be a problem as described here:

> Mostly the dancers are worried about getting some stamina together. After a very lovely week off, my body feels as if I've had two weeks off. Well we just have to … do the runs (of the whole show), daily to build it up.
>
> (*Catherine Quinn in* Dancer's Work log, *1999*)

These most basic physical attributes – alignment, flexibility, strength and stamina – are all under the control of that most fascinating part of the body, the brain and nervous system. This is attuned to respond to the ever-changing conditions of our body and surroundings. It is the instrument which fine-tunes the high degree of co-ordination and skills which dance demands. It is to this control tower that we now turn our attention.

Co-ordination

The skills of balance, control of energy and accuracy of action are the subjects of co-ordination in dance training. In order to increase skill levels, the nervous system must be finely tuned. Through repeated practice in class skills will improve. This may – for example, in balance – involve a decrease in the weight-bearing area. Increasing speed will result if the pace of an exercise is gradually increased.

The function of daily class is to practise technical skills. By movement repetition dancers build a link between commands and muscle memory. Gradually, as small memory pictures (*engrams*) are stored in the brain, skills increase, improve and become more automatic. Once memorised the dancer can focus more on the nuances of expression for performance. Computer software such as Life

Forms can be used to aid memory. Merce Cunningham uses it to store class exercises in a computer which dancers can check for clarification of co-ordination and sequences.

The nervous system consists of:

- the nerves/neurons;
- reflexes and receptors;
- the brain.

Together, these engage in a complex communication system which controls all human interaction in the internal and external environments.

There are two parts to the nervous system:

1 The *autonomic nervous system* regulates involuntary functions of digestion, hormones and the cardiorespiratory activity.
2 The *somatic nervous system* regulates both movement itself and our *perception* of movement.

Both systems are controlled by the brain via *neurons*. These are individual cells capable of sending messages to and from the brain and the rest of the body. There are two types of neuron:

1 *Sensory neurons* transmit messages about tension in muscles, tendons and ligaments, and about hot, cold, pain, orientation in space and co-ordination **to** the brain.
2 *Motor neurons* pass impulses **from** the brain to the muscles. The two types together allow you to put your finger on your nose without having to look at it.

THE BRAIN AND NEUROLOGICAL CENTRES

These centres comprise:

- the *midbrain*: the primitive control centre regulating physical reactions like sweating and cardiorespiratory activity;
- the *cerebral cortex*: the centre of fine motor control, involving decision-making for initiating and arresting motion. When new movement combinations are being learnt, the new information may cause a feeling of awkwardness. Gradually, in dance, most movement becomes reflex as motor memory develops;
- the *cerebellum*: this transmits information to the midbrain and cerebral cortex regarding the status of the body. It is crucial in maintaining upright posture and balance. When you miss the last step on the stairs, it is because the cerebellum has been misinformed by the eyes and so sends the wrong messages; and in turn, the wrong amount of muscle contraction required for ascent or descent is then executed.

RECEPTORS AND REFLEXES

In order for the centres in the brain to function, receptors must send information from muscles, tendons and joints about tension, co-ordination and spatial orientation. The brain then reacts by sending messages via motor neurons so that appropriate adjustments are made. Earlier in this chapter in the section on flexibility, the spinal reflexes affecting stretching were mentioned. These are muscular reflexes which are designed to protect the joints and muscles. There are three other such reflexes as shown in Table 1.6.

There are also reflexes relating to the senses of sight, touch and hearing: receptors in the eyes, skin and ears react to stimuli from the outside and send messages to the cerebellum, and appropriate adjustments are made on command from the brain. These reflexes are known as the *righting reflexes* (see Table 1.7) because they are primarily concerned with maintaining balance and orientation, and they comprise the *aural, skin and visual righting reflexes.*

THE PSYCHOLOGY OF DANCE TRAINING

As seen in the explanations above, there is a definite connection between mind and body: the mind can affect the way the body feels and reacts. In dance, where the focus is such a personal one as your own body, there is a need to avoid unhelpful, harmful practice when learning new co-ordinations. The concerns involved here are:

- tension and stress
- kinesthetic sense
- the use of imagery/feedback.

One look at a beginner's dance class will tell you how much of an increase in the overall tension level there is in order to achieve a desired movement. As we know, the cerebral cortex activity and other muscular reflexes are the reasons for this. It is incredible that the students can move at all when trying to use such

Table 1.6 *Muscular reflexes*

Name of reflex	Action	Applications
Flexor reflex	All flexor muscles contract when one is powerfully activated.	Increases intensity of abdominal contraction by accompanying it with flexors for hands, feet, knees – as seen in the Martha Graham style. When learning new skills, sometimes powerful flexions are accompanied by unwanted tightness in neck, shoulders etc.
Extensor reflex	Stimulates all extensor muscles when one is powerfully activated.	Explains 'bucking' when beginners start to jump. The powerful contraction of the extensor muscles of the feet, ankles, knees and hips causes an overflow of neural activity to the extensors of the spine, and the head and shoulders are thrown backwards.
Crossed extensor reflex	Activates the contracting muscle of the diagonally opposite limb, and facilitates the antagonistic muscles of the parallel limb.	For balance, when the right hip flexes, the left hip extends; and when the right shoulder extends, the left shoulder flexes. This is active in all balance and travelling. (See photo for Task Four.) In Graham-technique spiral exercises. In opposition – e.g. skips. Often, beginners flop about. The wise teacher may not mention arm position, but allows the body to 'take over', thus allowing the natural reflex to establish itself as the norm without the conscious control of the cerebral cortex.

Table 1.7 *Righting reflexes*

Name of reflex	Action
Aural righting reflex	Organs of balance in inner ear. Three semi-circular canals are filled with fluid and have hairy linings. As the fluid moves, the cilia (hairs) interpret messages to adjust balance. When infected, say, during a cold, there is a distortion in the feedback sent to the nervous system, and a loss of balance may result.
Skin righting reflex	Receptors called *exteroceptors* are sensitive to pressure, and send messages on where the body weight is placed. Whether lying or standing on feet or hands, the receptors in the skin are active. They can be of help to dancers on stage under blinding lights who may not be able to rely on visual righting sensations. These reflexes can be improved by practising movements with eyes closed.
Visual righting reflex	We depend on these mainly to maintain balance. Try standing on one leg with eyes closed. Activation of visual reflex is attempting to keep both eyes on the horizontal. This is not so appropriate during tilting, and so then the other reflexes may be of more use.

high levels of tension to perform relatively easy tasks. In addition, localised tension in fingers, face, shoulders etc. interferes. Known as 'Beginner's Paralysis', this does lessen as the dancer's general skill level and co-ordination increase. The ability to inhibit undesired movement in one part of the body is necessary in order to focus on a new skill. The paralysis may return with each new difficult skill, but gradually tension is lowered. In this trial and error process, the dancer may try different muscular combinations, and may encounter blockage in motor learning and co-ordination.

> You cannot help facing movement blocks that will stand in your way. No one can remove these blocks except you yourself, and only when you are able to remove them will you eventually discover yourself. This is the only way to improve . . .
>
> (*Hanya Holm in* The Vision of Modern Dance, *1980*)

Movement blocks to co-ordination vary, and are due to any of the following:

- specific weakness in the musculature – e.g. an inelastic antagonistic muscle;
- variations in potential according to body type (*somatotype*): *mesomorphs*, *ectomorphs* and *endomorphs* have preferences for different types of movement. The mesomorph prefers faster turns and jumps, whereas ectomorphs prefer a slower pace. All have different areas of weakness. Mesomorphs need to stretch their heavier muscles, whereas ectomorphs work to improve strength and stamina. Endomorphs work to improve their endurance and may need to control their weight.

Similarly, males, with narrower hips and a more direct connection between the femur and the pelvis than females, tend to be able to run faster but have less of an outward hip rotation. And other individual anatomical differences include different

lengths of torso and legs: those who have long legs and a short torso easily allow their limbs to reach out around them, whereas the long-torso and short-legged dancer would be more mobile in the torso and have a greater range of tilt, curve and bend;
- stylistic blocks: unfamiliar patterns between techniques – say, between Release style and classical ballet technique.

The emphasis should be, whenever possible, on relaxing and allowing natural reflexes to guide the way. Once the conscious use of the cerebral cortex cuts in, the intuitive powers of the dancer have less of an influence, and stress and tension start to mount.

How you treat your body can influence your thoughts and feelings. Regular exercise makes one feel good, builds body awareness and should build confidence and an overall sense of health and well-being.

Tension, stress and the dancer

Constant demands to have utmost physical control results in high muscular tension, sometimes in specific parts of the body. This can cause muscular imbalance, pain and a subsequent *spread* of the tension. The specific demands of dance can increase levels of neuromuscular tension for dancers, making this a major cause of injury in dance training. An overanxious dancer may have high levels of neuromuscular tension, and this may have any of the following effects:

- There is more injury than usual (the accident-prone dancer).
- The dancer starts to imagine injury and then feels actual pain.
- A dancer pretends to be injured in order to avoid a stress situation.
- There is a loss of flexibility.
- There is a loss of smooth co-ordinated movement.
- There is an increase in the heart rate and blood pressure.

A relaxed dancer will have better co-ordination, circulation and respiration. Tight muscles can constrict blood vessels and so impede blood flow, cutting down the exchange of O_2 and CO_2. Any long-term effect of anxiety which impedes performance – like pretending to be injured – needs firm handling.

Pre-performance nerves, butterflies, breathlessness, nausea, dry mouth and a need to sit on the lavatory, are all normal nervous responses associated with an increased release of adrenalin into the blood. Once the dancer is on stage, however, the fear vanishes and the show goes on.

Sometimes, after a long intense period of training or rehearsal or a tour, dancers become stale. All the hours of repetition and practice are suddenly gone, and fatigue and depression follow. A dancer may be injury-prone at this time.

Injury itself may cause further anxiety. Injured dancers instead of treating symptoms early on, may continue to work until eventually they have to stop completely.

> Dancers are afraid of being seen as lazy or unworthy ... Injuries should be seen as a positive opportunity to resolve the problem, not as purely negative.
>
> (*A dancer in Dr P. Brinson and F. Dick in* Fit to Dance?, *1996*)

Symptoms such as a loss of appetite, weight loss, depression, tiredness and digestion problems are common. A change of routine or environment or a few words of support may be simple but effective anecdotes to aid the recharging of the emotional batteries.

80% of learning difficulties are related to stress. Remove the stress and you remove the difficulties.

(*David Whiteside, Gordon Stokes, President,* 3 in 1 Concepts, *Burbank, California 1987*)

Often, a dancer will be *unaware* of neuromuscular tension until pain is actually felt: it will have been gradually building up, allowing the nervous system to tolerate its presence. Until the tension is released, the dancer will not even be aware of its presence: it has been successfully hidden for so long because it would otherwise have interfered with progress in training.

There are certain areas of high tension which are most difficult to release:

- An habitual posture is a learned habit often adopted in order to over-achieve in a specific skill (leg higher/more turn-out etc.).
- The tension has become part of the *expected* feedback during dancing, and changing it can cause real feelings of disorientation and disturbance.
- Emotional or physical pain from the past is often cloaked in neuromuscular tension, and so reducing it can cause fear, often related to a loss of control. This may manifest itself as nausea, weeping or exhaustion, and needs careful handling. The need for relaxation techniques such as yoga, 'release' and the Feldankrais and Alexander techniques is now widely recognised.

Let us take an example of neuromuscular tension in the shoulder joint. Raising the arms and 'keeping the shoulders down' is a learned co-ordination. Naturally, the *scapulae* (shoulder blades) will rise. In training, this involves constant contraction of the antagonistic muscles, and so the tension level may build. It is the *latissimus dorsi* which holds down the scapula. Careful stretching and relaxation will lessen the tension.

The shoulder joint (see Figure 1.16) is an area of great mobility, and special conditioning is needed before such skills as lifting are taught. There is perhaps more concern here for male dancers, although much post-modern work makes this a potential danger area for females too.

Figure 1.16 *(a) shoulder girdle (b) shoulder joint*

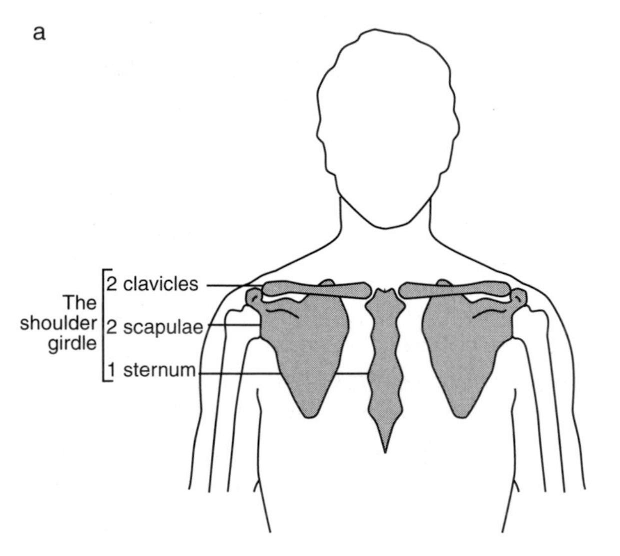

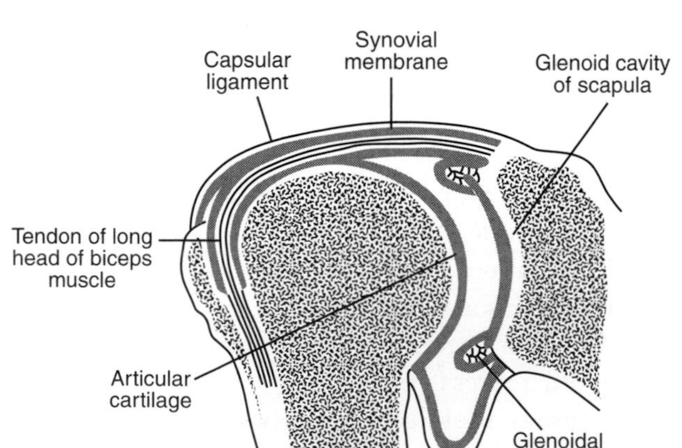

To show lifting: Nina Sorokina and Mikhail Lavrosky of the Bolshoi Ballet

A general strengthening of the following muscle groups should proceed by progressive overload to a point where more weight is being lifted than will be lifted in performance:

- the flexors/abductors of the shoulder: *deltoid*, *trapezius*, *serratus anterior*, *rhomboid major* and *minor*, *latissimus dorsi*, *pectoralis major*;
- the torso generally;
- the upward rotators of the scapula: *subscapularis*, *teres minor*, *infraspinatus*;
- the extensors of the knee and hip.

Six basic principles for safe lifting in dance

1. Maintain proper alignment.
2. Apply force close to the centre of gravity of the person to be lifted.
3. Apply force as close to the vertical as possible.
4. The lifter should lower their own centre of gravity with a plié in order to harness the powerful force from the knee and hip.
5. The lifted dancer should be kept as directly above the lifter's centre as possible.
6. Use the muscles of the leg, but the torso/back must also be strong and stable during the lift.

When lifting a partner above head height, abduction and flexion of the shoulders is important. There should be no backwards tilt in the lumbar spine. If the elbows or wrists are *swayback* (hypermobile), there may be an increased vulnerability to injury. In order to avoid injury, greater strength is needed.

Restriction of the dorsi-flexion of the wrists may also cause lifting problems.

Problems/injuries of the shoulder joint
The constant contraction increases tension deep in the muscle, and as a result the scapula will be pulled forward and eventually the muscles will go into spasm. This is known as *pectoralis minor syndrome*, and it may be painful to rotate the neck. There may also be numbness in the fingers and arm (on the *ulna* side). When the muscle is very tight, the nerve is pressed, in a way similar to *sciatica* in the hip. The source of the problem is mainly in the front in the *pectoralis minor*. Deep-pressure massage can relieve the pain, though it would seem that it takes considerable time for the posterior muscles – i.e. the *trapezius* and *deltoid* – to get the message that they can finally relax. *Pectoralis minor syndrome* is common in dancers because of the demands to keep the shoulders down. However, non-dancers such as typists, swimmers, flautists and string players are also susceptible.

Clearly, there are some complex co-ordinations and timings to be learnt in order to acquire correct lifting techniques. Learning any co-ordinations in dance has traditionally been taught by verbal instruction, 'monkey-see-monkey-do', and touching the dancer. This approach has been tried and tested over centuries of dancing. Relatively recently, however, a new school of thought has introduced alternative approaches which put more emphasis on the *inner self*. This holistic approach involves seeing life as a whole, with mind and body together; and it is an altogether more *internal* approach, starting from the inside out.

The kinesthetic sense, sensory feedback and imagery

The mind can work in a negative way in training, as we have read. It is only common sense, therefore, to assume that it can also be put to *positive* use – namely, by allowing our minds to use pictures and images that affect every cell in our bodies through sensory feedback. In the traditional list of the five senses – touch, taste, sight, hearing and smell – the forgotten *sixth* one is the *kinesthetic sense*. This involves the perception of *motion* and of *position*, and it depends on the proprioceptors and sensory organs involved in the righting reflexes. These send information to the central nervous system regarding muscle contraction, relaxation, joint position and speed of motion. Accurate kinesthetic perception requires the integration of this information with the perception of spatial co-ordinates, and it operates in the skills of balance, accuracy and the control of energy.

When the kinesthetic sense is operational, it can act as a link between mind and body in order to improve co-ordination. The receptors and brain centres can link up and use *imagery* to cause changes in, and to deepen the dancer's understanding of, movement. The post-modern dancer Remy Charlip called such release work 'bone meditations'.

> Take an image, let it hang in the mind, let the sensation of the thought dissolve through the body. Let the movement inside of the body . . . move the outside.
>
> (*Miranda Tufnell in* Body Space Image, *1990*)

- *Kinesthetic imagery* involves using feelings that accompany body movement, so that when a movement is performed correctly, it has a certain feel. For example, when doing foot 'pushes', use the image that the floor is covered with sharp pins to improve the use of the intrinsic muscles of the foot and the articulation of the arches and metatarsals. This exercise increases strength and mobility in the feet.

- *Visual imagery* involves a mind picture, maybe of a rainbow, which the fingertips may draw in the space above your head as you do large side-to-side triplets. It must relate to a *desired* shaping or placement of body parts, and be an image which you can hold in your mind's eye. Visual imagery can also be helpful for relaxation exercises. Set a scene in your mind which will be clear to you – say, a deserted beautiful beach where a warm soft breeze blows and the waves lap gently at the shore.
- *Anatomical imagery* can help with alignment; and as with all images, returning to the same picture or feelings each time a certain movement is executed should trigger the same muscle response, thereby improving accuracy and safe practice. Anatomical imagery is based on a sound understanding of body structure – of the size and shape of bones, joints and muscles.

TASK NINE

In pairs, play some quiet soft music in a warm quiet space. One person reads out the task slowly and quietly for the other who is lying in the constructive rest position:

'In a relaxed state, surround the head with a cushion of air, and let the jaw hang softly. Allow the brain to rest lightly in the bones of the skull. The brain is a control tower of information, sending and receiving, quietly humming, pouring, sifting. The brain sends messages that flow out into the spinal cord, down the spine and out to all over the body, networking to the six senses. Relax and listen to the world around you. Let the sounds and sights be felt and reflected through your body.

[Allow time here for the dancer to absorb these thoughts.]

'Open the body through the senses. Allow the body to move out amongst these sensations. Send these feelings back to the fluid-filled corridors of the mind where over 10 billion cells await the arrival of the information. Repeat this feeling of to-ing and fro-ing from brain, to body and outside a few more times.'

TASK TEN

Standing, let the shoulder girdle rest on a rounded ribcage. See the shoulder girdle like a ring circling, opening. See the scapulae like a pair of rafts floating on the ocean of the back. The arms hang from the scapulae. Imagine the scapulae as a pair of ears opening … listening out to the tips of the shoulders … down in the lift to the basement of the spine.

(*Based on an image in* Body Space Image, *Tufnell, 1990*)

- *Body image*. These days, the stereotyped image of the dancer's sylph-like body is gradually being eroded away. Yet, *anorexia nervosa* and related illnesses are still common. Dancers who have a negative body image, or who block out parts of their body that displease them, may be on the road to injury, failure and illness. A complete, clear and accurate body image is required for dance work. Too often these days we are bombarded with media-approved images of men and women. Whilst we know anyone can dance well, and whilst our teacher may encourage all the politically correct attitudes, there are still the magazines, television programmes etc contradicting what we want to believe.
- *Mental rehearsal:* this is an imagery technique that uses the body image to improve motor skills. You review the performance of an action in the mind. The aim is to see yourself executing the desired move effortlessly and accurately e.g. a pirouette. Many believe that this technique releases impulses over the neuron pathways and taps into natural movement. New co-ordinations result as appropriate muscles are triggered. Research has found that this technique produces action potential in the muscles.
- *Motor memory* is separate from the kinesthetic sense. It is stored in the cerebral cortex and *assisted* by the kinesthetic sense. Motor memory is developed by repeating movements in class or in rehearsal. As with any repetitive activity, the ability to pick up a movement quickly improves, and a larger and larger storehouse of movement pictures (engrams) to draw from is developed.

The mind is a muscle.

(*From the dance of the same name by Yvonne Rainer, 1966*)

The movement becomes second nature as it is memorised. The more experience you have in memorising movements, the easier memorising *new* movements becomes, because the greater the range of movements you have already memorised, the *smaller* the amount of new information that needs to be remembered with a new movement. So, just like the training of a muscle, the more you use the memory, the fitter it becomes. Indeed, the physical senses of experienced dancers are so well-tuned to their minds that they can later reproduce a movement learnt *by observation only*. This is one reason why repetition of movement in class is so important.

PHYSICAL SKILLS IN DANCE TRAINING

The concept of co-ordination in dance training is a complex one. It takes into consideration the many aspects of the nervous system in the psychology of dancers, as well as psychological strategies which can improve the quality of training. What are the actual skills which a dancer may improve by adopting such strategies? A general heading of 'co-ordination' covers a number of individual skills. These are listed below, and along with each is a task which adopts the use of psychological strategies as mentioned earlier. The skills are:

- control of energy
- balance
- accuracy.

Control of energy

The image of energy flowing from the centre of the body outwards is a vital one for dancers. In classical ballet, the lifted centre is the accepted norm. Learning to lift the weight up from the centre of the body, away from the pull of gravity, gives a look and feel of lightness, and also enables you to move, stop and change direction easily. (Do not hold the breath here.) Movements such as plié, falls, turns and jumps are all performed more safely and effectively with a lifted centre. In a fall, the centre keeps lifting as the body drops. This prevents too hard a landing and enables recovery for the next move (similarly for a jump).

A swing requires the dancer to drop with gravity on the downward phase. Too *much* tension/resistance will prevent the arc of the swing from giving in to gravity.

TASK ELEVEN

Standing, swing one arm back and forth. Notice how energy is required to lift your arm, but that gravity takes over on the downward phase. Try swinging other parts of the body – the leg, neck, hips, upper body from the waist. Too much resistance, as you will see, will block the natural swing.

Balance

This has to do with:

- alignment and stability;
- directing energies through the body.

Balance is developed as a dance skill through training. Stability is decreased by lessening the base on the floor – thus, balancing on, say, one foot makes it more difficult to keep the centre of gravity over the base. Energies are directed out from the centre through the extremities of all the limbs, and whenever one body part reaches away from the centre, an opposing part has to be stretched in the opposite direction in order to maintain balance. For example, on a rise (*relevé*), balancing is easier if you think about pressing down smoothly into the floor whilst sending energy up through the centre.

To show balance. Bedlam Dance Company 'In the Third Person', 1997. Dancer Rachel Krische. Photo by Chris Nash.

Make a drawing copying the figure in the photograph of Rachel Krische. Fill in arrows which show the direction that energy is being directed to maintain balance.

As mentioned earlier the *crossed extensor reflex* is a natural muscle co-ordination. It is crucial to maintenance of balance in many movements. Look back to the dancer on the left in the photograph for Task Four and you can see it in action. Her left arm and shoulder are in diagonal opposition to her right hip and leg. Often beginners in dance class can become so confused and tense that they lose touch with this natural reflex so you can see walking actions take on a rather awkward robot-like look. As the cerebellum overloads with too many new co-ordinations, movement becomes over conscious and contrived, cutting out the usual natural reflexes. Similarly dance styles may deliberately cut out such reflexes for expressive effect. This occurred when Nijinsky used parallel actions to give the two-dimensional look in his *Rite of Spring* (1913) and required the dancers to 'unlearn' their trained oppositional skills.

Dancers mainly use the eyes to maintain balance, e.g. when spotting turns, but blinding stage lights may lessen their effectiveness. This is when the other *righting reflexes* come in handy. The aural organs of the ears and the skin *exteroceptors* are both essential to good balance. In class try doing some movements with eyes closed in order to sharpen your awareness of the other righting reflexes.

Being *centred* is crucial to achieving good balance. Centring is both a physical and a psychological concept: it refers to the *physical* centre of gravity and, psychologically, to the satisfying *feeling* of being whole and grounded.

In ballet, the placement of the centre is fairly stable in order to enable multiple pirouettes and so on, but in modern genre the centre shifts more frenetically as the body tilts, curves, falls, bends and extends continuously.

Accuracy

The dancer must be able to move not only well but also accurately. This comes about with the ability to reproduce movement that has been seen in a demonstration. Beginners need to see movement in terms of placement, shape and direction. As dancers become more experienced in co-ordination, they are able to see more of a whole picture and yet be sensitive to detailed positioning at the same time.

Dancers also need to develop sensitivity to changes in dynamics and spatial orientation, so that these may also be performed accurately each time. For dance, the fullest movement potential of each individual dancer should be developed, and whatever the genre, this entails controlling movements more efficiently, harmoniously and expressively. This makes them more pleasing to watch for the audience, safer for the dancer and, for the choreographer, presumably more capable of expressing the intentions of the dance.

The use of breath with the movement can help accuracy. It also adds vitality and reduces tension in the body. And it further assists with the control of active muscles and with the relaxation of those not required. The overall effect is to give movement an effortless look and a greater expressive quality – in phrasing, rhythm, balance, jumping and stretching. *Restricted* breathing will limit both the movement of the thorax and stamina.

Tasks Twelve and Thirteen offer a few things to try which show how breathing can either enhance or restrict movement.

TASK TWELVE

1 Lie with arms above head, but half-bent, and legs relaxed. Check with your hand to see how much arch there is in your thoracic/lumbar spine. Breathe in through the nose, stretching your arms away from your feet. Breathe out forcefully, making a hissing sound, allowing arms, legs and back to relax. Imagine your lungs to be two balloons emptying and filling. Repeat three times. Check to see if the spine arch has lessened – i.e. relaxed.

2 Stand with your weight on both feet, arms abducted to your sides. Lift one leg directly in front of your body to a comfortable height and exhale at the same time. Release the breath beyond the toes.

3 Improvise and compose a short original phrase of movement. Practice it until it is memorised. Repeat it, trying out different patterns of breath until you find one which is most suitable for the movement.

4 From standing, collapse down and exhale. Rebound up, and inhale. Repeat a few times. Now reverse the breathing pattern, and choose which of the two worked the best for you. (Note: in general, dancers inhale when a movement suspends and exhale when giving in to gravity.)

Well-timed breathing also reduces stress and tension which are a major cause of injury in dancers. Relaxation techniques can play a crucial part in safe practice, and it is ultimately each dancer's responsibility to ensure adequate rest and relaxation for themselves. This may be a regular daily routine attached to a class or rehearsal schedule, or participation in yoga or meditation or some other relaxation-based technique. A lack of it can produce staleness and proneness to injury (real or imagined).

TASK THIRTEEN

Work in pairs. Lie down flat, and close your eyes. Allow your partner to take one arm; do not resist or assist as it is lifted a little by the hand. Allow it to be moved up, down and sideways and rotated, giving the full weight to your partner. Where resistance is met, this is a likely point where you hold neuromuscular tension.

Repeat with the other arm and legs, and as you work, note where points of tension are discovered in your body.

CO-ORDINATION – A SUMMARY

In training, the dancer is clearly engaged in a complicated day-to-day workload, not least of which is to improve the many complex co-ordinations of the nervous system as demanded by any dance style or genre. Be it ballet, modern, post-modern, African or South Asian, all ask a great deal in terms of co-ordination. Control of energy, balance and accuracy are all essential when performing any dance actions.

General body maintenance

To be fit for dance, all the aspects mentioned in this chapter are essential. What is required is a balance of exercise, training in skills, rest and relaxation, and finally an adequate diet.

DIET

> You are what you eat.
>
> (*Brian and Roberta Morgan in* Brain Food, *1987*)

So what are *you* then? A can of diet coke? That means you're sweet but go flat too quickly. A chocolate bar? Fatty and satisfying but prone to constant cravings. A fresh mackerel? A cool alert customer. Recent research has proven that eating oily fish regularly provides the right chemicals to improve transmission between brain cells. So the old wives' tale that fish is brain food is true! Therefore, if you wish to improve your co-ordination in dance training, then cut out the junk food and settle for the fish.

Dancers are notorious for food abuse, and possibly even more so for pretending that it is not happening. Mention the word 'diet' to a dancer, and the response will be cloaked in terms of *eating less*. 'Diet' should be a term which implies eating a sensible range of foods adequately. Enough calories, vitamins and minerals etc. must be consumed to keep you healthy now and in later years.

Basic considerations are:

- what to eat
- when to eat
- how to eat
- eating disorders.

> We need to reeducate dancers and get them to establish good nutritional habits. They should be eating carbohydrate and eating every three hours. We want the dancers to be slim, but with healthy, strong muscle tone so that they can resist injury.
>
> (*Tony Geeves in* New Scientist, 25 *December/1 January 1994*)

Appearances can be deceptive. You may look thin, but snack-based high-fat diets produce underdeveloped muscles which leave space for a substantial layer of fat on a seemingly slim body.

What to eat

An ordinary person with a quiet lifestyle needs 1,500 calories daily just to maintain normal body functioning and minimum activity. It is only reasonable, therefore, to assume that dancers need more in the region of *2,000* calories daily. About two-thirds of calorie intake is needed just to maintain the normal functioning of muscles, organs and body temperature. The rest of the day's activities – eating, walking, dressing, working, playing – need about 800 calories. The equation is easy – whatever calories we use up day-to-day come from food. If you consume more calories than you use, you put on weight. If you consume fewer calories than you need, you lose weight.

The following are essential components of a healthy diet:

- *proteins* – for building up the body;
- *carbohydrates* – to provide energy;
- *fats* – for energy and flavour;
- *vitamins* – small but essential;
- *minerals* – for bones and blood;
- *water* – for basic physiological functions.

Table 1.8 *Essential components for a healthy diet*

Nutrient	Sources	Needed for	Amount per day	Lack of: the effects
Proteins	Lean meat, fish, dairy, bread, cereals, beans	Muscle and tissue development and repair. Normal metabolism	40 g per day – 400 g bread or 200 g meat	Loss of muscle. Illness – e.g. flu – causes loss of protein
Carbohydrates (sugars, starch, cellulose)	Sugar, potatoes, wheat, rice, cereals	Energy	50–60% of food intake	Fatigue – weakness, headaches, irritability, poor co-ordination, nervousness
Fats	Dairy, meat, eggs, oily fish, cooking oils/fats	Improving the taste and feeling full. High energy source = high calories! Carry vitamins A, D, E & K		Too much is more the issue: heart disease, high level of cholesterol in blood
Vitamins	Most foods, particularly vegetables	Proper body functioning	Small daily amounts; e.g. 30 g vitamin C, 1 g vitamin B12	Vitamin D: rickets, bones soften. Vitamin C: scurvy. Too much: vitamin A: harms eyes; Vitamin D: upsets metabolism
Minerals	Most foods	Producing enzymes and hormones which control a number of functions in: blood, bones, teeth	Some, like calcium (in dairy products), are needed in large amounts. Others, like zinc, sodium, potassium, in smaller amounts	Lack of iron (18 g): anaemia. Lack of iodine: low metabolic rate, energy loss, weight gain. Lack of calcium (1200 mg daily): long-term brittle bones
Water	Water! Tea and coffee are diuretics and increase fluid loss. So does alcohol	Physiological processes, e.g. flush waste from kidneys maintain blood volume, sweating	Drink plenty daily	Dehydration, muscle fatigue, cramp, injury, exhaustion

The reduction of specific fatty areas, like under the upper arm, can be brought about by certain strengthening exercises for targeted spots. For example, lots of abdominal curls will remove fat from the abdomen; and similarly with strengthening exercises for the hips, thighs and upper arms.

Starvation diets are dangerous, and not likely to succeed. They cause dehydration and long-term damage to basic body tissues and functioning if followed regularly. Similarly, the spot reduction of weight in specific sites such as the thighs is not helped by wearing plastic trousers. These do not reduce fat, and in fact promote a loss of fluid and so can cause dehydration and heat stroke; they are only useful for keeping warm. The best way to lose weight is a calorie-controlled diet in combination with aerobic exercise. Burning off fat from all over the body by breaking it down for use as energy is the result of aerobic exercise.

Losing weight should be a carefully monitored affair. Height and weight tables are not the best way to gauge whether you are over- or underweight. The use of skin-fold callipers to measure fat on, say, the triceps are recommended and the fat here should not exceed 8–10 mm in women and 6–8 mm in men. Losing weight is a long-term process: it takes months.

Remember, the calories required for energy will vary with the individual metabolic rate. *Muscle* tissue burns off calories more quickly than other forms of tissue because it has a higher metabolic rate. It is also heavier than *fat* tissue. There is a possible cause of confusion here. Through exercise, muscle tissue builds up, and therefore weight increases. Weight loss is thus not an indication of fitness. Although muscle weighs heavier, it also burns off more calories, so weight loss is easier! With regular exercise, dancers who burn calories slowly can become high calorie burners (there is a general increase in the metabolic rate as muscle increases), and fat stores are reduced more rapidly. More muscle and less fat results in an improvement of body shape and general fitness, but not necessarily weight control.

There is nothing nutritionally wrong with being vegetarian; in fact, nutritionists favour such diets. However, the recommendation is to eat foods from all food groups. Eating more carbohydrates or protein than fats will ensure fewer calories and more energy.

When to eat

An important consideration here is that when the body is digesting food, the blood flow moves away from muscles to the digestive system. Obviously, this would not, therefore, be a good time to be exercising. Pre-performance eating needs careful scheduling. A small meal at least two hours before the show gives enough time for digestion. Foods like pasta or a sandwich, containing complex carbohydrates, are best because they will allow a steady release of energy throughout the performance. Concentrated sweet fluids are to be avoided because their absorption is too slow to enhance energy levels. These fluids may produce a peak of glucose in the blood (the body will release a burst of insulin to deal with this) and then a fall and a trough (see Figure 1.17) below the normal level which will make the dancer feel fatigued. And obviously, a tired dancer is one prone to injury. The daily rush and demands on a dancer can create a tendency to skip meals. Several small meals daily – 'grazing' – is an effective eating regime to accommodate such schedules.

Figure 1.17 *Changes in blood sugar level after drinking sweet liquids*

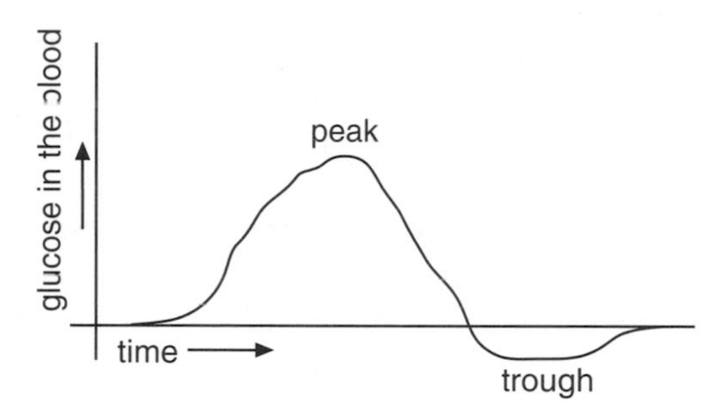

TASK FOURTEEN

Make a large (A3-size) poster which gives advice to dancers on what to eat. Use drawings, magazine cuttings, food labels etc. Make it bright and informative. Research the calorific values of food to include on the poster.

How to eat

Weight loss and weight gain are often concerns for dancers, and this reflects the preoccupation with abnormal thinness that permeates today's society. Gymnasts, models, some athletes and more and more men are targets of this 'look'. The eating disorders which arise from these unreasonable demands will be discussed below.

Read the quotation below and think very carefully about what this dancer is *really* saying. The definition of a 'good' dance student may be considered dangerous and harmful to methods and aims of dance training:

> Some critics abroad ... they do take the rude word – take the piss about me, how I am fat. I take it like a good student. I know ballet is aesthetic ... if I do a prince I have to look like a prince. But it's not completely up to me. I can become anorexic, but please give me more shows so that I can become anorexic quicker. Rather than sit at home and think, 'Hmmm, you big thing, don't eat ... I know it's wrong to say this, but here (UK) it doesn't matter how girls look as long as boys are tall and thin. I see many girls here not quite correct to be a dancer. In Russia they would never even be accepted into the company.
>
> (*Irek Mukhamedov in interview with Ismene Brown*, the Daily Telegraph, *May 1998*)

So what do princes, (or princesses) look like? Whose choice is it? Who is it 'up to', if not each individual dancer? Should a dancer consciously choose to become anorexic? He complains that the male dancers have to conform to an anorexic look and, even more incredibly, doesn't question this but insists that this so-called 'correct' appearance should apply to the females. Good grief! These are rather thoughtless words which require careful scrutiny. They are loaded with serious, and on occasion life-threatening, implications.

TASK FIFTEEN

Keep a food diary over two weeks of all the foods, and their weights, that you eat. From this you can work out the total calories taken in and divide this figure by 14 to obtain your daily intake. Compare your food diary with an *activity* diary for the same period. You can then work out the daily expenditure of calories per 24 hours. Then you will know the average number of calories you will need daily to maintain your present weight. If weight loss is desirable, decrease your daily intake by 500 calories - which comes to a weight loss, per week, of 2 lb or 900 g. If weight *gain* is required, *add* 500 calories daily to give 2 lb or 900 g weight gain per week.

Eating disorders

> Ballet dancers have a notoriously high incidence of anorexia and bulimia eating disorders in which dieting becomes an obsession.
>
> (*Tony Geeves*, New Scientist, *25 December 1993/1 January 1994*)

Anorexia nervosa is self-starvation and *bulimia* is a related disorder involving binges of eating and then vomiting, the abuse of laxatives or diuretics, or fasting. Both of these disorders will disrupt menstruation and give a long-term risk of *osteoporosis* (thinning of the bones). The first conference about osteoporosis was held in 1993. Many findings were brought to light. Here are some of them:

- Poor nutrition may be a contributory cause to hormonal imbalance; and when hormonal imbalance is combined with intensive exercise, the menstrual cycle may be upset. Any dancer weighing less than 47 kg (7 st 6 lb) is at risk. (This information was supplied by Dr Ashley Grossman, Professor of Neuroendocrinology (nerves, glands and hormones) St Bartholomew's Hospital.)
- In adolescence, 50% of the bone mass is acquired. Loss of bone density correlated with missed periods over a five-year span. Adequate nutrition is essential if stress fractures are to be avoided. (This information was supplied by Dr Victor Grossman, GP to Birmingham Royal Ballet.)

As always, prevention is better than cure. Taking extra calcium and avoiding smoking, drinking and drugs are advised. Oestrogen therapy for younger dancers can help alleviate loss of period and fragile bones later in life.

> In the next decade it is not inconceivable that a dancer who becomes crippled with arthritis or suffers an osteoporotic fracture will sue her company or school for knowingly exposing her to undue risk, in the same way as sufferers from repetitive stress injuries do now. Will it take the threat of litigation to make the companies' artistic directors, choreographers and teachers take this problem seriously?
>
> (*Fiona Dick in* Dance Theatre Journal, *1994*)

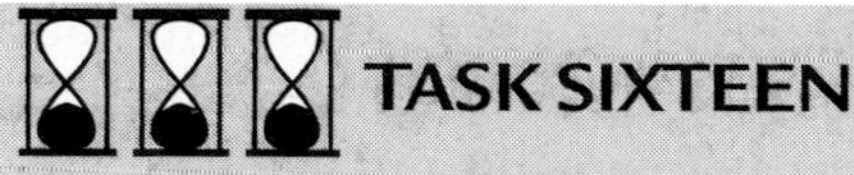

TASK SIXTEEN

Improving Own Learning and Performance

You could do this task at the start of every term as part of an ongoing self-improvement programme.

- Target three areas that you need to improve on from the list below. You may need to consult your teacher to identify them.
- Describe your strategy for improvements and the progress in anatomical detail. Again you may need to consult your teacher or a friend to help you monitor changes. You should evaluate how effective your programme is.

Area targeted for improvement	Describe strategy	Needs improvement	Working towards	Achieved
E.g. Flexibility of hamstrings	– A regular routine of reciprocal stretching. Monitor improvements regularly.	✓ 2nd Sept. Unable to touch toes. Hands at calf level.	✓ 2nd Nov. Have kept to routine once every two days. Hands now a little lower – lumbar spine feeling more relaxed. ✓ 2nd Dec. Didn't keep up routine regularly so not much more progress. ✓ 2nd Jan. Christmas – Blew it! New Year's Resolution – to keep to routine.	✓ 29th Feb. I am writing this whilst stretching. Mission accomplished!
Copy this table into your own portfolio. Select and enter three target areas.				
Strength of				
Stamina				
Alignment of				
Co-ordination				
Control				
Balance				
Accuracy				
Motor memory				
Attention to:				
▮ warming-up				
▮ cooling-down				
Diet				
Smoking				
Understanding and safe use of Technical terms e.g. turn-out				
Safe practices; clothing/floors				
treatment of injury				

In extreme cases, both disorders can be fatal. If you think that you have such problems, or that a friend does, then it is important for you or your friend to talk about it and seek help. Some symptoms are: obsessive preoccupation with weight, guilt about eating, unrealistically high expectations of oneself.

Diet – a summary

The food you eat should be organised to give you:

- maximum energy;
- minimum body fat;
- enough variety to ensure efficient body functions and so avoid injury.

This chapter should have given you enough

information in text, pictures and practical assignments to increase your understanding of what your body needs and how it functions. *You* have the main responsibility for its maintenance. Be good to it, and it should last you a lifetime of dancing and living.

References and resources

BOOKS AND ARTICLES

Arnheim, D. D., *Dance Injuries: Their Prevention and Care*, London: Dance Books, 1992

Blakey, P., *The Muscle Book*, Stafford: UK Bibliotek, 1992

Brinson, Dr. P. and Dick, F. *Fit to Dance?*, London: Calouste Gulbenkian Foundation, 1996

Dance UK (ed.), *The Dancer's Charter for Health and Welfare*, London: Dance UK, 1992

Dancing Times, *Study Supplement 5 'A' Level Anatomy* (A. McCormack) *Dancing Times*, LXXX 953, February 1990

Dick, F., 'Fit but fragile', *Dance Theatre Journal*, vol. 11, no. 2, 1994 (article about osteoporosis)

Ellfeldt, L., *Dance from Magic to Art*, Iowa: William C. Brown Company, 1976

Foley, M., *Dance Spaces*, Arts Council of England, London, 1994

Geeves, T., *The Difference Between Being Warm and Warming Up*, Dance UK Information Sheet No. 3, Dance UK, 1991

Howse, J. and Hancock, S., *Dance Technique and Injury Prevention*, A. & C. Black, 1988

Morrison Brown, J., (ed.), *The Vision of Modern Dance*, London: Dance Books, 1980

Ryan, A. J. and Stephens, R. S. (eds), *The Healthy Dancer*, Dance Books, 1987

Sweigard, L., *Human movement potential: its ideokinetic facilitation*, New York: Dodd, Mead & Co, 1974

Tufnell, M. and Crickmay, A. *Body, Space Image*, Dance Books, 1990

Vincent, L., *Dancer's Book of Health*, New Jersey: Princeton Book Co., 1988

Vincent, L., *Competing With the Sylph*, New York: Andre and Mckeel Inc., 1979

VIDEO

Ballet Floor Barre by Nicole Vasse, New York: Dance Videos, 45 mins, £15.99, 1995. Includes warm-up, work on turn-out and pelvic control, flexibility and cool-down.

WEB SITES

- For anatomy/injury treatment, causes and prevention

www.eskeletons.org – interactive learning with human anatomy, great fun!

www.sportballet.com – the ABC's of injury prevention and fundamental movement mechanics.

www.enteract.com – Stretching and Flexibility – everything you ever wanted to know, Brad Appleton.

- For 'alternative' techniques to improve safe and effective movement:

www.alexandertechnique.com
www.feldenkrais.com
www.pilatesfoundation.com
www.skinnerreleasing.com

- For general interest in dancers working in class and rehearsal:

www.danceservice.co.uk/dancers-log – Follows Catherine Quinn in rehearsals for Siobhan Davies Dance Company. Very informative for any aspects of dance training, making, rehearsing and performing dance.

www.danceuk.org

www.ndirect.co.uk/chrisnash – dance photography

TWO

THE CONSTITUENT FEATURES OF DANCE: MOVEMENT AND DANCERS

With every new ballet that I produce I seek to empty myself of some plastic obsession and every ballet I do is, for me, the solving of a balletic problem.

(*Sir Frederick Ashton in* Dance from Magic to Art, *1976*)

Composing dances may be said to be a process of *problem-solving*. Dance training prepares the body for the physical demands of dance and improves co-ordination skills. The next step may be making your own dances. Using the physical intellect imaginatively to compose dance involves learning about the components that make up a dance. Making dances, as outlined in Figure 2.1, is the focus of this chapter. The rehearsal process is further examined in Chapter 6.

Figure 2.1 *Process of composing a dance*

Idea (content)
Research
↓
Experiment with putting ideas into movement (improvisation)
↓
Select the most appropriate movements
↓
Refine and organise the structure and form a cohesive whole
↓
Rehearse, perform and evaluate success

As choreographer, you must be able to make clear for your dancers exactly what movements you require. This will help you to collaborate with the dancers and bring out their best in performance. Therefore, you need to be able to observe and analyse in order to find the most appropriate and successful movements. You also need a sound knowledge of the rules – even if only to go on to *break* them successfully.

TASK ONE

(This is a good task to do if you happen to be injured or ill.) Watch a class of dancers perform a taught phrase. Choose three of the dancers, and make notes on:

- individual differences in how they perform the phrase;
- individual differences in how *successful* they are in performing the phrase.

In addition, evaluate *why* some are more successful than others, and suggest how those who are less successful can improve their performance.

Figure 2.2 is a mind map showing the various constituent features that all dances, of any genre, possess:

- the movement components;
- the dancers;
- the physical setting;
- the accompaniment (the aural setting).

The last two features will be discussed in Chapters 3 and 4. Let us now analyse the first two in detail.

The movement components

The basic movement components are:

- actions
- space
- time
- dynamics.

THE SIX DANCE ACTIONS

There are three basic anatomical actions that the body is capable of performing: flexion, extension and rotation (see Chapter 1). The dancer in training will use these three basic actions in endless combinations to produce the six dance actions. These are:

- travelling (locomotion);
- elevation;
- turning;
- gesture (isolation);
- stillness;
- falling.

Travelling (locomotion)

Walking is a fundamental human activity, one which takes us from A to B.

> Every time you step you fall only to catch yourself from falling . . .
>
> (*Laurie Anderson from the album* Big Science)

The natural human walk involves heel down first. The endless other possibilities – rolling, knee walks, sliding, crawling etc. – are where choreography begins.

TASK TWO

- Walk slowly, feeling the moment of loss of balance as your centre shifts forward.
- Gradually accelerate to a fast walk – feel the natural walking action of heel down first (*dorsi flexion*).
- Change to a stylised dance walk: toe down first (*plantar flexion*).
- Carefully explore and experiment with different walks: on heels; on toes/balls of feet (*metatarsal arch*); on the outside of the foot; on the inside of the foot.
- Walk on different levels.
- Walk in different directions.

Figure 2.2 *Mind map of constituent features of a dance*

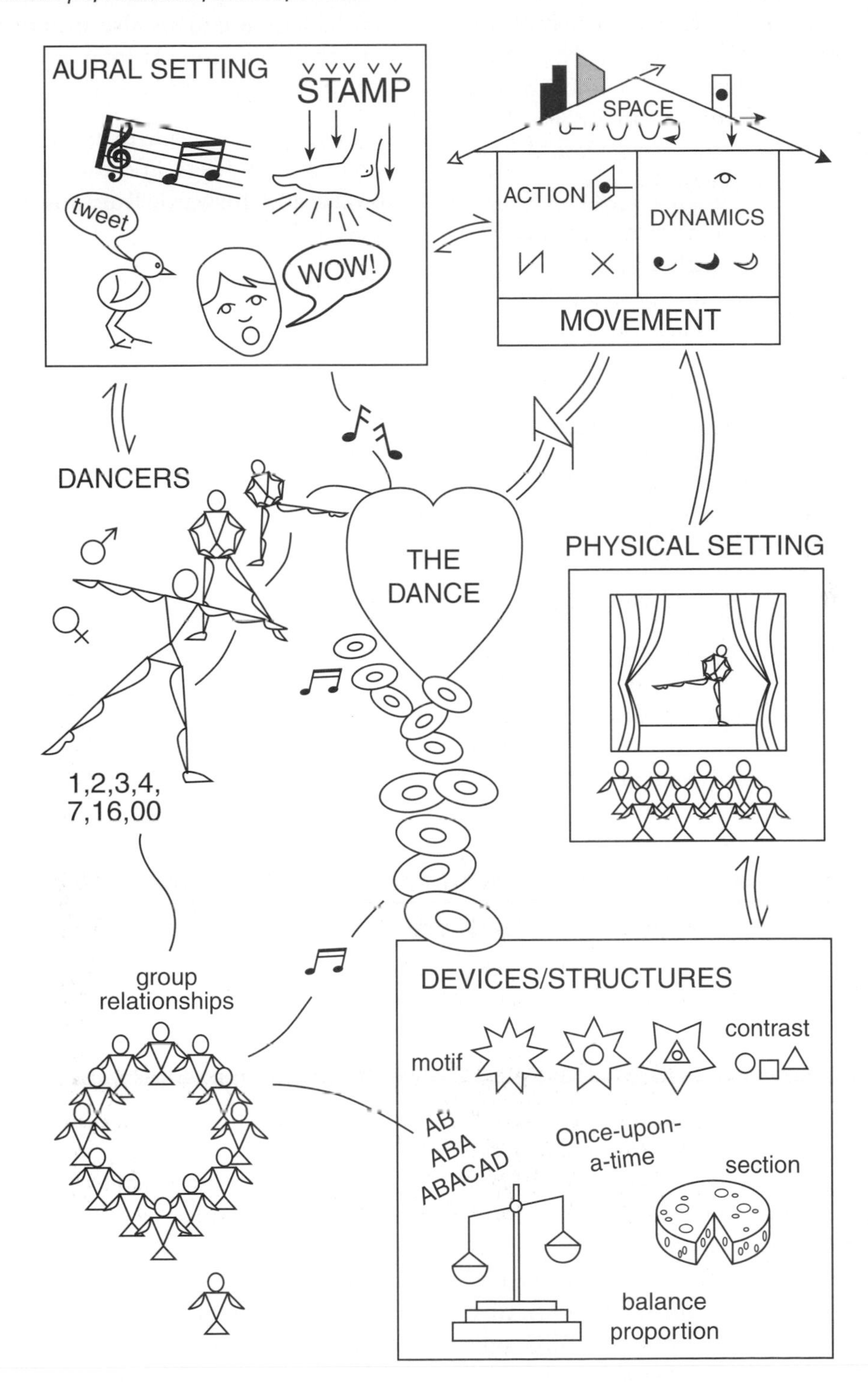

Walking involves an even rhythm. The ankle must extend to push off the back foot and shift the body weight forward. The centre needs to pull up to maintain a smooth, even quality. The eyes should focus on eye level, not downwards, and the arms should work naturally in opposition to the legs.

A *parallel walk* is more common in modern dance, while walking with *turn-out* from the hips is more usual in classical ballet - although the famous classical dancer and choreographer Vaslav Nijinsky caused a sensation by breaking this rule when he used a parallel walk in *L' Après-midi d'un Faune* (1912). Nijinsky wanted to give a look of classical Greek friezes in two-dimensions. So he used parallel legs and arms also unnaturally parallel to the leg action. At its première, the audience at the Paris Opera rioted!

Running is a fast walk using a greater extension of feet and legs, and the emphasis here is upward and forward. Running also involves an even rhythm.

Runs, triplets and prances are all variations of walking. Triplets are in a 3/4 waltz time signature, with the accent on the first downward step. Prances are runs which emphasise the upward knee lift sharply with a sudden extension of the foot.

TASK THREE

Select three from the following: walking; runs; triplets; prances; skips.

- Combine them to make a phrase which can be repeated on alternate sides continuously. Keep it simple - i.e. no arms, jumps, falls.
- Practice the phrase until you have it very clear and accurate.
- Repeat it four times.
- Notate it to show the repetitions.

When a number of steps are patterned together, they become recognisable dances. Frederick Ashton's use of folk steps in *La Fille Mal Gardée* (*The Unchaperoned Daughter*, 1960) includes clog dance, maypole dancing and a Morris dance.

Matthew Bourne often uses social dance steps and styles. In the 'Country' section of his *Town and Country* (1991), he makes a reference to Ashton's *La Fille* when peasants do a clog dance. But Bourne's is humorous satire of the upper classes who hunt and shoot around the peasant dance and the whole parodies the unrealistic, romantic view of nature. In *Late Flowering Lust* (1994 for BBC television) he used Morris Dance and social dances of the 1930s such as the Charleston and the Turkey Trot.

Other types of travelling, such as walking on the hands, are used in dances. In *Strange Fish* (*DV8*, 1992) a male dancer walks on his hands rising to the challenge of his macho identity. Rolling and sliding are used to travel by the ghost characters in Christopher Bruce's *Ghost Dances* (1981). Choosing these travelling movements expresses that they are creatures of the underworld.

Elevation

Elevation involves rising from the floor, in a jump or in relevé on a half-toe or en pointe. This is an exciting part of any choreography.

To show travelling on the hands: V-Tol Dance Company in 'And nothing but the truth' (1998)

Here we are again with both feet planted firmly in the air.

(*Hugh Scanlon, British Trade Union leader*)

TASK FOUR

1 In Figure 2.3, a number of folk steps are shown in Labanotation (see p216). Read and then dance the scores.

2 With a partner, compose a short duet which uses a variety of contacts – e.g. ballroom hold, link arms, hold waist, hands on partner's shoulders. (Music suggestions: Cajun music by Balfa Brothers' *Arcadian Memories*, Malcolm Arnold's *Dances*.)

Every human movement has three phrases:

1 preparation

2 action

3 recovery.

These are particularly clear in the action of jumping:

1 Preparation: bend knees; lift centre, rib cage and head.

2 Action: extend feet and legs strongly and

Figure 2.3 *Notation for Task Four*

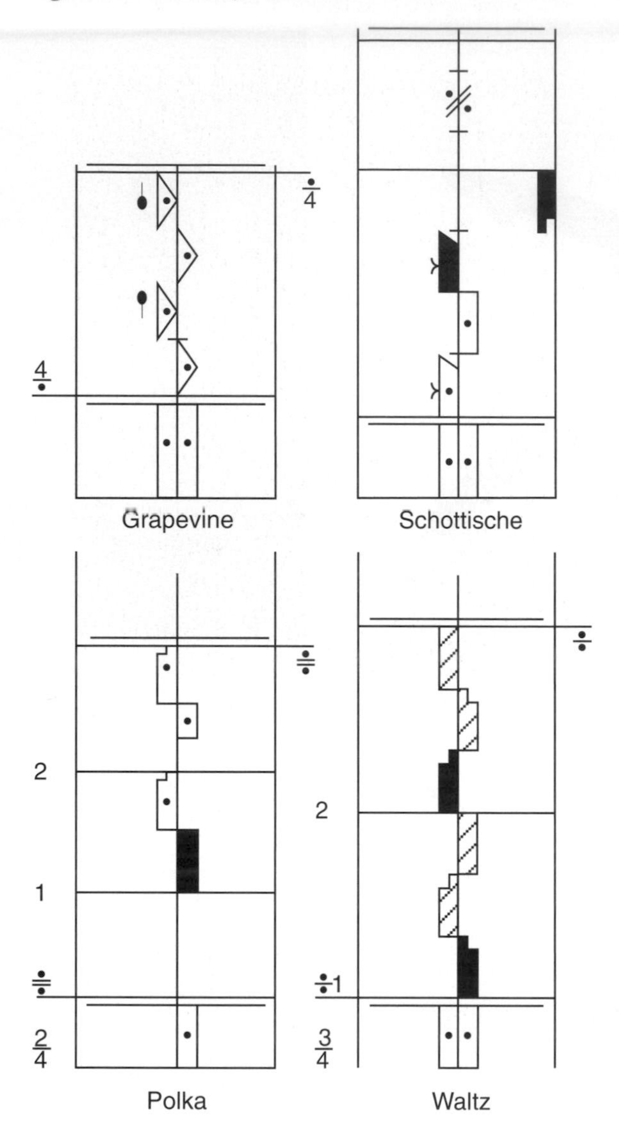

suddenly to take off – lifting arms may assist upward thrust; breathe in; lift focus.

3 Recovery: for safety and the protection of the Achilles heel, always land 'through the foot' – i.e. toe-ball-heel to floor; bend knees; maintain alignment and lift from centre on landing. Extend legs to standing.

As noted in Chapter 1, sometimes beginners, in an effort to take off, over-contract the muscles of the body, and a 'bucking' effect is seen in the air. Encouragement to *relax* in the air is needed here.

Jumps can be identified by whether the take-off and landing are on one foot or both. You only have two feet, so clearly the permutations are:

- *hop:* take off from one foot, land on the same foot;

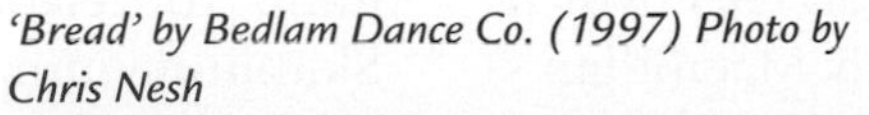

'Bread' by Bedlam Dance Co. (1997) Photo by Chris Nesh

- *leap:* take off from one foot, land on the other foot;
- *jump:* take off from two feet, land on the two feet;
- *sissone:* take off from two feet, land on one foot;
- *assemblé:* take off from one foot, land on two feet.

TASK FIVE

1. Notate the above five jumps, and label them by name.
2. Compose a phrase of movement which contains these five jumps in any order. Add steps and repetitions as desired.

Other details – like rotation of the legs, the use of the free leg(s) in the air, flexed or extended feet, the arm position, turning, travelling and so on – give jumps endless expressive potential. Jumping can burst upwards suddenly, propel powerfully forwards or sideways. A jump may soar, like leaps arcing through the air, or use arms swinging in opposition to enhance the effect of suspension. When combined with runs, the leap has a spectacular look. Landings can differ too. A rebound into *another* jump gives a bouncy effect and expresses something quite different from falling to the floor on landing. (What might the latter type of landing express to an audience?)

In *Nympheas* (1976) by Robert Cohan, two-foot-to-two-foot jumps with deep pliés on landings are used effectively in one section danced by the men, and give the impression of frogs springing between the pads of waterlilies.

In *The Drinking Song of Earthly Sorrows*, which is the first section of Kenneth Macmillan's *The Song of the Earth* (1965), six men leap and jump to celebrate the joys of the world. Skimming jumps are seen in Siobhan Davies' *White Man Sleeps* (1988).

TASK SIX

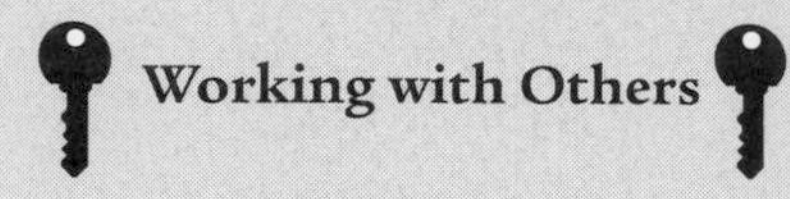

1  Combine lively jumps with travelling close to the floor (crawl, roll, slide, knee walks etc.) to create a short solo of surprises. Try to incorporate sudden changes of level and attitude. (Suggested music: *The Mission*, Ennio Morricone, CDV2402 - various tracks.)

2  Combine your solo with those of two or three other dancers to make a short trio. Ask spectators to describe what they see and to suggest titles.

Turning

> Turning is almost a dervish exercise with the world going around and you feeling calm and quiet.
>
> (*Hanya Holm in* The Vision of Modern Dance, *1980*)

The belief in the power of turning in the Sufi religion of the Middle East is so great that the dervishes' hours of spinning, they feel, connect their being to the heavens and the earth, centring them and empowering them to overcome any dizziness. This is, as such, a strong element for expressive movement. Turning strictly refers to rotating the whole body around with a change of front, or a full or multiple rotation. *Twisting* is also rotation, but refers to movement within a joint e.g. turnout of the hip. There are many different types of turn: full, half, quarter, multiple, inward and outward, jumping, travelling, on- and off-balance, pivot, spin and so on. These all require good placement and alignment to avoid a loss of balance or orientation. When beginners first start, they may feel as if their whole universe is moving, and this can cause great insecurity. Constant practice is therefore required. The eyes must focus straight ahead, not downwards, for balance. In classical ballet, 'spotting' is often used. This involves fixing the eyes on one spot for as long as possible and whipping the head round as quickly as possible. This helps to avoid dizziness. Modern and post-modern genres sometimes deliberately remove spotting, and the skill of retaining orientation then becomes internalised, not unlike the whirling dervishes. A practical example is *barrel turns*, which in ballet are performed outward, leaping sideways around and spotting on a mental image of a centrally placed barrel. Originally a favourite of sailors, this is an exciting explosive jump to watch. The post-modern version may be performed inwards, with less sudden upward feel and more skimming in soft curves along a straight pathway. The deliberate removal of spotting gives an even, lifting quality.

Turns can also start in different ways. Lifting the weight onto a half-toe rise (relevé) or en pointe allows the body easily to rotate around the axis. This may be continued in multiple by using the free leg to extend and flex in retiré (drawing the leg up in a bent position so that the toe touches the inside of the

Hove and Brighton Youth Dance in full spin

support leg) to give added momentum on each 360° turn. The weight of *throwing* an arm, leg or head may also initiate turning. The *Rose Adagio* in Marius Petipa's *The Sleeping Beauty* (1890) features multiple pirouettes. Princess Aurora turns swiftly as she accepts a rose from each admiring prince. And the post-modern work *Rotary Action* (Arnie Zane and Bill T. Jones, 1985) makes a clear use of cartwheels, rolls, turning around a partner, and the rotating of hips and shoulders in a simple but effective interpretation of the title.

TASK SEVEN

 **Working with Others and Communication** 

Choreograph a trio/quartet using the idea of transport. With turning as your dominant movement theme, ideas which may be useful for improvisation will include: the wheel, the Highway Code, traffic control, behaviour behind the wheel, bicycles, trains and the behaviour of passengers in train stations or at bus stops. (Suggested music: 'Whirling', from *Contemporary Dance Rhythms*.)

Gesture (isolation)

> Graham's knee comes up to her chest, her back curves slightly forward, and now her leg, knee leading, juts inward, circles out, in, out again, while her arms swoop through the air like a bird's wings. ... Graham speaks of the turbulent emotions lying deep within Judith's body.
>
> (*Elinor Rogosin in* The Dancemakers, *1980*)

The powerful language of gesture is all around us everyday. Waving goodbye, folding arms, pointing fingers, raising eyebrows, a nod and a shake of the head are ordinary body language which we all use to accompany speech. These everyday forms of movement are a rich source for choreography - as we note in the quotation above, where the gestures tell of the deepest vengefulness and passion. Gestural movement does not involve any transference of weight. Gestures are usually movements of single parts in isolation, and the *rotation* of the joints can play a significant part in subtle communication. In Labanotation, the facing of a palm on the hand is as shown in Figure 2.4. Similarly, rotation of the legs in the hip sockets in turn-out, parallel or turned-in (see Figure 2.5) opens up a range of expressive possibilities from humour to lyricism.

Bharatha Natyam from India uses a large amount of hand, arm and facial gestures called *mudras* in a complex language to tell rich narratives of myths and stories. Elements of this genre are visible in the work of post-modern choreographer Lea Anderson for The Cholmondeleys and The Featherstonehaughs. Anderson also uses sign lan-

Figure 2.4 *Notation for palm facings*

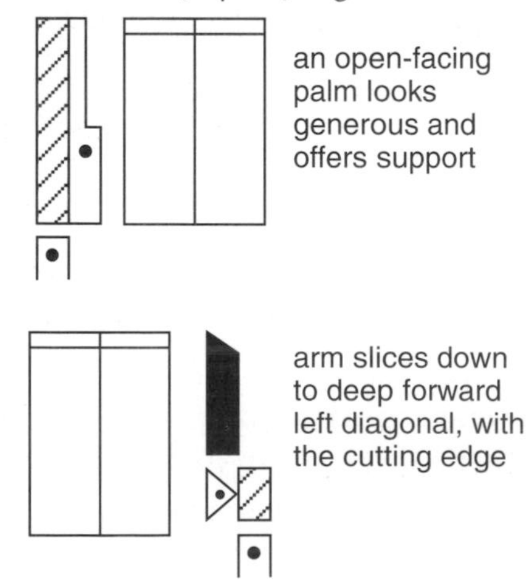

an open-facing palm looks generous and offers support
arm slices down to deep forward left diagonal, with the cutting edge

Figure 2.5 *Notation for leg rotation*

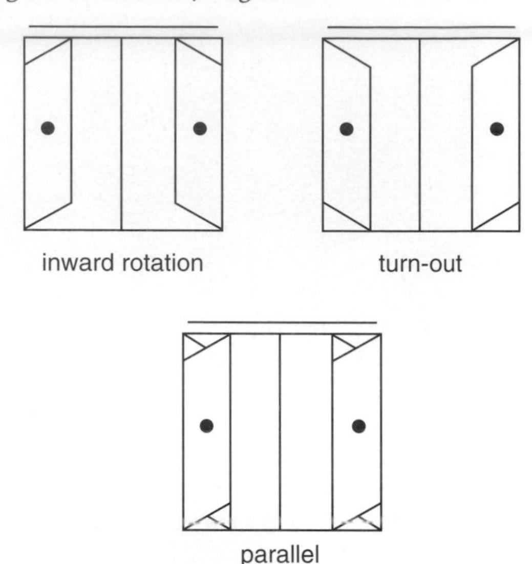

guage to give her work a characteristic quirky, detailed look.

> I became riveted by a single striking resemblance, which was simply their extraordinary range of gesture and facial expression. Their hands ... seemed to have a life of their own tracing elaborate, decorative patterns in space or spinning memories; ... while their faces had an even more eloquent repertoire of pouts, stares ... and glances.
>
> (*Judith Mackrell in* Dance Theatre Journal, *1986*)

Shobana Jeyasingh works in contemporary Indian dance, combining Bharatha Natyam's intricate gesture and steps with western influenced post-modern style.

> ... her sensibility owes as much to London or New York as it does to Madras.
>
> *The* Guardian, 2000

Even Richard Alston, better known for fine footwork, incorporated hand gestures like clicking fingers and clapping to show disgust or rejection in *Pulcinella* (1987). The gestures have an Italian feel such as when Pimpinella first enters. Amongst the bourrées and the brisés her hands gesticulate rapidly to her bothersome husband. In reply he jumps in second position whilst tapping his forehead as if to exclaim that she is mad.

Mimetic gestures are used in classical ballet to tell stories and make clear the relationships between characters. Jean Georges Noverre (France, 1727–1810) describes his thoughts on reform for ballet in his *Lettres sur la Danse et sur les Ballets* (1760):

> ... study how to make your gestures noble, never forget that it is the life-blood of your dancing ...
>
> (*Cyril Beaumont* in Dance Horizons, *1966*)

Later, in the nineteenth century, Marius Petipa (1818–1910) used long passages of mime as a kind of sign language so that obvious meanings were clear. For example, shaking a fist meant anger, while placing the hand on the heart meant love. Other gestures were less direct, like pointing to the heavens to declare everlasting love, or circling hands and arms around each other and over the head to symbolise dance.

The Cholmondeleys in The Cholmondeley Sisters

TASK EIGHT

1. Using as many different parts of the body as possible, isolate and improvise with gestural movements. Some of these may be recognisable everyday gestures, others more quirky.
2. Select a few everyday gestures and a few less common to create a dance entitled 'For a small space'. (Suggested music: 'Ballet of the chicks in their shells' by Moussorgsky, from *Pictures at an Exhibition*.)

Such mime is used rarely in modern ballets but is seen in the classics. In Petipa's *The Sleeping Beauty* (1890), Princess Aurora greets the four princes. In turn they support her in attitude and turn her as she holds the balance. When each releases her hands she raises both arms above her head to make a crown. This arm gesture means princess and it is repeated almost as a 'How do you do, pleased to meet you' greeting to each prince in turn.

Similarly, Carabosse mimes anger at being uninvited to the princess's christening in a death threat. Bringing up the arms to the side of the head and then down quickly with fists clenched so that they cross in front of the torso mimes death.

Stillness

> Stillness is not an absolute point. It is an ever-receding depth of understanding.
>
> (*Mary Fulkerson in* The move to Stillness, Dartington Theatre Papers, *1981–82*)

Being still is *active*! It requires strong control. There is muscle activity in a pause, a feeling of ongoing energy. Stillness contributes to rhythm, acting a little like a full stop in a sentence, and it gives the onlooker a chance to reflect on what has just been seen. It may also act to highlight what is about to happen, and it is often used as the ending for a dance.

The skill of balance may be involved if the body is being held still on a small area like the toes, and this requires strong control and co-ordination. The part on the floor pushes down whilst the rest of the body pulls upwards and sends energy outward to the extremities. This counter-tension outwards and towards your centre holds the body lightly over the base.

Good balance, say holding an arabesque or attitude, is helped by breathing and good alignment of pelvis and spine. Eyes and the balance organs in the ears help too, so do the proprioceptors.

In Richard Alston's *Soda Lake* (1981) stillness is used extensively, and is clearly appropriate to his study of the vast open spaces of the Mohavi Desert in North America. The silent, motionless 'passive landscape' (as Alston described this desert in 1983 on *The South Bank Show*), as presented in a minimalist set, is a perfect vehicle for stillness. Alston chooses certain shapes and positions of rest for which the dancer in performance has to allow adequate time: holding such positions as 'the big bird' and 'the sentinel position' are demanding on a dancer's stamina and sense of timing.

In Macmillan's *Romeo and Juliet* (1965), a long pause is used most poignantly when the young lovers see each other for the first time in the balcony scene. It is held just long enough for us to almost hear their hearts beating.

Of course many dances start and end with stillness. From a dancer's point of view control over this action is therefore crucial. Balance and stillness are maintained as long as your centre of gravity is aligned over the part of the body which is bearing the weight. Once balance is lost and gravity takes over movement results and often this involves falling.

TASK NINE

1 In pairs, one person closes their eyes while the other makes a shape. Without opening your eyes, use touch to feel your way around your partner's shape. Your partner must keep very still. When you think you know the shape, make it yourself and then open your eyes to see how accurate your copy is.

2 

Find prints of paintings by the Impressionist artist Georges Seurat – either *La Grande Jatte* or *Une Baignade* would be appropriate. In threes or fives, compose a short dance which uses stillness as a predominant feature to punctuate the movement. Convey a feeling of calm and heat. (Suggested music: Claude Debussy's 'Snowflakes are dancing', from *Children's Corner No. 4*, or 'Passepied' from *Suite Bergamasque No. 4.*)

Falling

In classical ballet, the *high level* predominates, while one of the aims of early modern dance, by contrast, was to *show* the effort of moving against gravity, not to hide it. This latter trend increased the use of *falling* and of low-level movement. I like to consider falling as the sixth dance action.

Doris Humphrey, one of the early pioneers of modern dance, regarded the struggle against gravity (suspension, fall and recovery) to be the very essence of life and action – 'The Arc between Two Deaths'.

> Standing still before a mirror, I found that first the body began to sway. Then, letting myself go, three things happened. I began to fall, the speed increasing as I went down. The body made an involuntary effort to resist the fall ... I hit the floor.
>
> (*quoted by Ellfeldt in* Dance from Magic to Art, *1976*)

Falling requires skill and co-ordination in order to be performed safely, and like all dance actions, it requires practice. There is a moment when the pull of gravity overtakes and the dancer 'intentionally' gives in to it. During this descent, the abdominal muscles must pull-up; and landing on the knees, elbows, shoulder tip or sacrum should *always* be avoided.There are two types of fall:

1 a *collapse*: a relaxed, successive giving-in which happens over the centre of gravity and tends not to rebound.

2 an *off-balance fall*: the centre of gravity shifts off-centre, making falling unavoidable as the pull of gravity takes over.

Various actions may pre-empt a fall – jumps, swings, turns – and at the end of the fall action phase, recovery may involve stillness, a roll or a rebound to continue.

TASK TEN

1  Explore the feeling of walking, falling and recovering. At the ends of falls, try out different techniques: stillness; rebound; rolls. In addition: falling in different directions: forwards, backwards, sideways and diagonally; try out both *collapses* and *off-balance falls* (see above); and try adding jumps and swings into the falling.

After five or 10 minutes, join up into a large group.

2  Continuing to explore the above themes, select some of the more successful ideas, whilst also copying the variety of tempos, falls, shapes and rolls that the other dancers are doing.

3  Using landing/gymnastic mats, try to teach each other any falls and rolls which someone may have learnt in a martial-arts class – like a judo or karate session – or in a gymnastics class.

Repeated falls and recoveries are often used in the work of post-modern choreographers like Mark Murphy for V-Tol. Murphy's *Where Angels Fear to Tread* (1995) is concerned with issues in today's society and often these involve intense emotional relations. Dancers push, pull, drop and throw each other reflecting on how people can hurt each other in real life.

Modern ballet also uses gravity in a more natural way. In Kenneth MacMillan's *The Rite of Spring* (1962) collapses are common. He noted that he wanted:

> ... a primitiveness of my own invention ... I believe that the actions and feelings that are shown may still be observed in people today ...
>
> (*In* Ballet for All, *P. Brinson and C. Crisp, 1971*)

The corps de ballet are like groups of people who lack individuality. Their unison movement is desperate and wild. They celebrate the sacrifice of the maiden because her death is the renewal of their lives. After her collapse she is flung into the air in a dark celebration. This primitive vision is often associated with the work of the pioneers in modern dance.

TASK ELEVEN

Fall from a standing position, transfer your weight simply, smoothly, gradually and safely to the floor until lying flat. Then roll to stand. Practise until the phrase is very clear, and then notate it, showing clearly which parts of the body (see Figure 2.6) contact the floor in which order. Make sure weight transference is smooth throughout.

Notate a simple score showing which parts of the body take weight in the descent.

The six dance actions of travelling, elevation, turning, gesture, stillness and falling, which are the foundations of choreography, are further developed by using a variety of other considerations, namely the *where*, the *when* and the *how*, which will form the focus for the next part of this chapter.

The space component

> 'No room! No room!' they cried out when they saw Alice coming. 'There's plenty of room!' said Alice indignantly.
>
> (*From* Alice in Wonderland *by Lewis Carroll*)

Designing a dance in space helps the audience to understand it; and any dance must be organised in space in a way appropriate to the chosen idea or theme. Dancers work *in* a space – i.e. a studio, gym, stage – but they also dance *with* space: it is alive, like an active partner. Mary Wigman (1886–1973) was a German early-modern dance pioneer famous for the way in which she used space as an active element. Rudolf Laban (1879–1958) classified dancers by their preferences for moving on a certain level, high, medium or low.

Figure 2.6 *Labanotation signs for parts of the body*

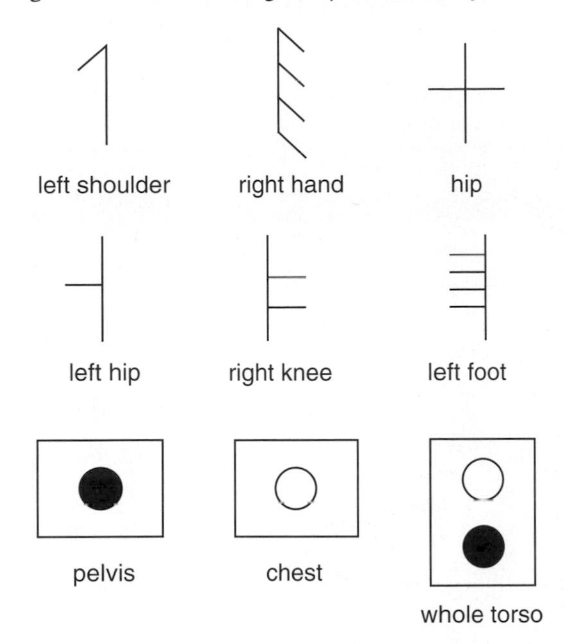

PERSONAL AND GENERAL SPACE

The space that lies around you as far as you can reach without moving off the spot is your own personal space bubble. In *Embrace Tiger, Return to Mountain* (Glen Tetley, for the Rambert Company, 1968), the dancers are placed bubble distance apart and go through ritual t'ai chi meditations. Later on, duets bring them into very close contact with each other, with touching and shadowing, and there is a feeling of agitation as their personal bubbles are invaded. Travelling out into the general space beyond your bubble opens up many spatial choices and possibilities.

FLOOR AND AIR PATTERNS

As they gradually reveal themselves to an audience, the *patterns* created by travelling on the floor (see Figure 2.7) and by gestures made in the air, be they curves, straight lines, circles, zig-zags, spirals or squiggles, will provoke different responses. Although it is difficult to pin down any exact responses, some generalisations may be made. Curving patterns are lyrical, gentle and continuous, whereas straight ones tend to come over as bold, more formal and strong.

Shobana Jeyasingh in the videodance *Duets with Automobiles* (1994 for BBC 2 TV *Dance for Camera* series, director Terry Braun), places dancers in a variety of interiors of modern London buildings. One section shows a solo dancer travelling down a long corridor. The dancer's floor pattern is one straight line and the arm gestures emphasise the long, thin, rectangular shape of the performing space.

Embrace Tiger, Return to Mountain *by Glen Tetley (a) to show dancers within their own space bubbles (b) later in the dance the dancers begin to overlap*

(a)

(b)

Figure 2.7 *To show notation of floor pattern*

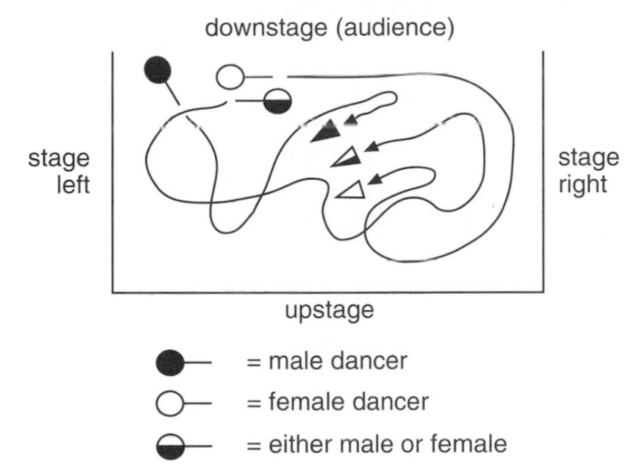

DIRECTIONS

As with different patterns, different *directions* – forwards, backwards, sideways, circular, up, down – may also provoke different reactions. Advancing forwards is positive, assertive and authoritative, whereas the backwards retreat possibly more defensive. Jumping up is lively, while there is an opposite feel to falling down. Sideways may be seen as sneaky.

At the end of Richard Alston's *Zansa* (1986) as dancers crawl backwards a soloist rushes forward across the front of the stage. All the previous tensions and crossings of duets and soloists are echoed here by an opposite in direction and level which brings the dance to a timely and appropriate end.

TASK TWELVE

Use the words below to create short phrases of improvised movement which use direction, pattern in the air and on the floor, and personal/general space in a way appropriate to the meaning of the words.

- Up one minute, down the next.
- Far-reaching effects.
- Neither here nor there.
- On the straight and narrow.
- Draw the line.
- At loose ends.

DIMENSIONS AND PLANES

Movement can be described in three dimensions:

- *height:* up and down;
- *width:* side to side;
- *depth:* forwards and backwards.

When two dimensions are joined together, *planes* are produced:

- the *horizontal plane* (also called the *table plane*): joins width and depth; opening and closing;

- the *vertical plane* (also called the *door plane*): joins height and width; rising and falling;
- the *saggital plane* (also called the *wheel plane*): joins height and depth; advancing and retreating.

Movement which emphasises the width dimension can appear flat, perhaps mechanical or puppet-like. This kind of movement would be appropriate when dancing in a *mask*, because of the inhuman, two-dimensional look which, like a mask, it conveys. The opening of *Ghost Dances* (Christopher Bruce, 1981) uses the width dimension to great effect. The dancers' tilting head gestures, sideways leaps and extensions into stillness create an unreality in our minds. They place hands on each others' shoulders and move in unison in a side-to-side folky step, presenting an image of power which is ominous and threatening to us mere mortals. These movements also serve to emphasise the death masks and the body paint which create the effect of flat skeletons hanging in the gloom. As soon as the mere mortals enter, we are drawn into the latter's more three-dimensional world - and into their vulnerability - by the way they travel slowly along the depth of the diagonal (up stage left to down stage right). By adding depth to the original movement, Bruce places these mortals in a more real, human world. The audience is drawn into a place where two worlds meet, and an accompanying sense of danger is conveyed.

LEVELS

Levels are an aspect of the height dimension. In classical ballet, the emphasis is often on the high level, whereas the low floor level is a feature of modern and post-modern dance. Martha Graham's earthy relationship with gravity was also a feature of the work of Doris Humphrey; and we also see it today in the post-modern work of Lea Anderson, for the Cholmondeleys - in 'Knees', the end section of her 1989 work *Flesh and Blood*, the dancers seem earth-bound, weighty.

> From the vertical to the horizontal, from standing, kneeling and lying, her cast explore the different levels between high and low, as if making contact with the unknown.
>
> (*Ann Nugent in* The Stage, *1989*)

In Matthew Bourne's *Swan Lake* (1995) there is an ingenious use of level playing on the set design. As the young prince lies asleep swans, as if in a dream, appear from deep underneath the oversize bed. Later in the same scene the swans gather on the bed, putting themselves higher up than the prince, who is now on the floor. They loom, menacing and dangerous, from their perch warning of the tragedy which is about to follow.

The middle level is our everyday one. Falling out of or rising above this level offer obvious expressive possibilities for choreography.

To show use of varied levels: Swansong (English National Ballet) Photo by Bill Cooper

THE SIZE OF MOVEMENTS

Tiny hand gestures, large sweeping arm gestures, a single step, travelling all around a space – these movements will communicate different sensations to onlookers; and the contrasts involved here should be explored by all choreographers.

Again, this factor is shown clearly in the work of Lea Anderson in *Flesh and Blood.* The small movements of eyes, noses, fingers and heads which draw the letters J, O, A and N in the air are later developed by *enlargement*: they travel and transform into arm gestures in the second section, 'Movement choir'.

In *Carnival* (1982, Siobhan Davies) the Saint-Saens music *Carnival of the Animals* produced some contrasts in movement size. The 12 dancers travelled fluidly and swiftly around the stage space in wide sweeping pathways in the *Aquarium* section, reminiscent of shoals of tropical fish. In contrast the lovelorn cuckoo uses repetition of a restricted arm gesture depicting his beating heart. The predictable repetition to match the bird call in the music is sad but very amusing, especially when he misses one. The very restricted movement of the elderly tottering tortoises (danced by Davies and Spink) travelling precariously across the stage adds another range to the expression.

TASK THIRTEEN

In groups of four or five, find as many objects which can be used to place dancers on as high a level – e.g. chairs, ladders or stage blocks – as you can. Use movements which emphasise the difference between high and low levels, and explore the possibilities individually – include the simple lifting and lowering of each other.

Experiment also with moving the objects so as to change the way in which planes and dimensions are used – you may prefer, at this stage, to stand out in turns and *observe* the resulting changes.

Finally, add the option to use *tiny* and *large* movements which others can pick up on by copying you close by or far away, by using large gestures to 'involve' other dancers across the space, or by travelling together.

This improvisation does not need to produce a finished dance, but it is advised to use outside onlookers to give feedback on the results.

THE FOCUS

This constituent feature of a dance composition can mean different things at different moments during a dance. Indeed, it can involve any of the following:

- *where* the dancer is looking: up or down; at a part of the body; at another dancer; at the audience;
- which way the body is *facing*: for example, does a certain shape look better facing on a diagonal or flat to the audience than it does facing sideways on?
- the performing skills of a dancer: these may have to do with facial expression, or with the dancer's attention to how to perform a certain movement (e.g. which part of the body to focus on in order to create a full expression). This factor, which will be dealt with later, is of concern to choreographers, because it is they who are trying to bring such skills out of their dancers.

These are important considerations when composing dances. A dancer looking inwardly, on the self, will clearly convey a different image from one focusing on the far distance, on an object or on another dancer on the stage. Choosing an appropriate focus for dancers is therefore vital.

In *Sergeant Early's Dream* by Christopher Bruce (1984), the dancers' focus is often thrown out to sea which is painted on the backcloth. This draws the attention of the audience to the dancers' longing for their original homeland which is full of memories and nostalgia.

The use of focus in the ball scene of Bourne's *Swan Lake* (1995) adds dramatic tension. As the lead males, the Prince and the 'Swan', dance their gaze is drawn to each other repeatedly. Sometimes on their dancing partner, or on the movement itself, but always drawn back to look at each other.

BAD Dance Company showing the use of focus

SHAPE AND VOLUME

The body can create a variety of shapes – curled, straight, wide, twisted and so on – and the spaces *around* and *between* bodies also need to be sculpted. In visual art, this latter space is often called the *negative space.* In dance it is seen during stillness, but also in the transitions from one shape to the next, and when it is enclosed by boundaries, it creates a feeling of *volume.* For example, when a dancer places the arms in front of the body, as if curving them around an imaginary beach ball, the sensation of volume is clearly felt.

Different shapes have different expressive potential. In classical ballet, it is so often *curving* lines which are used. These have a sense of the lyrical and the romantic, and an ongoing flow and grace. In contrast, the harsh angular and straight lines of early-modern dancers are hard-edged, tough and strong, and these have held the potential for expressing the social upheavals of their times.

> The modern dance as we know it today came after the World War. This period following the war demanded forms vital enough for the reborn man to inhabit . . . All life today is concerned with space problems, even political life. Space language is a language we understand. We receive so much of sensation through the eye.
>
> (*Martha Graham in* The Vision of Modern Dance, *1980*)

Similarly with *symmetrical* and *asymmetrical* shapes: the former giving impressions of regularity and stability, and the latter coming over as more unpredictable and insecure.

> If symmetry should be used sparingly in choreography because of its calming effect, then asymmetry, which stimulates the senses, is the area to court and understand for dancing.
>
> (*Doris Humphrey in* The Art of Making Dances, *1959*)

Further consideration about the use of space is to be found in later sections. In Chapter 3, which deals with the physical setting, there is an analysis of how to use a stage space, and of how different physical settings affect spatial design. The arrangement of groups of dancers in space is examined under a separate section in Chapter 5.

TASK FOURTEEN

1  Individually, choose four contrasting body shapes.

- Place them in an order and link them up with movements.
- Find a way, whilst holding each shape, of making it turn or travel, or both.
- Experiment with giving the shapes different facings so that an audience sees them from different angles – e.g. above, sideways etc.
- Experiment with changing the focus of the eyes during both stillness and travelling – e.g. moving from a focus on different parts of the body to a focus on the room around you.

2 From the above, choose movements to create a short solo piece entitled either:

- 'Distortions', or
- 'No way out', or
- 'Metamorphosis'.

(Recommended music: *The Big Blue* film soundtrack, by Eric Serra.)

As we move through space, we also, of course, move through *time*, and this will be the next constituent feature of dance that we will examine.

The time component

> 'If you knew time as well as I do,' said the Hatter, 'you wouldn't talk about wasting *it*. It's *him* ... I dare say you never even spoke to Time! ... Now if you only kept on good terms with him, he'd do almost anything you like with the clock.'
>
> (Alice in Wonderland, *by Lewis Carroll*)

Time can seem to have a life of its own. We have all experienced waiting for the kettle to boil, and how, when we are in a hurry, it seems to take longer. As choreographer, you may alter how an audience perceives time by the way that you yourself manipulate it. Like design in *space*, time plays an intrinsic part in the organisation of movement for choreography. It orders and measures, but it can also be a slippery customer, so, as the Mad Hatter cautions, it is advisable to be on good terms with it.

Patterning movement in time gives it form and rhythm, and makes it interesting for the onlooker; and the performing dancer, on their part, requires an accurate feel for the *temporal* boundaries of the choreography. This will be analysed further later in the book. Similarly, the analysis of time and rhythm in music will be examined in more detail later. Here we are concerned only with the simpler aspects of time as a constituent feature of dance composition.

SPEED AND DURATION

> Dance is concerned with a single instant as it comes along.
>
> (*Merce Cunningham in* Dance from Magic to Art, *1976*)

Sudden or sustained, and fast or slow, are the two most simple ways of analysing a movement, in terms of how much time it actually takes. Sudden movement can produce a sense of urgency in the onlooker, in contrast with an indulgent, gradual feeling that a slower and more sustained movement can create. If you compose a three-minute dance which is made up of 12 slow movements, it will have a leisurely feeling. Pack it with 200 movements, on the other hand, and the onlooker will feel rushed along at a breathless pace.

As choreographer and dancer, you need to build up your sensitivity to the duration of movement. Merce Cunningham and others often work with a stopwatch, which allows the speed and duration of a movement – which, after much rehearsal, always stays accurate – to be measured independently of the tempo of the music. One of his dancers, Karole Armitage, once said that he had taught her to recognise exactly how long a movement takes.

In composing dances, it is likely that you will mix slow and fast speeds. The way that you mix these will reflect your personal sense of time and the content of the dance idea.

A good example of this is in Alvin Ailey's *Blues Suite* (1958). It is set in a cheap brothel in the southern states of the USA where life is hard for the women who work there and for the men who visit. Each room of the house has its own story and the dance is made up of several scenes. The third section is a mostly slow tempo piece for a female trio. However, throughout all the sections faster desperate movement interrupts repeatedly. These frequent and sudden contrasts in tempo create a feeling that for these people fun is only fleeting, and that for them life is a struggle.

PHRASING

Single actions joined together make up *phrases*. Finding your own inner rhythm that will guide you to form phrases is an ongoing process which itself may take a long time. Phrases usually have a feeling of unity, logic or completeness about them. Each is a simple unit with a beginning, middle and end. The individual parts have a physical logic which connects them and makes sense. Phrases are grouped together, and build up into longer sequences and sections. In this way, their individual and group timings give a dance its *form* and allow the audience to find a visual sense. Unphrased movement is like a blurred photograph: very difficult to make sense of or to watch for any length of time. Phrasing occurs naturally both in life itself and in other art forms like music, poetry, painting and film.

In technique class you will learn phrases which, by challenging your physical skills as a dancer, contribute to your dance training. These are not necessarily of the same kind as phrases found in choreography which has as its main aim *expression to an audience*. It is important that you, as a dancer and choreographer, learn to be sensitive to the differences between these two kinds of phrase.

Phrase length

> Phrase means length in time. Breath length if you're angry, it's a short breath, it's a short phrase. If you are in a love

scene, like Tristan and Isolde, it goes on forever, you're in a l-o-o-ng phrase.

(*Martha Graham in* The Dance Makers, *1980*)

A phrase may be of any speed or duration, and there will be a mix in any one dance. When music is being used, the phrases are usually based on the underlying beat or musical form. Finding a movement's natural timing/phrasing allows you to alter it to suit whatever the expression demands. As Graham points out, breath can be a strong influence in phrase length - a forceful, sudden exhalation or panting, for example, will produce its own kind of phrase length. Increasing the depth of your breathing can give you a strong sense of where the phrase begins and ends. Each deep breath is a short phrase.

- inhale: rise, expand;
- hold: suspend, high point;
- exhale: fall, collapse, release into an action.

The length of a phrase is determined by its *content.* If a short punchy effect is required, the phrase will be a corresponding length.

So within one dance there will be phrases of differing lengths. Consider Richard Alston's *Soda Lake* (1981). Danced accompanied by silence the phrase lengths are very clear as there is no sound to distract us other than noises made by moving. The phrases vary from lingering and sustained to explosive whipping releases. The phrases are punctuated by long pauses giving the whole form the feeling of the original stimulus, that is the sculpture and the panoramic sparse landscape of the Mohavi desert in the USA.

TASK FIFTEEN

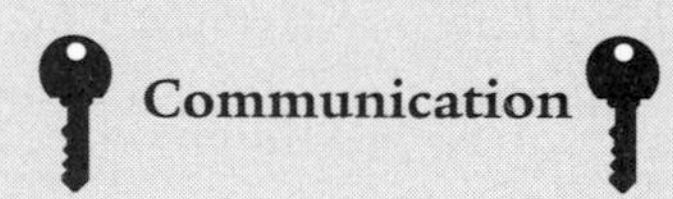

This task asks questions which relate to the constituent features as covered so far in this chapter; action, space, time, dynamics and phrasing.

- On video, watch *Soda Lake* (Richard Alston, 1981).
- Watch the first section again. It ends when the dancer runs back under the sculpture for the second time, sinks, rolls and holds in the lying 'rest' position.
- Use repeated viewings and pauses to answer the following questions about the first section of the dance:

1 There are four different phrases in the first section, How do they differ? (3 marks)

2 Name the five different actions used in the first phrase (5 marks)

3 In section one the dancer uses differing amounts of space at various moments. How would you describe the differing uses of space? (2 marks)

4 The action of stillness is used a great deal.

(a) How does it shape the phrases in section one? (2 marks)
(b) How does it reflect the idea that the dance is based on? (1 mark)

5 **(a)** Describe two contrasting ways in which the dancer uses focus. (2 marks)
(b) Suggest what these may express. (2 marks)

6 Suggest three ways in which the movement relates to the sculpture. (3 marks)

Total 20 marks – answers are on page 82.

Phrase shape

The content of the phrase determines not only its length but also its *shape*. Our breath phrases, for example, will differ in shape. The deep breath has a clear high point, but the panting phrase is shaped, with no real high or low points.

The shape of a phrase is mapped according to where its low and high points are. These may occur at the beginning, the middle or the end. The high point may be structured through an emphasis on any aspect of space, time or dynamics. It may be faster or stronger, or more expansive in space. And these changes can come about gradually or instantaneously.

Stillness may also be used in shaping. A catch of breath or a moment of hesitation or anticipation may provide time both to reflect on what has just happened and to heighten the impact of what is *about* to happen. A pause or a longer hold can help both to capture the attention of your audience and to increase their interest in your composition.

Time affects the dynamics of any movement. If you change the time taken by a movement, you change the *quality* of that movement. And furthermore:

> Accuracy of time is necessary to maintain the desired space. Change the space and the time changes, unless the speed of the particular phrase changes in order to keep the time the same. Change the time and the space and the movement changes.
>
> (*Carolyn Brown in* Merce Cunningham, *1975*)

TASK SIXTEEN

Using sudden and sustained speeds, stillness, and different levels and sizes of movement, make three phrases of different shapes using the following words as guides:

- melt, float, collapse;
- erupt, crawl, pulsate;
- sparkle, float, fade.

Use breath as an accompaniment when possible – it may add to the shaping of the phrase. Improvise individually on this task. You might like to draw the shapes of the different phrases.

(Recommended music: *Diva* film soundtrack.)

TASK 15 ON *SODA LAKE*; FIRST SECTION.

(Answers similar to those below are acceptable).

You may note here that the four phrases in section one are as follows:

Phrase 1: Slow rolls, arm gesture, roll, stillness, rise to sit, stillness = 49.36 secs.

Phrase 2: Rise to stand, quick steps, turns, tilts, return to sculpture, 'wing spread' = 22.74 secs.

Phrase 3: As for phrase 1 on other side of body = 48 secs.

Phrase 4: As for phrase 2 plus balance in attitude then run to sculpture, 'wing spread' = 17 secs.

1 The phrases differ: in length (long and short) (1 mark)

in weight (light and strong/heavy) (1 mark)

in speed and duration (slow and fast) (1 mark)

2 Extension and contractions (of torso), travelling (rolling), gestures (arms and legs), stillness. (5 marks - 1 for each action).

3 Personal and General space - as seen in the movements close to the body and those travelling around the floor. (2 marks)

4 **(a)** Sometimes it ends a phrase. (1 mark)

It marks a part of a phrase. The energy in the body is continuous throughout a pause and so gives certain phrases their unique shape. (1 mark)

(b) It echoes the idea of landmarks such as rocks, plants and telegraph poles, which are in the desert landscape. (1 mark)

5 **(a)** Inward and outward. (2 marks)

(b) The feelings of being 'in' the land held by gravity and of looking out across the landscape, marking territory, guarding. (2 marks)

6 The movement: travels away from and towards the sculpture (1 mark)

occupies the space under the 'hoop' (1 mark)

reflects the idea of the balance or quality of suspension that the sculpture has. (1 mark)

The dynamic component

Every moment varies *dynamically* along a range from light to strong. The dynamics and textures of a dance are like the colours of a painting. They create interest and contrast, as well as conveying much of the choreographer's intentions. In classical ballet, especially in the romantic tradition, the dominant dynamic is that of the sustained and the effortless. The tradition of modern dance, by contrast, emphasises heavy falls and suspended recoveries. Whatever genre is being used, the choreographer needs an understanding of the terminology and analysis involved in the dynamics of dance.

Energy is the potential for action which gives the 'Go!' In dance training, finding the right amount of energy to perform a movement efficiently is a priority. In composing dances, the task is to find out how to use energy in a way that is most appropriate to whatever it is that is being expressed.

Energy remains neutral until a *force* is applied which *releases* it. Depending on the intensity of the force applied, the resulting movement will vary in its *weight* from strong to gentle. 'Weight' is a term used specifically by Rudolf Laban in his analysis of *effort*, but it is also a term used in the dance world generally.

When force and time act together, *dynamics* result, so there may be a sudden *strong* dynamic or a sudden *light* one. Some dynamics are quite specific and are named 'qualities' – like swing, collapse, vibration or percussive (sudden, strong, sharp, staccato) movement.

Laban defined a wide range of specific qualities which he called *efforts*. These are described by the way that space, time and weight are combined – see Table 2.1. In Laban's analysis, space refers to the pathway of a movement through the air.

The broad spectrum of dynamics which is available for choreography should be explored to the full. In *Nympheas* (Robert Cohan, 1976), sustainment and suspension are first emphasised. Impressions of waterlilies floating and of the gentle movement of the water are conveyed. Contrast is then provided in the storm scene when the dynamic becomes stronger, more sudden, wild and free.

The range of dynamics can also be used to portray *character*. Even in the world of classical ballet, with its dominance of smooth effortlessness, subtle changes can still be used to great effect. In Sir Frederick Ashton's *The Dream* (1964), the characters are identified by the individual dancers' own inherent dynamic qualities. The original Puck, danced by Keith Martin, has robust, bouncy, driving character, well suited to the impish spirit.

Table 2.1 *The Eight Basic Efforts*

Effort	Time	Weight	Space
Punch	sudden	firm	direct
Float	sustained	light	flexible
Flick	sudden	light	flexible
Dab	sudden	light	direct
Press	sustained	firm	direct
Glide	sustained	light	direct
Slash	sudden	firm	flexible
Wring	sustained	firm	flexible

BAD Dance Company in In A BAAAAD WAY, *by Linda Ashley. Try to describe the contrast in dynamics in these two photographs.*

TASK SEVENTEEN

Individually improvise to create a phrase which presents images from the landscape of a rainforest. These images may include: the sun rising above high mountains; waterfalls crashing down into a calm pool; rare orchids opening, and humming birds darting and hovering around them; the tilt of the high, cool mountain peaks; the sway and swing of a tree canopy; bathing and floating in the cool river; the crash of destructive bulldozers. Make sure the phrase has a clear length and shape, and a variety of dynamics. (Suggested music: *Spirit of the Rainforest* by Terry Oldfield, New World.)

MOVEMENT COMPONENTS – CONCLUSION

The movement tasks outlined above have given ample opportunities to use a variety of stimuli as starting points for improvisation, composition and analysis.

In all aspects, the movement components involved in dance - as analysed above - are only as effective and expressive as the *dancers* who perform them, and it is with this point in mind that the next section of this chapter examines the choice of dancers.

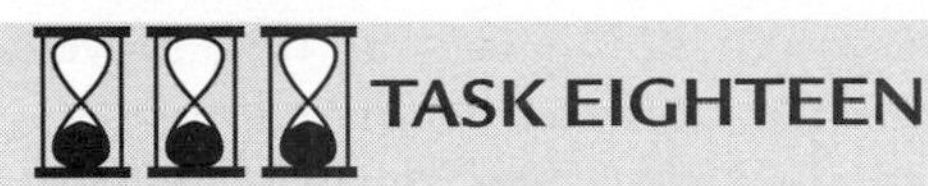

Improving Own Learning and Performance

You could do this task at the start of every term as part of an ongoing self-improvement programme.

- From the list below choose three areas that you need to improve on. You may need to consult your teacher to identify them.
- Always try to describe your strategy for improvements and the progress in anatomical detail. Again you may need to consult your teacher or a friend to help you monitor changes. You should evaluate how effective your programme is.

Area targeted for improvement	Strategy	Needs improvement	Working towards	Achieved
Example: Control of falling Copy this table into your own portfolio. Select and enter three target areas. Travelling – target/name different steps and combinations ... Jumping – safe practice ... Control of stillness ... Co-ordination of gestures ... Control of turning ... Spatial clarity ... Dynamic range ... Control of time/tempo ... Phrasing ...	– Ask teacher to help me find a programme of falling which will help me improve my confidence and skill level.	✓ 2nd Sept. I am very unsure of myself when I fall. I know that there are skills to work on. My teacher suggests that I try to build from falling in a half-sit position and gradually build up to standing. I think I'll use a mat at first!	✓ Sept 9 After class I have been spending 15 mins experimenting with loss of balance sideways from a half sit. Now I feel able to transfer weight smoothly, safely and sequentially to lying on my side. ✓ Sept. 16. I can now fall safely and confidentlyfrom a high kneel sideways. No mat! ✓ Sept. 23. Today I experimented with feeling loss of balance from standing. I can feel my centre of gravity shifting sideways and the point when gravity takes over. If I use a stretch away from the pull I find that I can control a smooth fall to lying on my side.	✓ 2nd Oct. I can do a controlled fall (pretty good one actually!) and from one leg on the ball of my foot. Like this: 1 2 3 Now I'm going to set a new target of falling backwards and forwards which seem to be more difficult in co-ordinating the various body parts.

The dancers

Choosing Dancers

We may wonder why certain dancers are chosen for a particular company or dance. There are a number of basic factors which we can pinpoint that influence the choreographer's choice:

- the number of dancers required;
- the particular role they are dancing;

- their physique;
- their gender.

Each of these will be considered in turn.

> A choreographer ... has no way of expressing himself but through movements which he must implant in the muscles of other dancers.
>
> (*David Lichine in* Ballet, *1947*)

> Alvin looks for dancers who will bring some special quality and who can make a strong statement on stage. He is really quick to see if somebody's personality is the kind of personality that will give ... Alvin has a good eye for how we'll all look together.
>
> (*Elinor Rogosin on choreographer Alvin Ailey, in* Dance Makers, *1980*)

> That's why Balanchine is such a marvellous choreographer. He has a concept of his dancers ... he knows each of them so well that he can propose something for them to try that they might not be aware they can do.
>
> (*Twyla Tharp in* Dance Makers, *1980*)

The statements above reflect various opinions about the choice of dancers. Most professional choreographers have a large number of dancers to choose from, and they will choose the ones who most suit their own personal style. This may mean that a certain dancer's *physique* will be right for a particular kind of technique; for example, Balanchine was famous for choosing very thin dancers in order to show off the lines that he required. Other choreographers may choose dancers for their *inner qualities*; for example, Lea Anderson prefers dancers of all shapes and sizes, but is concerned that they also be *thinking people*:

> When you're doing lots of tiny movements that need to be linked or performed in such a way that the dancer looks as though they know why they're doing everything. Each movement has a reason behind it ... I'm constantly looking for things for dancers to be thinking on stage.
>
> (*Lea Anderson in interview*)

When choosing dancers, you need to be clear about how they can enhance your dance.

There are those occasions when a dancer and a choreographer act as a mutual 'spark' for each other. Richard Alston and Michael Clark worked together in this way in various works including *Soda Lake* (1981) and *Dutiful Ducks* (1982). Clark's training in ballet and in the Cunningham technique equipped him with fast foot work, an ability to change direction quickly and an open torso which curved with ease and fluidity. All these technical strengths suited Alston's style perfectly.

The number of dancers

The *number* of dancers that is chosen should be appropriate to the choreographic idea. A large corps de ballet is clearly going to have different visual impact from that of a trio or duet. Nineteenth-century ballet works usually involved large numbers of dancers and soloists. In modern dance the groups tend to be smaller, and the performance of the group as a whole tends to be just as important - if not more so - than that of a soloist in any given piece.

Generally speaking, the more dancers there are, the more dramatic possibilities there will be. In a duet, the possible relationship - or conflict - is 1 vs 1. With four people, there are five possibilities:

- 1:1:1:1, or
- 2:1:1, or
- 2:2, or
- 3:1, or
- 4 together.

The possibilities do not end here, however, because *different* dancers may, at *different* times, act as the odd one out, and that increases the number of possible relationships again. In total, there are *15* possible combinations for a quartet.

TASK NINETEEN

In fours, read the notation placings in Figure 2.8. Decide together on the order in which to make these group shapes, and link them up with simple walking and running. Can you now find what the 15 different permutations for a quartet are? Add your findings to the original five shapes.

Bearing in mind how complex the possibilities are, it is thus especially advisable to ensure that the number of dancers be appropriate for a particular choreographic idea. If your starting point is a large painting with lots of action and figures, it may be appropriate to have five, six or more dancers. And for a poem or story with a certain number of characters, the number of dancers may need to be the same.

In Robert Cohan's *Hunter of Angels* (1967), the choice of a male duet was ideal to tell the story of Jacob and Esau. It offered an opportunity to show the struggle between the twins, and it cleverly and economically involved one of the dancer's playing a *dual* role as both Esau and the angel which visits Jacob. The transition between these two characters was accomplished smoothly and convincingly.

The idea of a trio is, like that of a quartet, to weave the dancers together, as in Glen Tetley's *Pierrot Lunaire* (1962), where a couple is broken up by a third person (this work explores the classic story of relationships to its maximum). In ballets such as Sir Frederick Ashton's *The Dream*, 1964 and Glen Tetley's *The Tempest*, 1979 the Shakespeare stories hold many opportunities for different size groups

Figure 2.8 *Notation showing placings for Task 19*

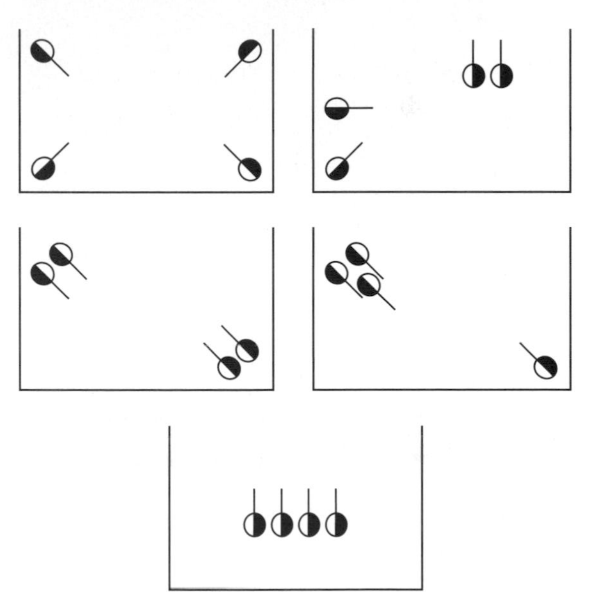

to be used in the various dramatic situations, and for the different characters. Again, choosing the correct number of dancers is crucial to revealing the narrative. Later in this book, more attention will be given to timings for and the staging of groups.

Role

Choosing those dancers who are appropriate for a specific role has already been mentioned in the previous section on dynamics. An

Pierrot Lunaire by Glen Tetley

individual dancer may have natural tendencies towards certain qualities and specific technical abilities which make them ideal for certain roles. In classical ballet, this may often be the case with characterisation – Lynn Seymour *is* Juliet in MacMillan's *Romeo and Juliet* (1965). Her gift as a dramatic dancer was reported to have propelled the action of the whole ballet. The same principle applies to post-modern works, but may not be so obvious. Speaking about the choreographer Rosemary Butcher, critic Stephanie Jordan points out:

> Her works, physically simple as they might appear, demand fine, experienced dancers and can be extraordinarily diminished in their absence.
>
> (*Stephanie Jordan in* Striding Out, *1992*)

Other post-modern choreographers like Bill T. Jones choose total 'non-dancers' as well as those with superb technique. In his *Still Here* (1994), Jones used people whom he had met through a therapy workshop for those who had lost loved ones through AIDS and other long-term terminal illnesses. Their taped testimonies, together with their role as actual performers in the piece, made the work 'undiscussible' for some critics (Arlene Croce in the *New Yorker*).

Similarly, Lloyd Newson's work with DV8 demands that dancers dig deep into their own life experiences to create roles and material for the works. This is an intense way of working and demands mental strength from the dancers in order to ensure in-depth exploration of the serious issues which are the main motivation of DV8.

Physique

Choreographers can tap into specific physiques sometimes. Lynn Seymour tells us how MacMillan used a particularly strongly built male dancer once whilst working on *Anastasia* (1967, Berlin). According to Seymour the pas de deux were:

> ... really difficult, because Macmillan wanted to use Rudolf Hotz's strength ... as much as possible so that the double-work became very strenuous.
>
> (*Lynn Seymour in* Making a Ballet, *1974*)

For performing lifts in pas de deux, body strength in the legs and upper body is required. Similarly, in the post-modern genre, where responsibility for lifting is often shared equally throughout the group, suitable physiques are more likely to make for safety and injury prevention, and the dance itself should also ultimately look better for the audience as a result.

The choreographic demands of the corps de ballet are such that a uniform physique is a prerequisite. This may also be observed in some mainstream modern dance companies. By contrast, in the post-modern genre we see the most diversity in physiques, as in The Cholmondeleys and The Featherstonehaughs.

Gender

A not dissimilar situation exists in choosing dancers for their gender. Certain roles in classical ballet demand specifically male or female performers, according to conventional stereotyping, and this may also be the case, of course, in some modern dance choreography. Take, for example, Martha Graham's 1944 *Appalachian Spring* which uses the heterosexual role model, with herself as bride and Eric Hawkins as groom (Hawkins went on to become her husband in real life). Merce Cunningham's works, by contrast, tend to be rather more *androgynous* in that his parts seem able to be interchangeable between males and females. This is a feature which we also notice in the work of post-modern choreographer Richard Alston. In *Soda Lake* (1981), Alston states quite clearly that it is a solo for either gender. Although originally choreographed for Michael Clark, in its later revival for the Rambert, it was danced sometimes by Mark Baldwin and sometimes by Amanda Britton. The nature of the movement is such that it has a gender-neutrality. It is the fact that the dancers have a similar training in Cunningham and ballet techniques that is the main reason for choosing them.

Post-modern choreographer Mark Morris also uses androgyny in his work, not through the gender-neutrality of the movement but by smashing the accepted norms of classical ballet and deliberately swapping roles around. This anarchic attitude to tradition and to gender stereotyping is best seen, perhaps, in his version of *The Nutcracker*, called *The Hard Nut* (1991)! In the dance of the snowflakes (a section well known to balletgoers), the stage is filled with dancers dressed uniformly, moving in unison en pointe and so on. Nothing unusual you may say, until you notice that these accomplished dancers are a mixture of men and women all executing the same movement, albeit with differing aplomb. The various qualities of the different genders render the movement a new richness and excitement. This tendency in post-modern choreographers to reject traditional gender stereotypes reflects a concern for political correctness in sexual politics. Choreographers like Lloyd Newson, with his company DV8, are concerned with such issues as homophobia, and he casts the dancers appropriately. For example, in *Strange*

Fish (1992), the opening image is a naked female Christ on the cross. Matthew Bourne is another whose work follows a similar approach to gender issues. The Fairy Godmother in *Cinderella* (1997) is danced by a male and the Ugly Sisters who are traditionally danced by men revert back to 'type' and are performed by women. This is a stark turn around where the men now play the goodies and the women the villains. Similarly, Lea Anderson has a concern for breaking down traditional stereotypes:

> The way I choose to show people is very conscious. I choose not to use very stereotypical role models and I choose very carefully what gender does what. It is deliberate. I'd never show a bloke chucking a woman about … I've seen enough of those. …
>
> (*Lea Anderson in interview, educational resource pack on Flesh and Blood*)

Put at its simplest, there are two obvious possibilities when choosing dancers. You could first choose the dancer and then build the choreography around their individual characteristics. Or you could choose a dancer whose style, physique and personality already suits your own choreographic idea. Alternatively perhaps the dancers may choose the choreographer who they think suits them best.

For more information on working with dancers see Chapter 6.

Strange Fish *by DV8 Physical Theatre*

References and resources

BOOKS AND ARTICLES

Brinson P. and Crisp C., *Ballet for All*, Newton Abbot: David & Charles, 1971

Crisp, C. and Clarke, M., *Making a Ballet*, London: Studio Vista, 1974.

Ellfeldt, L., *A Primer for Choreographers*, London: Dance Books, 1988

Hayes C. in *New Dance*, no. 42. October 1987

Humphrey, D., *The Art of Making Dances*, New Jersey: Princeton Book Co., 1959

Jordan S., *Striding Out*, London: Dance Books, 1992

Klosty, J. (ed), *Merce Cunningham*, Clarke, USA: Irwin & Co. Ltd., 1975

Nugent A., *The Stage*, November 30th, 1989

Mackrell J., 'Cholmondeleyism', in *Dance Theatre Journal*, vol. 4, no. 2, 1986

Rogosin, E., *The Dance Makers*, New York: Walker & Co., 1980

VIDEOS

From www.dancebooks.co.uk

Ballet Rambert, *Different Steps: Three Approaches to Choreography*, Rambert Dance Co.

DV8 Physical Theatre, *Strange Fish* and *Dead Dreams of Monochrome Men, Swan Lake*, Bourne, M., *The Hard Nut*, Morris, M.

Soda Lake, Alston, R., 1981

From National Resource Centre for Dance. www.surrey.ac.uk

WEB SITES

Companies

Adventures in Motion Pictures www.amp.uk.com

DV8 www.dv8.co.uk

Shobana Jeyasingh www.shobanajeyasingh.co.uk

General Information

www.ballet.co.uk

MUSIC

The following have lots of tracks between 2 and 3 minutes long:

Morricone, E., *The Mission*, Virgin Records, CDV 2402-257994, 1986, recommended for Task 6

Malcolm Arnold, *English and Irish Dances*, Polygram 425 661 2LM, 1990 recommended for Task 4

Contemporary Dance Rhythms, 1996 available from John Jalib Millar at Shamal Studios, 65 Bayham Street, Camden, London. Tel.: 0207 388 8205, recommended for Task 7

Tomita, I., *Pictures at an Exhibition*, by Moussorgsky (electronic version), RCA ARL1-0838, 1975, recommended for Task 8

Serra E., *The Big Blue*, soundtrack to the film *The Big Blue*, Gaumont/Virgin CDV 2541, 1988, recommended for Task 14

Soundtrack from the film *Diva*, Discovery Label, CD950622 recommended for Task 16

Terry Oldfield, *Spirit of the Rainforest*, New World, NWC 195, recommended for Task 17

THREE

THE CONSTITUENT FEATURES OF DANCE: THE PHYSICAL SETTING

The movement and dancers are a main consideration, but of course, the complete picture also includes the choices of:

- the performing space or venue;
- the set;
- lighting;
- costume;
- props.

These will be the focus of this chapter.

The performing space

The type of space that a dance is performed in will affect the design of the choreography. The dancers themselves will also need to relate to the environment in which they are dancing. With both the dance and the dancers actively relating to the performing space, the audience should have a clear view of the performance in all its aspects. The following quotation makes this clear.

> My first piece *Tank Dive*, was made for a small room ... that is actually a little auditorium ... and the whole piece is predicated for that space; I mean one of the walls was curved, so a lot of patterns had to do with that. It has very much to do with site lines.
>
> (*Twyla Tharp in* The Dance Makers, *1980*)

Although we usually expect to see dance on a stage, nowadays choreographers work in many different types of venue. Dances can even be seen in enormous outdoor spaces – such as in Lea Anderson's *Sportorama* (1999). The site for this dance was the huge arena at Crystal Palace, with both her companies The Cholmondeleys and The Featherstonehaughs plus 160 other performers. The audience sat along one long side of the hall and watched epic size scenes. A variety of group formations portrayed different sports. On occasion the performers moved among the audience. In the post-modern era, dancing in airports, tunnels, art galleries, museums and gymnasiums, and on rooftops and beaches, have all been considered to be suitable for performance.

THE PROSCENIUM STAGE

When you go to the theatre, the picture-frame *proscenium* stage is the traditional set-up. This is the one most often used for classical ballet, and it offers rich possibilities for showing things clearly if it is used correctly.

The historical context

In the fifteenth century, Italians staged lavish indoor spectacles. Theatres dating back to 1580 can be found in Italy. These were fairly open so that the performers, often courtiers, could move easily from the auditorium to the stage. Sometimes, the *audience* would perform too.

The placement of dancers

Placing and moving dancers around on such stages must take into consideration the fact that different areas have differing degrees of *power*. Dancers placed upstage will appear *distant* (in space *and* time) for the audience, whereas downstage has a feel of more intimacy, and can be used for comic effect. The stage is divided into named areas as shown in Figure 3.1.

Figure 3.1 *To show stage areas and their possible uses*

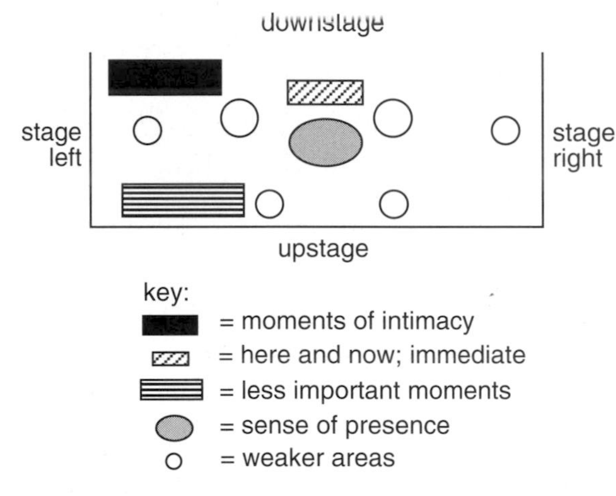

Matthew Bourne uses the up- and downstage areas to great dramatic effect in *Swan Lake* (1995). The Prince, after writing his suicide note, makes his way upstage and contemplates the lake from the very back centre of the stage. It is as if he is about to become a part of the past. In contrast, comic moments like the walking of the Royal Corgi dog and the hilarious perfumed ballet interlude are all performed at the very front of the stage.

Kenneth MacMillan's *Song of the Earth* (1965) ends with the figures of Death and the Man and Woman travelling forward slowly as the curtain falls. There is promise of afterlife and renewal as they move into 'present' time in the downstage area.

To show a stage from Florence 1616

The movement of dancers on pathways in the stage space

Similarly, the *diagonals* on the stage are very powerful. According to Doris Humphrey, if a figure walks down from upstage right to downstage left, this action:

> ... will clothe this figure with heroic strength, all made merely by the use of architecture of stage space.
>
> (*Doris Humphrey in* The Art of Making Dances, *1959*)

On this pathway, the dancer will pass through weaker and more powerful points of the stage space – not least of which is centre-stage, where the presence will be at its strongest. Approaching downstage, the dancer will then become more human, someone we care about. This device is used in *Giselle* (1841, Coralli, Perrot) when Hilarion is being thrown into the lake by the *wilis*. Starting downstage left, bottom corner, Myrtha, Queen of the wilis, seals his fate by ordering him to his watery grave, the lake. He is propelled along the line of the corps de ballet stretching the whole length of the diagonal to the far upstage right corner. The other dancers seem almost invisible, their fine arm gestures, so effortless, stirring the air as he is blown along. Then, he finally exits. Gone from the human world, he is now forever in the distance of time and space, in the immortal world.

There are always exceptions to the rules, however, and choreographer Merce Cunningham, although acknowledging the stage space as such, chooses to ignore the above considerations. He makes it the responsibility of the *audience* to decide what to select to watch in dances that scatter over the space like leaves blown by the wind. There is *no* central focus of power. This is particularly noticeable in his dance *Tread* (1970). The electric fans, designed by Bruce Nauman, are regularly spaced across the front of downstage, causing not only an interruption in the audience's sight lines but also a breeze in the first few rows. This puts the viewer in a situation where, as in real life on the street, you must make choices as to what to watch and when. You could focus on the entire stage, or on just one small area between two fans, or on Cunningham's interrupted journey across the stage. It is almost as though the picture frame has gone and the stage is filled with dancers in any number of places, all of equal importance. Cunningham's attitude to space is similar to that of American modern painters of the 1960s and 1970s, like Jackson Pollock whose technique of dripping paint randomly onto canvas gave the effect of a continuous flow through the space.

> Cunningham inherited a stage space ... a formula of perspective unchanged since the Renaissance. As a result, stage space implied a class society in which centre stage was regal. ... The sides, the back and corners? Strictly plebeian, home of the brave corps. ... There is no *best* spot on a Cunningham stage. ... The stage is not merely decentralised, it is demagnetised.
>
> (*James Klosty in* Merce Cunningham, *1975*)

When working in venues with an audience on two, three or four sides, Cunningham would give different dancers different fronts. This would create more of a three-dimensional look – one well suited to the next physical setting which we are looking at.

In-the-Round: The Circular Stage

The 'in-the-round' physical setting, which dates back to the ancient Greek chorus set-up, and even before that to circles in ritual dances, alters our whole attitude to – and concept of – design; and even nowadays, it is difficult for some to make the adjustment to the circular setting. Consideration must be given to spatial design in the choreography – particularly in the placing and facings of the dancers. This, as just mentioned, would pose little problem for a Cunningham choreography – unlike for most ballet and modern dance works, which may have been framed for the proscenium stage.

Obviously, circle patterns and circular group shapes will work well, and this makes for many possibilities: to face the centre and give a feel of a magical magnetic centre; to spiral around to and from the centre, like the Snail formation in a mediaeval *Carole* (line dance); to place the dancers' backs to the centre and acknowledge the outside space; to proceed around the edge of the circle in a ritualistic manner; to crisscross the circle with other geometric formations like triangles, squares, lines or less formal clusters of dancers. Acknowledging the power of the circle can lead to much choreographic interest. Using it in an uninformed way, on the other hand, may lead to a drab design which does not allow the audience 'in', either because it comes over as two-dimensional or because too much use is made of inward/centre facings. (It is interesting to observe how young children's or beginners' first attempts at choreography often involve working in an inwards-facing circle. All that the audience can then see are their backs, obscuring any interesting movement which may be happening.)

The videodance of Shobana Jeyasingh *Duets with Automobiles* (1994 for BBC 2 *Dance for Camera* series, director Terry Braun), places dancers in a variety of interiors of modern London buildings. In one section the eye of the camera places the audience in the centre of a circular space and creates a feeling of being in-the-round. The camera also looks through the eyes of the dancers from windows which overlook down into the space.

In Robert North's *Troy Game* (1974), the circle is used to emphasise the amusing atmosphere of sparring and competition between soldiers. The group travel around the circle in a motif which allows them to acknowledge the audience, the centre of the circle and each other. It has an alive, three-dimensional qual-

To show use of circle formations: Nureyev and Fonteyn in La Bayadère

ity. By manipulating the turns and the timing, they rotate and try to catch each other out by a sweeping leg gesture, rather like a football tackle to the opponent's lower leg. Each soldier jumps over this tackle just in time. Thus, the circle continues to 'hypnotise' and to amuse the audience simultaneously.

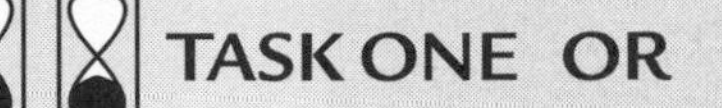

TASK ONE OR

In groups of six or eight, work together to compose a dance entitled 'Black holes, shooting stars, the planets and their spinning moons'. Choreograph it with a view to performing it in-the-round. (Suggested music: 'Alienscape' on *Dancetechnic*, by David Harry, 1992.)

OTHER STAGES

As well as the performing settings mentioned above, there are others which also require consideration about the placings and spacings of dancers in choreography. Although similar to the proscenium stage or in-the-round, they each have their own individual characteristics:

- *End stage:* there is no frame or arch, and the stage and the auditorium continue into each other.
- *Apron stage:* part of the stage projects into the audience.

In any of these, *where* the audience is seated – in terms of above or below the stage – will affect what they see. If they are lower than the stage, then the front vertical lines will be emphasised. On the other hand, the movement in the horizontal plane, the floor pattern and the formation will be stressed if the audience is seated above the stage.

THE SITE-SPECIFIC PERFORMANCE SPACE

We may think that dance performances out-of-doors are something quite avant-garde and post-modern, but before the courts of Europe introduced the proscenium stage they held spectacles of quite a different type: the wealthy Italian aristocracy of the High Renaissance held spectacular pageants out of doors as well as inside the palaces. Centuries later in the 1960s, dancers and choreographers returned to outside settings as an alternative to the theatres. They also looked for alternative indoor venues in which to present dances which used their environment as a rich source of stimulus for the imagination. And now, dances are performed anywhere and everywhere. The choreographers Lea Anderson and Rosemary Butcher typify the attitude of choosing unconventional performing spaces.

These more informal environments pose very different problems for choreographers. As Rosemary Butcher became aware, in her out-of-doors work, the dance can tend to get lost in the surrounding architecture, or amongst passers-by. For this reason, she later used the perspectives and distances of specific sites to her advantage. In *Passage North East* (1976), Butcher first placed the dancers in the distance: on the far side of the harbour to the Arnolfini Gallery, Bristol. Then, they crossed

Site-specific dance in the Natural History Museum, London,
Dance Umbrella *1996 Stephan Koplowitz's 'Genesis Canyon'*
Photo by Chris Nash

To show outdoor spectacles of the Renaissance, Alcina's Island, *1664, in the grounds of the Palace of Versailles. It uses the lake as part of the set. The island in the centre back was burnt in a huge firework display. The wings are supported by guy ropes*

by boat to end up dancing to the audience in front of the gallery. In North America in the 1960s, many other artists also experimented with these more informal settings, both indoors and out. One such artist was Anna Halprin. Halprin had influenced the Judson Group, New York (started 1962), which comprised dancers who were working as a cooperative. This set a trend later in the UK when X6 set up a similar group in London in 1976.

> We don't accept the theatre as a conventional place where the audience is here and you're there, but it is a place. ... You don't have to be on the stage separating here from there. ... Everything we do is dance somehow...
>
> (*Anna Halprin in* The Vision of Modern Dance, *1980*)

Such informal indoor and outdoor settings offer different ways for the audience to relate to the choreography. In X6, choreographers like Madee Dupres experimented with how she could build an easy relationship with the audience in these settings. Her audiences were asked to comment or even to take part sometimes. In *Choice and Presence* (1977), they were invited to make noises of their own choice when she raised a foot. Thus, the audience was involved not just visually but also audibly and sometimes physically. They would also raise and lower blinds as she improvised the dance. Clearly, this way of choreographing is *not* concerned with the rules and sight lines of the picture-frame proscenium stage!

In 1996 the Dance Umbrella Festival staged its first site-specific work. Set in the Natural History Museum main hall *Genesis Canyon* by Stephan Koplowitz used 38 dancers and three singers. It emphasised the Festival director's belief about site-specific work:

> ... it offers the possibility of erasing the belief that dance is for a selected few who have been educated to understand it.
>
> (*Val Bourne in* Barefoot in Jurassic Park *by Allen Robertson, The Times, 25 September 1996*)

Sometimes the audience are inadvertently involved, as in Lea Anderson's *Out on the Windy Beach* (1998)

> Perhaps the man who ambled drunkenly up to the raised stage at Brighton's Hove Lawns thought he was suffering from a particularly bad bout of delirium tremens when he saw six fluorescent creatures ... Staff diverted him away, but for a few brief moments he had shown signs of adding welcome spark to Lea Anderson's new alfresco show.
>
> (*Nadine Meisner in* The Sunday Times, *31 May 1998*)

Architect Mark Foley, who has collaborated with choreographers in designing dance venues, thinks that dance is a unique way for architects to experience space. More and more choreographers are relating their work to architecture. Shobana Jeyasingh thinks that dance and architecture both 'sculpt space'. Her classical South Indian dance vocabulary can be seen as fluid geometry.

 **TASK TWO OR** 

Walk around your campus and find a place you feel that you could dance in. Spend some time there, and discover what parts of it draw your attention – a space between the buildings, a tree, a staircase, a bench . . . Watch, and listen. What type of people use this space? Do they leave certain energies behind them that may add atmosphere to your dance?

Gradually add things to this place – in movement, or in objects, costume etc. – that make clearer the special qualities of the place. They might echo the buildings, shapes, light, sound, memories evoked. Develop movements which draw attention to your discoveries about this place. What is special about it? Is it dangerous? Is it fun? Is it busy or calm? It is a place for travelling or waiting? What makes it different?

The basic physical setting may be transformed by whatever a choreographer may choose to place in it. This will be the next aspect of the physical setting to be considered.

The set

In the outdoor environment, of course, 'set' is often already present, and the choreographer may choose merely to add to it. On the stage, however, the choice of set is individual to each dance and to each choreographer, and involves anything from leaving the stage plain and bare to covering it with plastic carnations or dead leaves as Pina Bausch did in *Carnations* (1982) and *Bluebeard* (1977). (The trampling of the flowers under the dancers' feet is Bausch's way of telling us that people often crush each other in their relationships; and the dead leaves similarly remind us of a couple whose romance is gradually fading.)

The history of ballet shows how sets gradually evolved alongside the development of technique and choreography.

THE HISTORICAL

By the sixteenth century, the set began to become important. The theories of Roman architect Vitruvius were revived, and three types of stage set emerged:

1 *scena tragica*, showing objects suited to monarchs;
2 *scena comica*, showing ordinary houses;
3 *scena satyrica*, showing pastoral scenes.

These would underline the messages which the entertainments contained. This is particularly clear to us when we notice the use of complex machinery to make gods and heroes appear from the heavens. Note that at the time of the Renaissance, amazing the audience was the stamp of authority of the ruling families. It would function to enforce their power over others. It was also an acceptance of Aristotle's belief that theatre existed to release the emotions. As the sixteenth century progressed, backdrops became interchangeable through a variety of ingenious devices. The use of perspective to add to the illusion gave events like *Le Ballet Comique de la Reine* (1581) a focal point in the auditorium –

which is where the royals would sit, centre front row. This has influenced the design of proscenium stages in theatres ever since.

By the seventeenth century, wings had also been invented, and theatres now sprang up – particularly in Italy. The proscenium became properly established, and a splendour of machinery, colour, light and dance exploded.

In the eighteenth century, luxurious Italian and French spectacles were set against meticulously painted backdrops of staggering architectural realism. These larger-than-life sets marked the pinnacle of neoclassical theatre dance in the late eighteenth century and early nineteenth centuries. Respect for order, antiquity, heroism and nobility were the characteristics of theatre design, particularly in Italy. People like Sanquirico designed sets with perspectives painted with mathematical precision, giving an ordered appearance. The French Rococo design was particularly outstanding at this time, and there was also a growing taste for the exoticism of China and the East – as seen in *Les Fêtes Chinoises* (1754) by Jean-Georges Noverre in Paris. This fashion was combined with a move away from seventeenth-century formality in favour of a more natural look. This was in the context of a growing curiosity about freedom of expression both in society and in the other arts generally.

The rebellion against the cold logic of neoclassicism, which itself was a reaction against the more frivolous Rococo style, finally resulted in the great era of romanticism in society and all the arts. Revolution in *society* was a main influence here. The French Revolution was about to explode, and with it the ordinary people were to become leading lights in society, replacing the European aristocracy in the bid for power. As such, they became part of the romantic backdrop from which writers, musicians and painters could choose elements when telling stories.

Ballet was a late arrival to the romantic movement. The writings of Victor Hugo and others began to influence ballet. The breakthrough came with *La Sylphide* (1832). With Marie Taglioni in the lead role and designs by Ciceri, an atmosphere of magical moonlit forest glades and floating sylphs was created. In the nineteenth century, the painted backdrop of the romantic ballet – with its realistic trees and even *real* plants, and its mirrors placed to look like lakes, as in the original *Giselle* (1841) – became the new fashion.

The decline of this burst of freedom of expression in the middle and the end of the nineteenth century affected the design of sets as well as the standard of dancing and choreography. Set designs now became largely mindless and decorative, with little meaning or originality. One outstanding exception to this was the Shishkov design for Petipa's *The Sleeping Beauty* (The Imperial Ballet, 1890). He used a theme of the grand reign of Louis XIV as a clear homage to the theatre's patron, the Russian Tsar. The design enhanced the brilliance of the ballet itself. It contrasted two historical styles: an architectural backdrop with vistas of sixteenth-century, Versailles-type magnificence (Act 1), and the eighteenth-century Baroque-style triple arch (Act 2), where Petipa placed the god Apollo, in Louis XIV-style costume. Only in Russia were standards upheld, and even there tradition was becoming stale. However, it was from here that ballet was to be reborn in glittering glory, like the phoenix rising from the flames, when a rich Russian patron of the arts, Sava Mamontov, commissioned painters to design sets for his private operas. From this, Serge Diaghilev was inspired by the painters Bakst and Benois to found the Ballet Russes, which became a hot bed of innovation. The closeness of designer, composer and choreographer, insisted on by Diaghilev, led to explorations into creative new ideas and ideals for all aspects of the ballet. Diaghilev employed names like Picasso (*Parade*, 1917) and Tchelitchev (*Ode*, 1928) – the avant garde of European painters. Thus, ballet began to look forward once more.

During World War I Europe was in turmoil, and in this context the Ballet Russes took on the break with the past, as did cubism in painting and discord in the new music of such composers as Stravinsky and Satie. It was a meeting point and a melting pot for ideas which struck out in new directions. Consequently, stage design took on many different functions and identities: the humorous novelty of moving skyscrapers in the cubist *Parade* (Massine), where costumes became so extreme that it was difficult not to see them as sets rather than as dancer's clothes. In Massine's *Ode*, the revolutionary use of phosphorescent costumes, neon lighting, puppets and film to tell the story of eighteenth-century Russian court spectacles and revels was astonishing to audiences of that time. The Ballet Russes, from its Monte Carlo theatre, was reaching new heights of innovation. Diaghilev brought in the new wave of French artists such as composer Eric Satie, artist Jean Cocteau and designer Coco Chanel. In Russia the new politics of communism interested Diaghilev. Along with this went artistic developments like constructivism. This movement

La Chatte, *designed by Naum Gabo*

was influenced by cubism but focused on making constructions which explored space and form for their own sake. The famous constructivist Gabo designed the set for *La Chatte* (1927, Balanchine). The transparent mica sculptures on a black floor and backdrop were uniquely original in that time.

Simplicity and paring things down to their very basics was one of the innovations of the hard-hitting modern dance works of Martha Graham in the 1920s and 1930s. Talking about the difference between traditional painted backdrops and modern dance decors, she says:

> ... basically a painting enlarged for the stage ... at best can only be an accent for the dance.... Dance decor can ... serve as a means of enhancing movement and gesture to the point of revelation of its content.
>
> (*Martha Graham in* The Vision of Modern Dance, *1980*)

In her collaborations with the Japanese sculptor Isamu Noguchi, in dances such as *Frontier* (1935), the set became integrated into the choreography and served to enhance the meanings in the movements. In *Frontier*, a six-minute solo, Graham appears as a young woman living in the wild western lands of the USA. The set is a section of a fence, from which two large ropes fly out and upwards like the railway track disappearing into the vast open spaces which surround her home. The dance is about the North American pioneering spirit on one level, but it also touches on how the space makes the woman feel. She marks out a square pattern on the floor – almost like the fence bordering a ranch – using tiny steps.

THE PRESENT DAY

World War II ended in 1945. It had restricted dance and theatre greatly. Once over, companies such as The Royal Ballet were back in business and the traditional classics were restaged, often retaining the traditional grand style. The reopening of The Royal Opera House, Covent Garden in 1946 was marked by a new production of *The Sleeping Beauty*. Olive Messel's set designs for the Sergeyev version showed off the elegance of the Petipa ballet. They were the essence of fairy tale enchantment, and much needed in the depressed times. Still highly regarded today the set design may be seen to have influenced later versions. The later and very different Victorian Gothic look of Henry Bardon's 1968 production (Ashton) was thought to have dominated the dancing. The 1975 Georgiadis design for a Nureyev production (The London Festival Ballet), based the look on a sound historical basis with its mediaeval castle.

From this point onwards, a rich variety of set designs opened up. Merce Cunningham's collaborations with famous avant-garde painters has produced some intense and remarkable moments of choreography. In *RainForest* (1968), the dancers moved among helium-filled silver pillows designed by Andy Warhol. This is typical of the unpredictable element in Cunningham's work. The design, music and dance are all independently created, only coming together in performance. This is designed not only to surprise the audience but also to add to the environment in which the dancers are performing. The dancers in

RainForest move around and between the pillows with ease and with little concern. The dance and the pillows may be connected or not: the decision lies with each dancer and with each member of the audience. This is a very different attitude from that of Martha Graham whose sets supported the symbolism and emotional meanings of the choreography.

The legacy of commissioning contemporary artists such as with Kenneth MacMillan and Australian painter Barry Kay continues. In Kay's design for *Anastasia* (1971, Royal Ballet) a wide range of settings, from a picnic scene to a hospital, are contained simply and economically in a modern style. He suspended large semi-transparent scrolls, then by adding props or film projections he varied locations from lyrical to visualising fearful memories of the Bolshevik massacre of the Imperial Russian Revolution.

Richard Alston in such work as *Soda Lake* (1981) features sculpture by Nigel Hall. Alston's background in visual art often shows in such collaborations. *Wildlife* (1984) is another example of his more formal style of which he says;

> ... it would be silly for them (the 'kites') to just sit there and say 'Look here's an artwork and we're underneath it ...' They had to be involved in some way and he (designer Richard Smith) invented motors which were able to turn them and also flew them up and down. So they get right into the space.
>
> (From *Rambert Dance Company video,* Different Steps, *1985*)

These are abstract works, intellectually cool. They link to infuence from the Cunningham style.

In Britain's New Dance movement, post-modern choreographers were exploring the set as a part of their overhaul of the values and strategies of dance. They presented dance as simply as possible and so *no* set was often the choice. We should remember that the choice of a bare stage is a 'something'.

> Miss Wigman owes curiously little of her success to externals. She has no scenery at all beyond curtains.
>
> (*Herman Ould in* The Dancing Times, *1926*)

The choreographers of New Dance chose to focus more on the movement for its own sake. Site specific work was experimented

RainForest *by Merce Cunningham*

with at this time. Where set, props or costume were used they often carried political meaning or were used in surprising, unconventional ways. The plethora of props and set in Fergus Early's *Naples* (1978) were used to exaggerate the spoof of Bournonville's 1842 *Napoli*. The original romantic fishing village becomes a twentieth-century Naples with a cast of comic caricatures of Italian life on lambrettas, with football fixations and eating Italian spaghetti and ice cream.

Matthew Bourne's use of set design by Lez Brotherston is bright, energtic, pantomime-like in wit and colour. In *Highland Fling – a romantic wee ballet* (1994), characters disappear up the chimney and the whole is suitably set for Bourne's parody and comic narrative.

Lloyd Newson uses a great deal of split-level set design. In *Strange Fish* (1992) various entrance and exit points through side doors, windows and hatches are combined with a tank of water to create a world where dancers are isolated and immersed in their subconscious. The set by Peter J. Davidson is active. It falls apart and its architectural structure required dancers to have lengthy rehearsal with it so that set and movement were integrated.

The use of film as set is popular nowadays. Mark Murphy (V-Tol) integrates specially made film clips into his dances to support the narrative, not just as background. *Without Trace* (2000) has large projections so that dancers are performing within 20-foot images of themselves. Siobhan Davies has been collaborating with film makers since 1986. Catherine Quinn in 'Dancer's log' describes how the designer David Buckland watches rehearsals of *Wild Airs* (1999, Siobhan Davies Dance Company) to decide which sections to film and where he wants stillnesses projected so as not to detract from the live action.

TASK THREE

(Extra time is also needed to collect the boxes.)

In a large group, collect as many different-sized cardboard boxes as possible. Mix them with blocks, chairs, ladders, benches and any other structural objects to hand, and arrange these in unexpected angles to create an environment. Explore ways of moving under, over, around and through the structure.

Compose movement around ideas selected from the following:

- restriction
- shape
- escape
- change
- hide and seek.

A set may enhance choreography by reinforcing the images which are being used or by acting as a complementary dimension in time and space. Or it may act simply to accompany the movement as an independent element on the stage. Whatever its function within the dance, the set may itself also be changed and transformed by the use of different *lighting* effects. This other aspect of physical setting is the next one which we will look at.

Lighting

From minute to minute in our everyday lives, we respond to changes in the light around us. This is a natural reaction exploited to the full in the theatre. From the earliest days of classical ballet, through the discovery of the use of ether for stage lighting, to the spectacular possibilities of today's lasers and other forms of technology, the use of changes in light has served to influence the audiences' reactions massively.

> Jack Thompson's work as lighting designer is crucial in creating strong atmosphere and highlighting meaning within scenes.
>
> (*Lloyd Newson in interview with Mary Luckhurst, from the programme note for* Bound to Please, *1997*)

A change in light triggers an automatic response in us. It attracts our attention, and it defines space. Atmospheres of warmth, danger, isolation and fear are here all possible. Boundaries between areas can be established. The use of projected slides, film and video can add to the technical effects.

THE HISTORICAL CONTEXT

During the Renaissance, and up until the middle of the seventeenth century, candles and daylight would have been the only source of lighting for any performances. With the invention of oil lamps and candelabra, however, more elaborate lighting effects became possible. These were then added to by the use of reflection in mirrors, and simple projection was also introduced. Fireworks displays further became common. But it was the invention of gas lighting in the 1830s which was to make a real difference. The romantic ballet could now be danced in a convincing moonlight. The gas itself, *ether*, became a source of fantasy for writers and poets of the day. Its effect on the mind was to produce hallucinations of mystery, and the word 'ethereal', meaning 'beyond the real, in the supernatural', was born. The ethereal included anything weird and wonderful. Spirits roaming in the dark, deepest forests, not unlike vampires, ghosts or ghouls – anything strange and exotic was the fashion.

In 1822 a designer named Ciceri staged a fairy opera *Aladin ou Lampe Merveilleuse* and first used gas lights. In 1831 he staged *Robert the Devil* at the Paris Opera. The moonlit cloisters, where white-veiled nuns emerged from their stone tombs, marked the beginning of many such scenes in the romantic ballets which followed. The famous Act Two of *Giselle* (1841) must have been a revelation for the audiences. Ciceri's forest glade was both dark and light but with a ghostly supernatural moonlight, and here the spirits of maidens who were abandoned on their wedding night roamed, vengefully seeking out victims, without pity for any man who may wander their way. In the gaslight, the wilis – as they were called – must have seemed to have been floating off the ground.

THE PRESENT DAY

Before going on to look at the modern-day use of light in dance, it is first of all worth considering a few technical aspects about lighting.

Different sorts of lights

- *Floods:* these give a general wash.
- *Battens:* these are rows of lights.
- *Spots:* there are two kinds: one gives a softer look – a *fresnel*; while, on the other hand, a *focus* gives a harder edge – i.e. a sharply defined beam. Both of these can have attachments which restrict the size of the circle of light: an *iris diaphragm*, and *barn doors* which reduce the spillage of light into unwanted areas.
- *Gels:* these can be slid into frames and fitted onto the front of the lights to give colour. Warm pinks and ambers, cooler light blues and steel or intense greens and deep reds and blues are all possible. Mixing gels will give other tints, like yellow (red + green) or purple (red + blue), but this will dim the brightness of the light.

When using lighting, the colour of the costumes must be considered. Costumes will usually look better if lit by a mix of pale, sympathetic tints. The choice of light colour can change the mood, create images and add a symbolic meaning to enhance the dance.

The *direction* from which the light shines is another important consideration. In dance, a side light at torso level works well because it gives depth and moulds the flexible body of the dancer.

Lighting for dance differs from other theatre lighting. Bodies are sculpted as they move in and out of the beams. Side light at low level 'lifts' the dancers whereas at a high level it creates shadows pulling the dancers forward. At a high level it also shines over the dancers' heads so it cannot be blocked by the moving bodies. So the most appropriate plots for dance use side and overhead light with pools, and any dark areas filled with front light.

It is always advisable to *cross-light*, that is, light an area from more than one direction. Large amounts of light from front-of-house above will give a stagey look, whilst light shone from a low level only can create eerie shadows.

The *intensity* of light can also vary to give effects like – at the end of a dance – a slow fade-down or a snap blackout. Similarly, at the start of a dance, the scene may gradually become visible, or figures may first appear just as silhouettes or as lit figures in general darkness. A *cross-fade*, where some lights fade up as others fade down, may be used to change from one scene to another – changing the atmosphere from, say, cool to hot.

The *cyc* is a light-coloured backdrop suspended from a batton. Light is thrown onto it so that a *wash* covers the back. It is lit by strip-lights in front and above it. It can be lit from the floor behind but this may put the dancers' feet in the dark. A black backdrop is often used but it is less flexible for lighting than a cyc.

Effects such as *gobos* (cut-out patterns placed in front of a light) can create patterns for dancers to move through – such as a forest glade. This can also be done by the projection of cut-out designs, a device which can distort the bodies of the dancers. Flashing lights, in turn, can give a lively, disco feel, and strobes and colour wheels can be useful too.

The work of Alwin Nikolais is renowned for its stunning and elaborate blend of light, slides and effects. Nikolais transforms the human shape of his dancers, makes them disappear, and then makes them reappear in kaleidoscope patterns of colour. His *Somniloquy* (1967) makes use of a slide projection onto a gauze curtain, in a setting like the mouth of a cave. Dancers appear behind this curtain, their faces lit by hand-held torches.

When they shine the torches onto the gauze, they make patterns on it. The projections change colour many times: blue, green, red, purple, silver. Finally, a projection of many *white* dots places the dancers in a snowstorm. Nikolais' concerns in his choreography are with the environment that we all live in. It changes, and *we* too change in a constant battle for survival.

In almost total contrast, the dance *Soda Lake* (Richard Alston, 1981) is daring in its simple use of plain white light. This post-modern solo is danced in simple black costume, accompanied by silence and by minimalist sculpture for the set.

Siobhan Davies' *The Glass Blew In* (1994) explored the differences between *human* qualities and those that have to do with shape and texture. The lighting was designed by Peter Mumford, and the original programme note says it all:

> The piece is a sensuous, poetic interplay of colour, pattern, dynamic and sound ... Mumford has marked out the stage with a rectangle whose floor is at different times, a wash of green violet or magenta. ... It gives full rein to Davies' fascination with borders. She presents her dancers not only inside the rectangle, but also on or outside its demarcation.
>
> (*From the original programme for* The Glass Blew In *by Siobhan Davies, 1994*)

The closeness of the dance and its lighting design is seen at its most intense here. Not only does the light support the mood, it also defines the actual space environment in which the dancers move.

In Lea Anderson's *Go Las Vegas* (1995, lighting by Simon Corder for the Featherstonehaughs), the audience itself contributed to the lighting. On entering the theatre, they were provided with small torches, and instructions were given in the programme, and verbally by one of the dancers, on exactly when and how these were to be used. At a signal, the torches are shone onto the dancer's phosphorescent silver suits, so that these light up whilst the dancers' faces and hands remain in blackness. The suits thus dance as if they have a life of their own. It is a fitting finale to a dance which has shredded the glitz and glamour of faceless showbiz – another direct hit at an aspect of our society which Anderson scrutinises.

> They're a pack of good time anarchists who take on the dance establishment with rambunctious glee.
>
> (*Review of* Go Las Vegas *in* Time Out *magazine, 1995*)

TASK FOUR

From the list of dance titles below, choose one and describe how you would light it. Make clear how it would start and end. Describe any changes which occur during the dance. Keep it simple.

Be sure to include notes on colour, direction, intensity and special effects.

- 'The corridors of power'
- 'Water scene'
- 'Silent movies'
- 'What goes around comes around'.

You may not have access to lights, but when next at the theatre or watching dance on video, be sure to keep an eye out for how the lighting is used to enhance the dance.

Costume

Any costume can be worn in relation to a dance. One can make the *most* of its restrictions, or one can use it to enhance both the general visual design and the particular ideas/concerns of the dance. In this sense, it is like choosing the right sort of lighting: it should be appropriate to, and should enhance, the overall purpose and expressivity of the dance. The following are the most basic considerations in the choice of costume:

- shape
- colour
- material.

THE HISTORICAL CONTEXT

In the spectacles of the late sixteenth and early seventeenth centuries, costumes were highly theatrical. Rich fabrics and fantastic designs were often used to enhance character. Some designs were grotesque and evil, others were harmonious, and the animal world was represented by the decoration of animal skins, the use of parrots and so on. Mortals and immortals mixed together in a world of magic and illusion.

By the middle of the seventeenth century, the world of fashion and very expensive clothes were a priority for the courts of Europe. The professional dancers of the court ballets had to dress elegantly and stylishly. The costumes were decorated symbolically so that the story was clear to the monarch and the court. After all, the ballets were usually about them, and so court dress with some decoration suited the occasion. According to the etiquette of the court, a dancer representing the monarch would be presented on stage for the monarch himself to admire! The way a man bowed or received bows told everything about him, and the audience too understood the symbolism of the costumes and choreography. The court life was thus presented in dance, and everything was done to support the power of the monarchy. Often, the ruler would be shown in the finale as the god Apollo or as the Sun, the supreme being within his domain. It must have been a fine line between who was

To show Berain design 1616, Habit d'Africain

just a performer and who was part of the *real* court, and hence the entertainments could make both political and imaginative statements at the same time.

The male dancers' designs allowed freedom of movement, but the females' skirts had to reach the ground. Masks were popular to show stylised characters such as sweet nymphs or hideous demons.

Gradually the court ownership over the theatres of Vienna, Milan and Paris weakened, and a more independent, professional dance tradition emerged. At the Paris Opera in the early eighteenth century, ballet found independence as a performing art. The success of *Les Fêtes Chinoises* (1754, Jean-Georges Noverre), revealed a new interest in the foreign and exotic. The rigid rules of costuming according to prescribed characters were less important, and as the need to move took priority, skirts shortened. In the 1730s, Camargo shortened her skirts from floor level to a few centimetres above the ankle. This enabled her renowned *entrechats* – the crossing or beating together of the feet during a leap in ballet – to be seen by the audience. In the writings of Noverre in the early eighteenth century, the major changes that were happening in ballet were clearly stated in his comments on costume.

> Obstinacy in adhering to outworn traditions is the same in every part of the opera; it is monarch of all it surveys. Greek, Roman, shepherd, hunter, warrior, faun ... all these characters are cut to the same pattern and ostentatious display rather than good taste has caused them to be spattered at caprice. Tinsel glitters everywhere. ... I would banish all uniformity of costume. ... I should prefer light and simple draperies of contrasting colours worn in such a manner as to reveal the dancer's figure. ... I would reduce by three-quarters the ridiculous paniers of our danseuses, they are equally opposed to the liberty, speed, prompt and lively action of the dance.
>
> (*Jean-Georges Noverre,* Letters on Dancing, *1760, translated by Cyril Beaumont, 1930*)

Noverre was against warriors who were dressed in their Sunday best, and he rejected masks as artificial. He was then moving towards greater natural design.

Around the corner lay the French Revolution and the new romanticism. Adoration of the exotic, peasant life and local colour, mystery and the supernatural was seen in Taglioni's *La Sylphide* (Paris Opera, 1832). The design, by Ciceri, included romantic, moonlit forest glades into which the white *tulle tutu*, fitted bodice, flowery crown and pink tights fitted perfectly. The invention of the *pointe shoe* allowed ballerinas to float over the earth, spirit-like. Costumes now also conveyed national identities from far-flung places – Scotland, Bulgaria, India.

The sumptuousness of the costumes towards the end of the nineteenth century is typified by the Russian Petipa's *Sleeping Beauty*. Some of the 1890 original costumes can be seen in The State Theatre Museum in St. Petersburg. They drip in gold and pearls and by today's standards would be very restricting on a dancer's movement. Also the tutus are longer than the style of modern ones. In the 2000 Kirov reconstruction of the original version, the costumes were redesigned to allow for greater freedom of movement, but in an effort to make the production authentic the costumes were still heavier than those we are used to seeing.

Ida Rubinstein in Schéhérazade; *costume by Bakst*

The influences of the artists Leon Bakst and Alexandre Benois produced a revolution of design and colour during the rebirth of ballet in the Diaghilev era at the start of the twentieth century. In the costumes for *Schéhérazade* (Fokine, 1910), there was a startling new use of intense, sensuous and powerful colours. The whole look was daring, vibrant and fantastic.

This taste for the shocking and avant-garde reached its height in 1917 with Picasso's humorous, absurd and modern designs in *Parade*. The movement of the Managers – the characters who ran the travelling show – was impeded under the heavy wooden frames of their skyscraper costumes. The dancers themselves were often a secondary consideration to the design.

THE PRESENT DAY

Shape

Costumes can often make life difficult for dancers (as we saw in *Parade*). Dancers usually rehearse in their most comfortable clothes, and when suddenly dressed in an unfamiliar costume, their whole sense of the movement may change. Costumes should move *with* the dancer, so that the dancer feels able to move with all the fullness required. Frederick Ashton had a favourite designer in Sophie Federovitch. He said of her:

> She believed firmly that nothing must hide the dancing or impede the dancers, and that the background should not distract.
>
> (*Sir Frederick Ashton in* Making a Ballet, *1974*)

Costumes for ballet tend to be more traditional in style than those for modern dance companies, and they usually flatter and enhance the dancer's classical lines. However, more adventurous attitudes to design for ballet costumes are perhaps more common now than they used to be. A modern dress version of *Giselle* (1996 Michael Pink, Christopher Gable) was staged by English National Ballet Company, with Charles Cusick-Smith the designer. It is set in 1939, with images of film stars and swish hotels. There is a clash of style, however, when a sword, such a crucial element in this ballet, appears. This is an anachronism: a gun would have been more likely in those times; and this is a problem also often presented with modern-dress versions of Shakespeare. In this instance, the sword is, however, essential for Giselle's suicide. The design for Act Two then brings us not a corps de ballet but instead an evil, undead, vampire-like hoard – truly romantic in its chilling horror and supernatural mystery.

The shaping of the zebra costume in David Bintley's *Still Life at the Penguin Café* (1988, The Royal Ballet) is effective in extending the lines and dynamics of the movement. A unitard with zebra stripes combines with face paint and head-dress which is like a mane running down the spine to the tail. Tassels are fixed to the arms connecting the dancer to the earth and emphasising the line of movement beyond the hands. The zebra skin is echoed in the women's dresses but they are frilly and manmade, posing the threat that an animal's fate may be to walk the catwalk next season.

A costume may be chosen deliberately to *distort* the lines and shape of the body. Alwin Nikolais combined this idea with his extraordinary lighting effects:

> In this piece a faceless trio, entirely covered by sacks, comes to life through various patterns of body pulsations. … They remind me of a collection of potato sacks pulled up over a mound of bubbling rubber.
>
> (*Elinor Rogosin in* Dance Makers, *1980*)

Nikolais is concerned with imposing *limitations* on the dancers, and with the way that this reflects the problems that humans have in managing their own environment. He rejects the Graham interest in Freudian psychodrama, heroines and national pride in favour of the relationships between human and nature. The question of the role of technology and a 'green' focus moves him to create, on stage, other worlds for our contemplation.

Similar distortions of the human form are found in the work of French choreographer Philippe Decouflé. *Decodex* (1995) has costumes which transform dancers into

Five Brahms' Waltzes in the manner of Isadora Duncan *by Frederick Ashton; dancer Lucy Burge, costume by David Dean*

chameleon-like creatures, microbes and praying mantis to name but a few.

> The show begins with a community of electrified frogs and you don't know whether their heads are up or down.
>
> (*Dominique Frétard in* Le Monde, *1995*)

Colour and materials

After the 1920s, there was a reaction against the opulence and excesses of the Diaghilev era. Designers restricted their use of colours to a more austere range, and shape too became pared-down. There was still fine traditional design for the world of ballet, but now also forward-looking designers for the new choreographers who formed the rebellious movement in modern dance. Isadora Duncan was the first to make a real impact, choosing to wear flimsy fabrics in the style of a Greek tunic – shocking to many at that time. This was beautifully reproduced in the tribute work *Five Brahm's Waltzes in the Manner of Isadora Duncan*. Danced by Lynn Seymour and choreographed by Frederick Ashton in 1975 (and later revived for Lucy Burge by Ballet Rambert in 1984), it too used the free, floaty fabric that had made Duncan famous. The material enhanced the freedom of the movement and its energetic patterns through the air.

The costumes for *Dracula* (1996, Pink/Gable) danced by the English National Ballet, are of lavish design in keeping with the classic story. Designed by Lez Brotherston (an Associate Artist with Adventures in Motion Pictures) the sumptuous fabrics, lush colour and beading are completed with the detail of sets of fangs.

Such partnerships as Merce Cunningham and Robert Rauschenberg also pared down costume and rejected decoration. Simple, all-in one, tight-fitting leotards, often in plain pastel shades of colour or – as in *Summerspace* (1958) – painted to match the background with tiny dots or soft sprays (design Rauschenberg), were used. These costumes would make the dancers appear not as if they were *in* space but as if they themselves *were* space.

The dance of Martha Graham was for austere times, and to be taken in a serious mood. Graham often designed the costumes herself, and they were frequently inspired by the movement itself. Take Martha Graham's solo *Lamentation* (1930) where the intense repetitive rocking and sorrow was moulded into the tight-fitting sheath. New fabrics like stretch jersey were now used for the first time. This use of costume enhanced the main idea of the dance.

The post-modernists of the 1960s onwards produced an enormous range of ideas on costuming dance. At first, they rejected all the achievements of their forerunners in modern dance.

> No to spectacle no to virtuosity no to transformations and magic and make believe no to glamour . . . no to style no to camp.

These are the words of iconoclast of the 1960s Yvonne Rainer, and natural everyday movements and simple street clothes were the final product. The dancers of New York, and later the UK, were working on shoestring budgets, and this factor had a significant influence on the look and values of dance.

From a choice of the dullest, most insignificant rehearsal clothes, we move to the imaginative designs of present-day French choreographers, Regine Chopinot and Philippe Decouflé. In Chopinot's *KOK* (1990), the costumes are designed by Jean-Paul Gaultier, the king of French avant-garde fashion. The final result is stunning and chic, with rich colour and pattern, as well as upfront sexuality.

In Shobana Jeyasingh's *Romance with Footnotes* (1993), the dancers wear terracotta in contrast to the bright iridescent set. The design of the clothes is traditional Indian and sets off those aspects of the choreography which are from the same geographical location.

Traditional Bharatha Natyam dancers wear bells around their ankles which function to weave the sound of the dancers' stamping with the accompanying drum beat.

In present-day Britain, costume design takes many and diverse forms – from the cool, simple cut of the Siobhan Davies company, as seen in the jeans and denim shirts of *Wyoming* (1988), to the leather jackets of the Cholmondeleys in *Metalcholia* (1994) or the long silver dresses made in the new Liquid Jersey in *Flesh and Blood* (1989/1993). Lea Anderson's choice of the metal, fluid, reflective fabric similarly *reminds* us of the chainmail of St Joan. Depending on the light, this latter fabric would change colour and texture during the various sections of the dance. This effect was also seen in Robert Cohan's work *Nympheas* (1976) for the London Contemporary Dance Theatre. Sections of Monet's impressionist painting of waterlilies were painted onto all-in-one leotards. The colour of the paint changed with the lighting, so that typical impressionistic changes in light and weather were reproduced on stage – from a calm blue summer's day to the sudden dark of a passing storm, the deep brown and greens soaking into the costumes.

In Richard Alston's *Wildlife* (1984), the sharp zig-zags of Richard Smith's set of moving kites are echoed in the strident designs and vibrant colours of the painted leotards. The dancers are in some imaginary deep forest, and their sharp, angular movements,

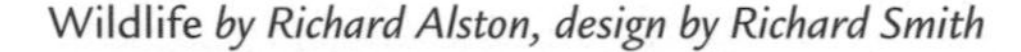

Wildlife *by Richard Alston, design by Richard Smith*

enhanced by the costume and set design, convey moments of animal instinct and their struggle for survival. There is an image of the broken lines of camouflage of animals in the undergrowth.

Masks and body or face paint offer other possibilities. These were particularly well used in *Ghost Dances* (1981) by Christopher Bruce for the then-named Ballet Rambert. The ghosts of South American myth appeared ghoulish and sinister in body paint which emphasised their skeletons, and in white eerie masks which hid any signs of mortality or human feelings.

Body paint is used to great effect on the swans in Bourne's *Swan Lake* (1995). The skin is whitish-grey and looks quite haunting. Combined with the black stripes on the head and face, the wild swan look is complete. The heavy 'feathered' trousers are the finishing touch.

We can say here, in summary, that costume may enhance the intentions of a dance by doing one of a number of things:

- emphasising the mood by choice of colour, shape, fabric, texture;
- enhancing the formal properties of movement through certain lines and shapes;
- clarifying character and story.

TASK FIVE

Fill a box with as many items of clothing and fabrics of different texture as possible. Place it in the centre of the room and let dancers take turns at 'Lucky Dips'. Whatever is pulled out of the box gives rise to movement ideas which everyone copies. The dancer passes on the item to another dancer who continues to improvise with it before abandoning it and dipping in for another. This idea can be further developed by making deliberate choices instead and then working in small groups to form short dances using the clothing chosen as a main source of movement ideas.

Props may also be added to the box if desired.

Props

As with set and costumes, props are an integral part of a dance. When used thoughtfully, they will not only serve as decoration but will also enhance the intentions of the dance and so add to the audience's appreciation.

Props may:

- enhance a character;
- have symbolic meaning;
- add to the movement itself;
- in the case of very large props, become almost *the set itself* as well.

Looking at a few examples will help you to understand the power of props.

PROPS WHICH HAVE SYMBOLIC MEANING/ENHANCE CHARACTER

The magic myrtle flower wand of Myrtha, Queen of the Wilis, in Act Two of *Giselle*, is *symbolic* of her all-powerful presence. In the Kirov version of the ballet, the wand actually explodes as she condemns Albrecht to dance himself to death, and it also moves of its own accord, thus adding to the narrative. And in Act One, the sword which Giselle throws herself onto (although not in many present-day versions) is symbolic of the sign of the cross. In committing suicide, Giselle places herself out of the protection of a grave within the churchyard. Hence, she is doomed to become one of the undead wilis. This is a custom which would have been well recognised by an audience in the 1800s.

Martha Graham is once again not to be overlooked, in her collaboration with sculptor Isamu Noguchi and the innovations which it produced. For them, sculpture coming to life on stage is part of the whole ritual, and it enhances both the meaning of the movement and the audience's emotional response. In *Night Journey* (1947), a rope binds together Jocasta and her son Oedipus. The rope is a symbol both of the umbilical cord and of sexual love. This Greek myth of doom and destruction is powerfully told from the women's point of view.

Following in the Graham style, work like that of Robert Cohan for the London Contemporary Dance Theatre in the 1970s and 1980s produced some delights, like *Waterless Method of Swimming Instruction*, 1974, where, in one section for the men only, huge rubber rings take on lives of their own, providing boats for the dancers to row and, when piled up on top of one dancer, completely entrap him.

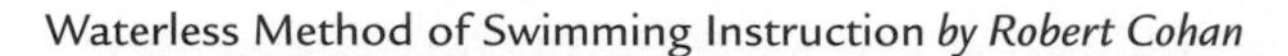
Waterless Method of Swimming Instruction *by Robert Cohan*

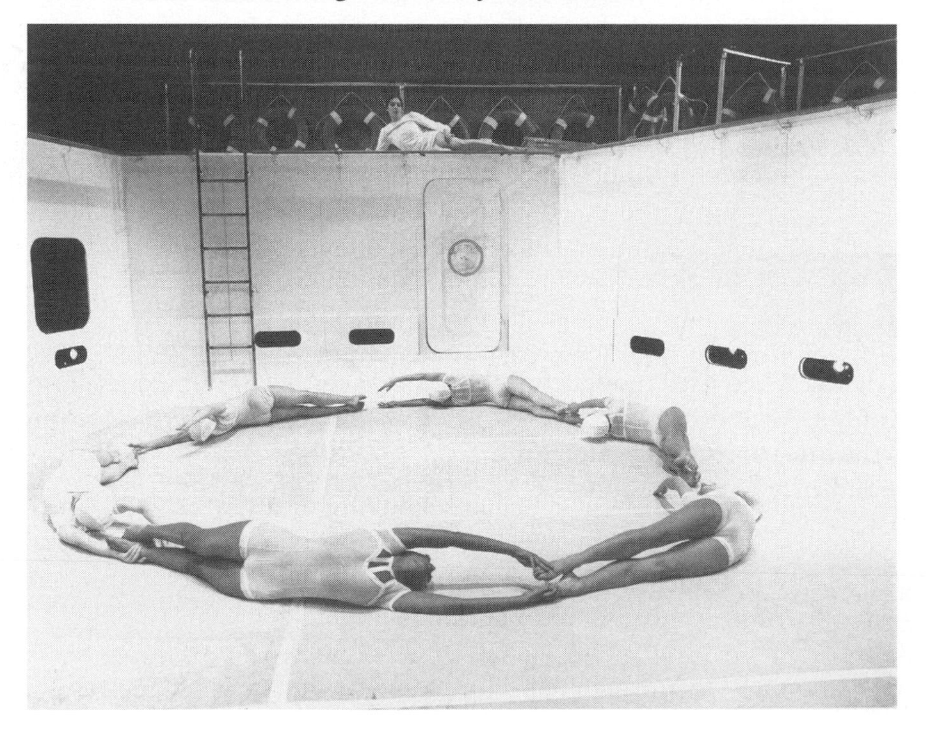

In Christopher Bruce's *Sergeant Early's Dream* (1984), the section entitled 'Geordie' uses the lyrics of a song which tells of a woman's lament for her hanged husband. Her scarf becomes the symbol of the hangman's noose in the final image of the dance, reinforcing the characters and the narrative of the song and dance.

A chair, red noses and canes are used as props in Christopher Bruce's *Swansong* (1987). They are manipulated by the guards and the prisoner to represent a wide range of images associated with interrogation. The canes double as accessories for tap dance and as weapons of torture; the red noses humiliate and panic the victim and the chair is a weapon, a shield, a comfort and prison bars.

THE PROP-SET

In 1928, the Russian artist Pavel Tchelitchev combined an innovative range of elements in his stage design for the Ballet Russes' *Ode*. This presented a modern view of the festivities of the Russian court of the eighteenth century. The dancers were covered entirely so that they became anonymous figures. They held cords which wove a web over the stage and were connected to lines of dolls at the back of the stage. Such were the interconnections here that it seemed difficult to know where the costumes ended and the props or set began. This kind of distortion also features in the later work of Alwin Nikolais where again props are simultaneously costumes, and it can be difficult to know whether or not they are also part of the set.

A prop-set in Glen Tetley's The Tempest; *(1979) design by Nadine Baylis*

Similarly, Georges Balanchine, in his design for *Orpheus* (1948), chose a white silk curtain to fall in a dramatic swirl like lightning, and a rope which, although a part of the costume of the Dark Angel, *also* became an integral part of the movement.

An early work of Robert Cohan, *Hunter of Angels* (1967), used a huge ladder which was both set and prop at the same time. This was moved around with great skill (considering its size and weight) to become the wings of an angel, a womb, a labyrinth and Jacob's ladder to heaven. In this way, it was, at different times, both an extension of the dancers' bodies and a set to be explored in countless ways for movement possibilities. The simple idea of rolling out the red carpet in Bourne's *Swan Lake* depicts the Royal Family very effectively by defining their stage space.

Study the photograph of *The Tempest* on page 117. How does the set add to the story?

PROPS WHICH ADD TO THE MOVEMENT

In a Graham-style work, the costumes, set, props and music are all integrated with the movement in a deliberately orchestrated attempt to reinforce the meaning of the choreography. This is not so for ex-Graham dancer Merce Cunningham whose approach is to make each element of the production a *separate experience* – as, again, in *RainForest* (1968), where the helium-filled silver pillows, designed by Andy Warhol, are met by the dancers in an unconcerned way.

In Act One of Petipa's *The Sleeping Beauty* (1890) the peasant corps de ballet dance a waltz using garlanded hoops which enhance the weaving pathways and circular formations.

Sometimes a prop can act as both a set *and* a costume. In a post-modern work of Steve Paxton's called *Music for Words*, a transparent 12-foot-square room was deflated around him until it became his costume.

Philippe Decouflé features a most amusing prop-costume in *Decodex* (1995). A solo is performed with one foot fixed to a square pedestal limiting every move and adding humour because of the enormous effort which the dancer must put into even the smallest step.

Choosing a diverse range of objects and then allowing improvisation with these to lead to performance is a common approach for post-modern choreographers. *Stories* may grow from these objects, or the objects may change the way that you *move*. The only limit is the imagination.

Rosemary Butcher's collaborations with visual artists have led to some surprising results. In 1981, in *Spaces 4*, the artist Heinz-Dieter Pietsch improvised with polystyrene as he watched the dancers. As the dance progressed, he built various objects which captured the *spatial* qualities of the dance, and the dancers in turn connected their movements to the installation, echoing corners and rough edges, or confirming boundaries. Following on in 1987, his props for *Touch the Earth* were metal rods which were *carried* during the dance. The dancers gently marked out their homelands which were reminiscent of various locations which Butcher associated with the plight of the native American Indians and the loss of territory. The poles are images of teepees or farming tools, and the movement is deeply reflective of a community in a state of sharing and supporting.

Tennis racquets are used to enhance the movement and meaning in Matthew Bourne's *Late Flowering Lust* (1994, for BBC TV). The racquets enhance the illusion that dancers are making contact with the ball. But the larger theme of a group of small beautiful young things enjoying their weekend house party in pre-war England has a darker side. They seem oblivious to the despair of one of the friends played by actor Nigel Hawthorne.

Choreography using sporting motifs goes back to Moliére's comedy of manners, *Les Facheux* (The Bores, 1661). Sports such as bowls and shuttlecock were featured as a platform for a satire on manners and social privilege similar to *Late Flowering Lust* some three centuries later. Valsav Nijinsky also choreographed using tennis as a metaphor for modern manners in the 1913 ballet *Jeux*. A version of *Les Facheux* by Bronislava Nijinska was choreographed in 1924 for Diaghilev.

The dance production now only requires one other constituent feature to complete the picture: the accompaniment or aural setting. This is an area full of possibilities and choices. What the audience *hears* also needs to be appropriately chosen to support your movements, sets, lights, costumes and props, so that what is heard and what is seen can be combined into an understandable whole for and by the onlooker.

Late Flowering Lust: Photo by Gabrielle Crawford

TASK SIX

Select a number of objects as props, such as:

- a pillow
- an umbrella
- a large pole or stick
- a large hoop
- a feather
- a picture frame
- a balloon
- a newspaper
- a doll
- a cardboard tube
- a large piece of silk or chiffon.

Experiment with how the object affects the way you move when, for example, you carry it or attach it to you. Let the objects become something *other* than what they are. For example, if they are heavy, let them become light, or if they have an obvious use, use them for something else totally different.

Finally, choose one object and let it lead to a dance; *or* arrange a few of them around the stage space and create a story or landscape or 'scene' with them. (Suggested music: *Underneath the Bunker*, by The Orb.)

References and resources

BOOKS

Au, S., *Ballet and Modern Dance*, London, Thames and Hudson, 1988

Clarke, M. and Crisp, C., *Ballet: an Illustrated History*, London, A. & C. Black, 1973

Cohen, S. J. (ed), *Dance as a Theatre Art: Source Readings In Dance History From 1581 to the Present*, New York: Princeton Book Co., 1992

Kirstein, L., *Dance: a Short History of Classic Theatre Dancing*, New York: Dance Horizons, 1969

Sorrell, W., *Dance in its Time*, New York: Columbia University Press, 1981

Spencer, C., *Leon Bakst & the Ballets Russes*, UK: Academy Educational, 1995, well illustrated

VIDEOS

Available from www.dancebooks.co.uk

Giselle – The Kirov Ballet, Vinogradov's production

Evening with the Rambert Dance Company, includes Christopher Bruce's Sergeant Early's Dream

Swansong, (Bruce) English National Ballet (1995)

Still Life at the Penguin Café, David Bintley for The Royal Ballet (1991)

Ghost Dances and Journey, by Christopher Bruce, the Houston Ballet

Available from www.surrey.ac.uk

Body as Site, Rosemary Butcher (1993) performance in Guilford Cathedral

Hunter of Angels, Robert Cohan

Making of Maps, and Romance ... with Footnotes, Shobana Jeyasingh

Without Trace ... Mark Murphy, V-Tol.

WEB SITES

Companies

www.merce.org – Merce Cunningham

www.sddc.org.uk – Siobhan Davies Co.

www.vtol.demon.co.uk – V-Tol, Mark Murphy

On the History of Costume a very wide ranging site is www.balletdance.about.com

www.nga.gov.au/russia – informative site of costumes of the Ballets Russes, 1909–1933, as exhibited at the National Gallery of Australia, Canberra. Well illustrated

www.artslynx.org/dance – huge range of dance information

MUSIC

Dancetechnic, by David Harry, available from Primrose Studio, White Cross, Lancaster, 1992, tel no: 01524 849622, recommended for Task 1 – This tape has many tracks which are useful for improvisation

Underneath the Bunker by The Orb, Polygram Island label IMCP219, 1996

FOUR

THE CONSTITUENT FEATURES OF DANCE: THE AURAL SETTING

Accompaniments for dance

There are many types of accompaniment (aural setting) to choose from for dance. The most obvious one, music, is often chosen, but it must be stated loudly from the start that it is also worth trying out others. The list of choices includes:

- silence
- the voice
- sound (both natural and found sound)
- music.

The final choice must be one selected, like the movements themselves and other constituent features, with great care. In the end, both what the audience receives *visually* and what it receives *audibly* should be compatible in some way, even if this is because these aspects are very *different*: the differences here may create interesting contrasts and clashes.

SILENCE

The early German expressionist dancers, like Mary Wigman at the start of the twentieth century, often chose silence as the accompaniment to their dances.

> Nearly all her most original dances are unaccompanied by music ... music is secondary, almost superfluous.
>
> (*Herman Ould* in Dancing Times, *April 1926*)

Without any sounds to hide behind, a dance must be clear, strong in content. It must have its own vibrant internal rhythms and form. Silence is the equivalent of the spaces in visual art or the stillness in dance. The apparently negative aspects of any art form are just as important as the obviously positive ones. They exist woven together: you can't have one without the other.

All kinds of movement and atmospheres are possible in silence.

Water Study (1928) by Doris Humphrey is an outstanding example of the use of silence.

> ... the dance without music ... increases concentration and attention onto movement to an astonishing degree. ... 'Water Study' ... was composed for fourteen girls whose bodies rose and fell, rushed and leaped like the various aspects of water, the only sound being the faint thudding of feet in running movements, reminiscent of surf.
>
> (*Doris Humphrey in* The Art of Making Dances, *1959*)

The use of silence in Richard Alston's *Soda Lake* (1981) enhances the complex rhythmical changes in the movement. There are sudden changes of speed, from quick allegro footwork to prolonged stillnesses. The enormous empty space of a *real* desert landscape exists in a vast silence, and in this work, the overall bare, minimal look is similarly well-balanced by an accompaniment of silence. There is a real atmosphere of quiet openness and solitude where the dancer performs.

Sometimes, a few seconds of silence at the start or end of, or during, a dance can add contrast and avoid predictability. It may also serve to highlight moments of greater importance by allowing the onlooker's ear to rest and thus to appreciate the movement more.

Siobhan Davies often continues the movement when the music has stopped. We see this in *White Man Sleeps* (1988). The female solo, at the end of part 3, continues echoing the last phrase of the music and eventually fading into stillness. Dancers also hold a stillness shape of the animal head motif while the music plays quietly. Both of these have an effect of maintaining pace and balance and holding the viewer's attention.

VOICE

When people move, they often accompany their movements with voice, in song or in words, quite naturally. Or there may be another person doing this, or it could be on tape. The accents and types of sounds could blend smoothly with, or they could act as a contrast to, the movement. The voice may use words, human sounds like giggles, sighs and so on, or song. The choice is wide-ranging, and involves the inner world of the dance. The speech may also be distorted, and it does not have to make sense. For example, it may sound like a rap with a repetitive rhythm (in the original text, the words may not have been repeated, and consequently, the sounds become like a musical score). *Dutiful Ducks* (1982), a solo for dancer Michael Clark by Richard Alston, used a sound tape (text score by composer Charles Amirkhanian) which repeated a few rhythmical phrases of words, like: 'Dutiful, d-d-d-d dutiful ducks, dutiful ducks ... in double L.A. Tree tops sway.' The phrasing, rhythm and accents of the movements all matched those of the text score. The sources of voice and text may be found in poetry, stories, diaries, newspapers and magazines.

Kenneth Macmillan uses poetry in a Mahler score in his *Song of the Earth* (1965). It does not literally translate the words into dance as he did in *Images of Love* (1964) which was based on Shakespeare's love sonnets. He said:

> I don't expect the audience to know what the words are about, although I'm pleased when they do ... the audience can take the ballet on any level ... I have to pick a poetic image that will go with the words rather than illustrate them.
>
> (*In* Making a Ballet, *1974*)

So how is MacMillan treating the words and voice? Perhaps the easiest way to think about it is that he is choosing images which capture the broad themes of the poems. These were enjoying and saying goodbye to the joys and beauty of the world, and the promise of renewal after death. An example of this is in the first *scherzi*, *Of Youth*, the dance is full of youthful energy, fun and beauty. As the poem mentions the reflections of the scene in a smooth, quiet pool the soloist is momentarily upside down.

Dancers' own voices are often used by Lloyd Newson. In *Strange Fish* (1992) Nigel Charnock's solo as a misfit at a party is accompanied by his voice. He babbles on, mostly about loneliness, people and being a 'party animal'. His interest, he tells us, is 'collecting people' and his rantings reveal deep down his despair and longing to be one of the 'crowd'. As his banter speeds up it sparks a chain reaction in the other dancers as they try to avoid him. It accompanies them as they run away and dive into each other's arms and he continues to chase them chatting incessantly.

TASK ONE

Choose a short fairy story. Photocopy it, and cut it up into separate phrases that make sense. Let each dancer choose at random one or two phrases and improvise them, saying the words at the same time as moving. Show each other the results.

Discuss how the phrases may be put together into a group dance using silences, repetitions of phrases and an understandable narrative. Try to add humour and drama so that the story becomes more than it was in the original version.

SOUND

Non-human sounds from nature and the environment can be very appropriate for some dances. The sounds of wind, water, storms, street activity, railway stations, birds, football crowds or telephones are just some of the possibilities. You could sample some yourself by taking a portable tape recorder out and about and making recordings. In Robert Cohan's *Forest* (1977), the sounds of wind, running streams, thunder, rain, bird calls and a wolf howl are mixed with an electronic score to create a forest atmosphere. The dance movement mixes images of the animals who inhabit the forest with their calls which ricochet around the space. When dancing in an outdoor location, the *found* sound can become the accompaniment itself. For example, the sound of passing traffic can draw attention to desired issues in a dance that is concerned with environmental pollution.

To John Cage (composer for Merce Cunningham) any sound or noise is music. He has given piano concerts consisting of sitting and not playing for 20 or so minutes, thus forcing the audience to listen to the everyday sounds around them. In his view, this is a way of experiencing the environment. The high level of technological advances now means that the dancers themselves can create their own aural settings as they move. In *Variations V* (1965) by Merce Cunningham, the dancers' movements activated antennas on stage which sent signals to the orchestra pit. Triggered by light intensity, the antennas set off tape recorders, radios, and so on, to make electronic sound. In this way, the dance was not at all dependent on the accompaniment – rather, the score depended entirely on the *movements*.

The sound of a train whistle is used as a link between sections in Alvin Ailey's *Blues Suite* (1958). It works well as a transition device to 'glue' the sections together, but it is more than that. The whistle also emphasises the expression and meaning of the piece because it suggests other ideas; where these people live, 'the wrong side of the tracks' and their poverty; the fact that the men who visit the cheap saloon are travelling workers. So a sound sets a clear social and expressive context for the dance. The sections of the dance are accompanied by Blues music, the words, tradition and atmosphere of which also set the tone.

The sounds the dancers themselves make can often serve as the accompaniment. Stamping, clapping and breath sounds all provide possible aural settings. Tap dance, Indian and flamenco all use the sounds of the feet and hands to enhance the rhythmical experience for the audience. Metal taps on the shoes, bells on the ankles and wooden castanets in the hands all serve to emphasise the aural aspect of the movement.

In Christopher Bruce's *Swansong* (1987), the idea of the interrogation of a political prisoner in a South American jail is cleverly brought to life. The feet of the interrogators and the prisoner tap out and shuffle question-and-answer conversations. Claps and finger clicks are also used. All of this is mixed into a sound and musical score that heightens the intensity of the plight of the tortured prisoner. They play cat and mouse with him, and in a macabre setting of red noses and music-hall song and dance, we feel that his fate is sealed.

MUSIC

The most obvious thing to do is to set movements to music, but this may make a dance totally reliant on the aural setting. It is the movement that should be the main concern of the dance. As George Balanchine once remarked, the audience should see the music and hear the dance. The relationship of dance to music is discussed in greater detail later in the book. What we are concerned with here is choosing music that has a positive influence on the dance. The dancer should feel able to be 'inside' the music, as if the air is full of it.

Choosing music

A poor choice of music can ruin a dance. Ideally, the dance and music should *support* one another. There are a number of things which should be considered when choosing music:

1 *Balance.* A piece of music which has large numbers of instruments or a rich production quality may not be entirely suited to a solo dance. On the other hand, some music is sparse in its style and so may not be ideal for a large group dance.

2 *Avoiding the obvious.* Music from the Top Ten, or old favourites which you enjoy listening to, are *not* always the best for dance. Similarly, some well-known classical music or hits from West End shows can also prove difficult because people know them so well that they already have their own set ideas about them, and this may mean that your choreography will be overpowered by their preconceptions. Often, much of this type of music is the wrong length anyway, and cutting it is not only illegal but also unartistic. After all, how would you feel if a musician cut off the last minute of your dance because it was too long to fit to the music? This shows a lack of respect for the artistry of the other artist.

   Of course, there *are* always exceptions to the rules! Michael Clark used the well-known song *Shout* by Lulu to great success. This can be seen in Charles Atlas' film about Clark, and in Clark's work called *Hail the New Puritan* (1986). Clark followed the simple structure of the song to the note. It was the unorthodox choice of movement style, involving his typical fast classical footwork and flexible torso combined with a sharp, clean execution in the dynamic range, that made for the success. Clark's highly technically accomplished dancers held their own with the music. The *contrasts* between the visual and aural features served to hold those two aspects in balance. Furthermore, the use of humour or satire in a dance may be enhanced by choosing music which holds within it many known clichés.

It is your responsibility as a choreographer to research the availability of music. These days, there is a massive range of music available. Explore this by visiting your local music library, and try listening to things with names on them that you may have never heard of. In this way, if you find something, you can buy it without having wasted money on a blind testing. There is no excuse for not finding the wildest wackiest of music for your work.

> I think that there's a difference between music that dialogues with dance and music that I might like to listen to at home.
>
> (*Shobana Jeyasingh in interview with Christopher Thompson in* The Stage, *1992*)

3 *Quality*. Whenever possible, it is important to use top-quality recordings. It is best to make a rehearsal tape, and not to use the original all the time but to save it instead for performance. Recordings full of scratches and jumps, or that are hardly audible, are unacceptable unless that particular effect has been chosen for a special reason. For example, if you wished to create the feel of an old black-and-white film, it may be appropriate to choose such recordings.

4 *Style*. Music set in a particular country or period of history needs careful handling. It is possible to mix and match modern music with, say, that in an Indian style – as Shobana Jeyasingh frequently does.

> We've got silence, fast tempos, slow tempos, we've got lyrics, we've got rhythm. It's all about changing moods and changing atmosphere ... It certainly works for me, on contemporary dance terms, any dance terms, on pure entertainment terms.
>
> (*BBC Radio 3's* Nightwaves, *October 1992 about Shobana Jeyasingh*)

On the whole, the overall styles of the dance and music need to be *matched*. Scottish, Spanish, Irish, African, Renaissance, mediaeval, impressionist, romantic, neoclassical and jazz styles are all useful if handled properly. If these labels are unfamiliar to you, then perhaps a little research into music would be helpful.

5 *Live music*. Ideally, live music should be used whenever possible, but of course access to this can be difficult. You may know other students who study music and who may be willing to play for you. You will need to provide them with copies of the score, and it may help to make a recording of their playing for you for rehearsal periods. There may even be some who can compose, and this could be very exciting. Improvising together can be great fun, and very productive. Using percussion instruments, dancers too can accompany each other in improvisation. It is important to let dancers and musicians *take turns* in leading. In the final choreography, the musicians may play an equal part in the performing.

Live music is played in *Without Trace* (2000, Mark Murphy for V-Tol). The musicians are on stage but only partly visible through the muslin screens of the set.

Using music

There are a number of ways that a dance may be formed with music:

- dance and music composed together;
- dance created first, then music composed for it;
- compose music first, then dance to it (most common);
- a dance sketched in, then either music composed for it or suitable music is found;
- music and dance composed separately, only coming together in performance.

When a piece of music is chosen first, you need to do a number of things to prepare for the creation of the dance:

- Listen to it over and over again, carefully.
- Improvise to it.
- Develop an understanding of its feel, form, meter, tempo, instrumentation and so on (use written notes to help your memory).

Remember, music and the dance do *not* have to match exactly. The dance needs a rhythmical life of its own which is not dictated by the music.

> Abstract dancing is analogous to abstract music. The same three elements are there – the tone, rhythm, melody and harmony, with the addition of the kinesthetic appeal only possible in the dance. This means that to a sensitive onlooker there is a constant stream of primitive excitement going on inside...
>
> (*Doris Humphrey in* The Art of Making Dances, *1959*)

Sometimes in rehearsal it is fun to try lots of different types of music for a dance. The results can be surprisingly successful!

The more complex the musical scores, the more demanding it is on the choreography. Thus, music by Schoenberg would be more demanding to choreograph than a short country and western song. One way of overcoming the difficulties involved is to use *dancer's counts*. These are not necessarily the same counts as the music, but are determined by the *phrasing* of the movement within the music framework. For example:

- Music: 8 phrases of 4/4 played fast = 32 counts.
- Dancer: 4 phrases of 6-6-8-12 = 32 counts.

In this way, the counts grow organically from the demands of the movement, and are thus more in tune with the needs of the dance and the dancers. This makes working with difficult – or for that matter *any* – music easier. Ideally, it should be possible for each dancer in a group to have *different* sets of counts to the same piece of music, and yet for all to finish with the music at the same time as each other. Doris Humphrey did this in *New Dance* (1935). The music played 6 phrases of 4/4 whilst the dancers moved on phrases of 7-7-10. The sum of both is the same. It is a satisfying moment visually and aurally for the audience, as both meet at the end after having had their independence.

Known for his method of visualising the movement on listening to the music Kenneth MacMillan once said:

> I have a reservoir of music in my head, things I've known for years, and about three months before I start working music seems to start to go round in my head which is relevant to the area in which I'm going to work.
>
> (*In* Making A Ballet, *1974*)

Even though he would mostly start with the music, sometimes – as in *The Invitation* (1960) – he found the musical style of Matyas Seiber fitted the idea. So he worked closely with the composer around a detailed outline which showed running times, character and emotions; the rest was written to fit. One section of the music was already written but the rest responded to MacMillan's request for such things as melody to enhance the emotional expression and for it to have a period atmosphere, so social dances, Polka and Gallop, were included.

The tasks below allow you to try new approaches to accompaniment and music that you may not have considered before.

TASK TWO

1 Find a copy of 'The Jabberwocky' by Lewis Carroll. Select certain key words and phrases which may be spoken by a narrator or by the dancers themselves. Decide on an overall format for a group of five or six dancers which is not too literal but may use certain atmospheres, moods, moments and meanings. The monster might be made up of many individuals and not just one. Also, the fighting scene could involve all the dancers fighting an invisible Jabberwocky. Notice here too the form of the poem itself, in that the first and last verses are the same.
Find some music or sound effects which the text can be easily woven in and out of. It may be music that creates a general atmosphere of fear and mystery without a particularly strong beat. (Suggested music: the soundtrack of the film *Diva*.)
Using text, music and silence, compose the group dance.

2 Using percussion instruments for an accompaniment, make three dance phrases of 5-5-8 counts. Dance them whilst accompanied by the group playing 6 measures of 3/4 in a steady tempo, accenting count 1 of each bar.
Take it in turns to dance and play.

3 Use k. d. Lang's song 'Big love' (from *Absolute Torch and Twang*). Listen carefully to it, then write down the number of beats and measures in the verses and chorus. Make movement phrases which have irregular counts that are not the same as the music but that add up to the same total at the end of each verse or chorus.
Practise until the two fit together. Start or finish with a silent section of movement.

Leaving the final word to a well-known and highly respected choreographer:

> I listen to a lot of music and I love it, but I don't often work with it. Or rather I work with it 'in private' in that I get many ideas about time, rhythm and time structures from music. ... I found at one time if I used music that I really liked I ended up creating something that was very enjoyable to do, but the movement tended to be banal and very simple, getting into nothing but steps, running around on the beat. ... I began working with ideas because body rhythms are different from musical rhythms.
>
> (*Richard Alston in* Making a Ballet, *1974*)

References and resources

MUSIC

k. d. Lang's song 'Big love', from *Absolute Torch and Twang*, Sire 7599-25877-2, 1989, recommended for Task 2

Soundtrack from the film *Diva*, recommended for Task 2

FIVE

Form in dance

> Tis to create and in creating live
> A being more intense, that we endow with form.
> Our fancy, gaining as we give the life we image. (*Lord Byron*)

In Chapters 2, 3 and 4, the basic building blocks – the constituent features – of dance were analysed, and we considered how to make appropriate choices of such constituents when composing dances. In giving dances a choreographic *form*, the movement components, dancers and physical and aural settings have all to be woven together into a tight web.

> The work as a whole must be one of stuff, as an emerald is all emerald – crush it to powder, and each tiny pinch of that powder will still be an emerald.
>
> (*Ted Shawn in* The Vision of Modern Dance, *1980*)

It is the overall *unity* of the dance which the audience sees and hears in performance:

> If you look carefully at *Scènes de Ballet*, you will see that there isn't a single step in it that doesn't relate to the structure as a whole. This is equally true of unassuming ballets like *Les Rendezvous* and *Les Patineurs*.
>
> (*David Vaughan in* Dance Now, *1995*)

This chapter examines how the various constituent features are organised so as to produce the final 'look' of the piece.

Form

Form, in its raw state, is all around us in the world we live in. Morning, afternoon, night, the four seasons, birth, life and death are all universal forms which everyone recognises. In making dance, music, poetry, painting or film, we take our sense of order and recreate it in an *imaginary* world.

> Form is the shape of the content. Form without content becomes form for the sake of form. ... The form should contain the original impetus out of which it was created.
>
> (*Hanya Holm in* The Vision Of Modern Dance, *1980*)

Form can thus put across *content*, like the meaning in the dance of Martha Graham, or it can be the message itself.

In rehearsal, the choreographer will be working around some basic ideas for the constituent features and for what the overall look may be. A gradual process of developing and structuring the materials – including, of course, the dancers themselves – eventually leads to a cohesive dance form which must satisfy the choreographer's own needs but also be clear to the dancers, and to the audience.

The ways in which the movement is manipulated, and the way in which the various constituent features interrelate throughout the dance, make each dance unique. As well as using intuition during the creative process, the choreographer needs knowledge about certain possible *procedures*. As in music composition, there are certain useful traditional devices and structures in choreography which comprise the skills of the craft, the tools of the trade. Like the physical skills involved in the training of a dancer - skills which add to the dancer's resources - these technical skills will increase the choreographer's own range of abilities. And again, as with the dancer's training, it is the physical *doing* which is crucial. *Participation* in the solving of choreographic problems, and in improvisations and compositional exercises, is the way to develop a wider range of choreographic skills.

Once experience and understanding is increased, these 'rules' will add both depth and a wider range of choice to the process of composition; and of course, they may be broken where justifiable. Without a knowledge of such choices, the choreographer may be stuck only with what they already know, plus what they have learnt through trial and error, and this situation may well narrow the individual's range of expression rather than enhancing and fine-tuning it. Practical experiences in the following categories are necessary:

- compositional devices;
- compositional structures;
- the relationship of the dance to the accompaniment;
- the organisation of groups in space.

The final finished dance should have a natural, organic feel. Each part of it should grow naturally, almost *inevitably*, into the next just as a seed grows into a flower.

Compositional devices

Motifs are a single movement or a short phrase of movement which embody the *style* and content of the dance. They are repeated, varied and developed by *manipulating* the movement. These manipulations usually involve some change in the movement components of action, space, time or dynamics (see Chapter 2).

Below is a list of ways in which motifs can be developed:

- Use different parts of the body.
- Alter the basic body posture, say from standing to lying, sitting, upside-down or twisted.
- Add actions or change the action.
- Change the size.
- Change the level.
- Alter the focus.
- Change the direction, dimension or plane.
- Alter the air or floor pattern - make the air pattern into the floor pattern, or vice versa.
- Increase or decrease the tempo - augment or diminish, i.e. make slower/faster.
- Vary the pattern of the beats of the rhythm.
- Change the accents.
- Retrograde it - reverse the order of the movements.
- Change the dynamic or quality.
- Fragment the motif - use only one part repeatedly or some parts only, or change the order of the parts.
- Alter any of the aspects of the physical setting.
- Mix bits from different motifs together.
- Combine any of the above.

(There are added considerations in motif development when dealing with group dances, but these are dealt with later under a separate section.)

Motif development is a way of producing a lot from a little, while also avoiding too much repetition – which may be boring for the audience. The phrases involved will also tend to lengthen into whole sections and organically provide logical development, contrasts and eventually *unity*. We all know those awful moments when inspiration just is not happening! Once, after much practice, you are able to do it spontaneously, motif development will help you to avoid drying up.

A good example of the use of motif repeition and development is clear in *White Man Sleeps* (Siobhan Davies, 1988). A key motif is described as the 'framing face'. It has a quiet, calm feel. It is first seen in the second part of section 1 when one dancer traces hands around another's face. Then later in section 2 it is danced as a solo repeating to become an accent and to emphasise pauses. It is also developed in section 3 when its dynamic softens, and again in section 4.

Figure 5.1 *Notation for motif development exercise in Task 1*

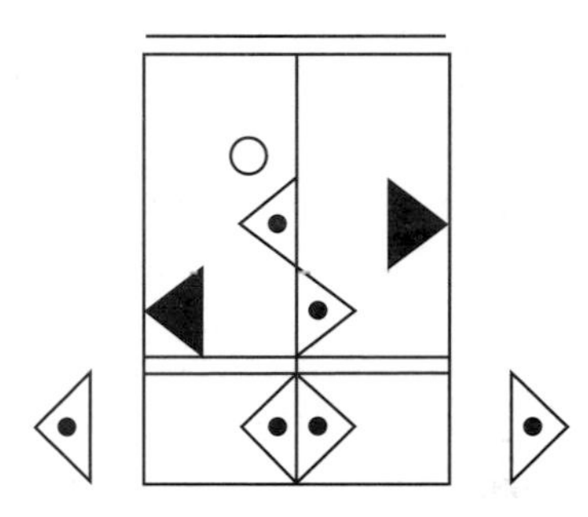

TASK ONE

Dance the motif from the notation given in Figure 5.1. Develop the motif as follows:

1 Repeat it.

2 Add an arm gesture as you sway.

3 Add another action on so that you now have 3 parts: the sway + arm gesture + another action (turn, travel, jump, fall or stillness).

4 Repeat just the sway.

5 Reverse the order of the 3 parts – i.e. retrograde.

6 Fragment the 3 parts by changing the order.

7 Dance all 3 parts, but add a new detail – i.e. embellish it.

8 Repeat one part 3 times.

Practise this whole sequence 1 to 8 until it is memorised.

Write a notation score for your developed version. You can use your own system or a recognised one. You can continue to develop in your own way from here. (Suggested music: *Strike the Gay Harp* by The Chieftains, 3 Claddagh Records.)

A similar manipulation of motifs is called *theme* and *variation*. This, however, is more of a recognised structure in music *composition*, and so it will instead be dealt with later, in the section on compositional structures.

CANON

The device of canon involves two or more dancers dancing one or more motifs at different times. It therefore only applies to duets and group dances. Motifs are here danced in succession. This may give rise to relationships between dancers of: leading and following; question and answer; co-operation and confrontation. In music, canon is seen as a preset structure, but in dance it is more usually used as a device for developing motifs. Thus, the group movement becomes organised in time.

Dancers moving in *unison* may do one of the following:

- the same movement at the same time;
- similar or complementary movements at the same time;
- contrasting movements at the same time.

Similarly, there are different types of canons:

- A *simple canon* will be in strict order. Each dancer dances an entire motif, then keeps still while another dancer takes over. This is the simplest type of canon, and it may be made more interesting by allowing the dancer's timings to *overlap* so that the dancers are always a few counts behind each other. This places demands on the dancers' skill at dancing in *groups*, for it requires sensitive timing with, and an awareness of, others.
- A *simultaneous canon* involves dancers doing the same motif at the same time but starting from different points in the phrase. So, Dancer 1 may do counts 1 to 8; Dancer 2 may start at count 6, dancing 6-7-8-1-2-3-4-5, and another dancer may start at 4, dancing 4-5-6-7-8-1-2-3; and so on. This creates a dense, coherent and interesting look.
- A *cumulative canon* is just what it says: cumulative. Each dancer joins in with the lead dancer at various stages during the dancing of a motif, and they all finish at the same time. This gives a look of an increase in force or power through an increase in emphasis on the movement.
- *Loose canons* offer more opportunity for the manipulation of a motif. There may be a use of different levels, facings or placements in the stage space. Adding stillnesses is also effective, as may be varying the dynamic or rhythmic elements.

TASK TWO

Take a short phrase you know well from technique class. In threes or fours, try the various canons in the list above. Be as accurate as you can throughout, and use your 'radar' (sense of timing and spacing) with the others sensitively.

CONTRAST

Contrast introduces new material which is noticeably different from anything so far seen in the dance. This can be introduced suddenly or gradually. For example, a light, slow motif can be contrasted with large fast jumps, and this can be done by gradually increasing the tempo and strength, or by switching from one to the other in an instant. In *I am Curious Orange* (1988) by Michael Clark, there is a clear use of contrast when a slow, balletic, lamentful solo is immediately followed by the dancer tearing off her pointe shoes and performing a frenetically fast dance. Similarly, the bright and dark characters in ballets such as *The Nutcracker* and *Sleeping Beauty* create dramatic tension in their conflicts. In *Swan*

Lake (Bourne, 1995) the whirl of the ballroom and shooting scene are in contrast to the scene which follows. The Prince is sedated by the team of nurses who perform a motif of minimal arm and hand gestures with frightening surgical precision.

HIGHLIGHTS

Highlights will maintain the interest of the audience and draw attention to particular features or images that the choreographer may wish to emphasise. Usually, a dance has a few moments which the audience remembers the most vividly. These therefore function to make clearer the *meaning* or *content* of the dance. Highlights inject *pace*. As the audience is swept along in the stream of consciousness of the piece, the highlights enable them to maintain a grasp on its overall direction more easily, and this clearly heightens their enjoyment, understanding and appreciation.

In an interview Robert Cohan once spoke about a dance lecture-demonstration which involved several days of choreographing of a new dance in the presence of a public audience. This nerve-wracking process produced a dance of continual highlights (one for each day!) which did not follow the correct proportion or pace that the sections of the dance needed for a balanced structure. He stated that he would not attempt that process again.

There are a variety of ways of creating highlights. One approach – similar to that found in the development of motifs – is to manipulate a movement component. One obvious technique here is to make use of rhythmical and dynamic accents. Highlights can be created by using a stronger dynamic, but they can also arise from emphasising a softer, gentler dynamic. A prolonged stillness, in anticipation of something happening, is also effective in creating tension and interest.

> Expectancy and the unexpected are both attention-getters, and the skilful uses of each are unbeatable.
>
> (*Doris Humphrey in* The Art of Making Dances, *1959*)

For dramatic and narrative structures, the creation of tension and pace is vital, and highlights can be useful to do this. One method used by choreographer Ian Spink in *Further and Further into the Night* (1984) was the repetition of motif. This dance is based on Alfred Hitchcock's classic thriller *Notorious* (1946). It is a story of romance and intrigue. Many of the motifs relate to movements from the film, so that everyday movement is used a great deal. At one point, the gestures involved in serving a drink are repeated over and over to various dancers. This creates humour and also tension.

An increase or decrease in the *numbers* of dancers may draw attention to themes like isolation, rejection or celebration.

A change of set, costume or light, or a prop placed carefully in anticipation of its later use – any of these alterations in the physical setting may cause various moments to be highlighted.

In *Swan Lake* (Bourne, 1995) a clever moment which keeps the pace of the action occurs when a statue is unveiled as part of the Royal duties. It turns out to be an almost naked male. This catches the audience's attention as well as contributing to the plot. *Ghost Dances* (Bruce, 1981) has highlights built into each section. Towards the end of each section the ghosts infiltrate the ordinary people. Their presence is ominous and threatening and they catch our eye and smoothly lead into the highlight of a section when they 'strike' and another person is killed or 'disappeared'.

Similarly, in the *accompaniment*, a sudden unexpected silence is as effective as a whole outburst of heavy rock music.

CLIMAX

There may be several highlights in a dance, but there is only one main high point: the *climax*. The dance should be organised to gradually build towards this, making it seem inevitable, organically right. This again involves a crucial pacing of the constituent features. Pacing is a balancing act which requires a delicate and subtle treatment of all the interconnected layers of the dance. It follows the logical progression and direction of the piece, whilst also continually providing enough interest and even diversion, so that the climax happens at just the right moment. When the final climax happens, it should confirm what the audience has expected and yet also provide a certain element of *surprise* so that it is not too obvious. It should sum up everything that has happened before it. The climax might be a fast and furious outburst of energy and action, or it could fade away to a gentle quiet, or it may be marked by the end of a particular story. Or, it may well be that the climax does not come at the end of the dance.

The actual ending of the dance is, however, the last thing that the audience will see, and they will remember it the best, and so it must be memorable - it must not disappoint or puzzle, or leave the audience uncomfortably up in the air not knowing whether or not to applaud. It is noticeable that the endings of Lea Anderson's works are often glitzy and fast. We see this, for example, in the shiny phosphorescent suits of *Go Las Vegas* (1995). And in the ending of *Precious* (1993), which depicts the process of alchemy turning base metals into gold. The dancers realise their dreams by changing their perspectives and states of being. Finally, they achieve the golden state of equilibrium, and the movement's pace increases to a furious tempo. In contrast Siobhan Davies's dances often end 'quietly'. *White Man Sleeps* (1988) ends with the dancers in turn gradually coming to stillness. A motif of a low hovering arabesque is the final lingering image.

Movements in 8 (1995), danced by the Phoenix Dance Company and choreographed collaboratively by Maggie Morris and Gary Lambert, has a dazzling climax where individual soloists jump, turn, fall and shift through space with breathtaking energy. But the end itself is a return to the soft, internalised style of the beginning. The dancers seem to be meditatively centring themselves, and slowly they exit, melting into the red sunset. There is a real feeling of the passing of a dancer's day: waking into the day's activities, performing in the evening, and slowly calming down into slumber. The exit of the dancers at the end leaves only the musicians on stage, and the ringing of a large gong finally resolves the whole dance.

It is clear from both of these examples that it is not only the movement components that are manipulated to achieve climax and the end but also the other constituent features of the physical and aural setting. The *imagination* is used to create a fusion that feels organically inevitable.

TASK THREE

'Surprise me!' Ensuring that you use contrast, highlights and climax, compose a duet which has a surprise for the audience. (This was set as a choreographic task by Robert Cohan in 1986 at the London School of Contemporary Dance. It proved to be very testing for all the choreographers present.)

BALANCE

The proportions of the sections of the dance need to be appropriate to the individual movement phrases and how they relate to each other. As phrases develop and lengthen, they become whole sections, and each must be an appropriate length for its movement to be appreciated fully. Similarly, if there is a *meaning* in the movement, enough time is needed for this meaning to be put across to the audience.

In rehearsal the choreographer will be making spontaneous and intuitive choices about how single movements grow into phrases, and about how long those phrases are, and how long the sections are that are the *sum* of those phrases. These are delicate decisions which will give the dance its final overall form. Throughout the creative process, the choreographer will be *organising*. As movement is developed, the process of giving the dance a balanced structure is occurring simultaneously. Sometimes, the order and length of motifs, longer phrases and whole sections is obvious early on in rehearsal, but at other times it may require some experimentation. Finally, the choreographer decides what is, for them, a sensible and appropriate ordering and length for all the parts. This will amount to the final balance and proportion of the dance.

Forest (1977) by Robert Cohan provides a good example here. The dance is based on three simple motifs:

1 the 'calling' motif;
2 the 'prowling' motif;
3 the 'pairing' motif.

Through repetition, variation and development, they combine in numerous ways to create the balance and form of the dance. Several sections become obvious to the audience as it watches. Many short sections overlap by means of frequent entrances and exits, making their beginnings and ends clear. The dance has nine sections which fall into four main parts (ABCD) during which various different moods are expressed: slightly romantic; the darker menace of a pack of prowling predators; calmness; tense nervousness.

There are perhaps interesting similarities in balance and structure between *White Man Sleeps* (Davies, 1988) and *Forest* in that the sections are linked by dancers' exits and entrances. Also the balance of content within the sections, solos and intimate duets mixing with faster groups travelling in canons are similar. Even the devices of motif repetition, development and variations bear some resemblances.

Marius Petipa was recognised for his talent of balancing sections in his ballets. In *La Bayadére* (1877) for example, the solos are echoed and enhanced in balance with and by the *corps de ballet*. The version staged by Nureyev for The Royal Ballet (1963) ran as follows: Entry of the *corps de ballet*; *pas de trois* for the three soloists; entry of Solor and

Nikiya; *pas de deux*; *corps* enter and Nikiya solos; Solor solo; variations by three soloists; Solor and Nikiya duet; Nikiya solo; *pas de trois* with *corps*; Solor and Nikiya *pas de deux*; Nikiya solo; Solor solo; finale.

TRANSITION

Transitions are the links between movements, between phrases and between sections of the dance, and as such they are an integral part of the dance. As one movement or phrase grows into the next, the organic and logical progression should also flow.

Transitions can differ in:

- length – gradual or abrupt;
- complexity – as simple as a plié for a jump, or involving a whole phrase of movement.

Transitions usually *correspond* to what they are linking, so that a transition between whole sections may be more complex than that which connects two simple actions. In *Septet* (1953) by Merce Cunningham, the dancers' exits and entrances at the end of each section use everyday movements like hand shakes, nods and waves. This draws attention to the gaps between the sections, making the transitions as important as the dance itself. Bourne's use of transition in his *Swan Lake* is often quite traditional, reminding us of a conventional ballet in that the front curtain may close between acts. This allows for complex scene changes and adds a sense of theatre. Other transitions include the use of set, for example, when the Prince's oversized bed is turned around so that it becomes the palace balcony from which the royal family wave to the public below.

Four Scenes (Christopher Bruce, 1998) uses a simple transition to link the sections. A soloist, usually in silence, dances briefly to link the four stages of life. Each solo provides a thematic link in its choice of motif, often echoing the previous section and/or hinting the next.

LOGICAL SEQUENCE AND PROPORTION

Sequencing a dance logically involves organising the natural progression from start to finish. Part of this process includes a consideration of the individual proportions of the beginning, middle and end sections. The final chosen order and length of the sections and their constituent features must give the appearance of a unified whole. It should also amount to the most expressive sequence and proportion for the corresponding expressive intentions of the choreographer.

The proportion of the beginning, middle and end not only of the whole dance but also of each individual section is also vital to correct pacing and the expression of the intent. For instance, a long, gradually building opening section leading to a shorter middle section and an abrupt end may well be suited to some dances. In other instances, a dance may be more suited to a fast short opening section, a long middle section of some complexity, and a gradually winding-down ending. Task four gives you a chance to work on these ideas.

TASK FOUR

1  Look at the titles below and choose appropriate proportions for their beginning, middle and end sections. Write these out in table form. Give brief descriptions of the length of sections and the general motifs and images used.

- 'The rebellion goes up in smoke'
- 'The river from source to sea'
- 'Obstacle race'.

2  In groups of four or five, choose one of the themes above and improvise around the chosen sections. (Suggested music: Side 2 of the Penguin Café Orchestra's *Broadcasting from Home.*) As you work, select the most appropriate track for your needs.

UNITY

No matter how complex the form of a dance is, it must still work as a whole unit. Too many unrelated components or ideas will be too confusing for an audience to comprehend. The flow of the piece, its peaks, troughs and conclusion, is what gives the piece its unity or overall form. The central concern of a dance helps to maintain the flow, giving it coherence. This may involve either a particular meaning or a concern with the movement for its own sake. The central theme is selected, then the process of manipulating and selecting appropriate constituent features follows in rehearsal.

Consider Petipa's formula for making a ballet as stated by Joan Lawson in *A History of Ballet and its Makers*, 1964:

> He examined each step of the classic vocabulary, assessing its merit and quality as it were, and allotting it to one of the seven categories of movement so that it could:
> **1** Be a preparation or provide a link between one movement and the next.
> **2** Add lightness, height, depth and breadth to the dance.
> **3** Add brilliance and sparkle, even wit.
> **4** Lend continuity to the flow of the line, help to the movement and complete the total pattern of steps.
> **5** Add speed and excitement.
> **6** Become the highlight or finishing point of an enchaînment or dance.
> **7** Lend the finishing touch to the total picture.

This can be analysed to reveal much information about the devices of transition, highlight, contrast, phrasing, climax and balance.

Contrast and variety are a part of the overall unity, and they too must be selected in a way appropriate to the central concern of the dance. Sometimes, even the most unlikely and incongruous ideas can work if these fall within the main purpose of the dance. Then, by their very differences they enhance the central idea and help the onlooker to grasp the main mood, meaning or inner vision of the dance.

> The structure of a ballet might be tight, compact, like the structure of a building; good ballets move in measured space and time, like the planets.
>
> (*George Balanchine in* Complete Stories of the Ballets, *1954*)

TASK FIVE

Allow at least three one-hour sessions for this task.

- Look at the pictures below. Use them as a score for a dance.
- Improvise and select short phrases/motifs for each.
- Memorise these, and teach them to three or four dancers.
- Randomly choose which order they appear in, asking the dancers to perform them so that you can observe. Continue to do this until you are able to select one or two of the orders as the most successful. Note that this will involve making transitions if there are sticking points.
- Gradually, by careful observation:
  - develop and extend the motifs so as to make sections;
  - decide on the length of the beginning, middle and end sections;
  - give consideration occasionally as to the climax and the end;
  - consider if there is enough suitable contrast and variety.
- At any point, you may like to consider trying out different accompaniments as you work, until you find one which is most appropriate.
- Give the finished dance a title.

The above task should produce a dance which could, after rehearsal, be performed, and it should have overall form and unity, the central concern here being the photographic images. The organic structure of the dance will have grown through the gradual manipulation and selection of movement and the use of choreographic devices.

Alternatively, choreographers may look to structures which are *pre-set* and are often derived from music or art or literature. In the next section, these structures will be examined in detail.

Compositional structures

Compositional structures are traditional frameworks which have set patterns. These frameworks are often found in music, literature or art, and fit into one of the following three categories:

1 sequential
2 contrapuntal
3 episodic.

SEQUENTIAL STRUCTURES

These contain themes which progress in a definite order. Letters of the alphabet are used to label each theme or section. The simplest sequential structure is AB. Choosing the structure which best expresses the dance idea is essential. Unity is still necessary between the themes A, B, C etc. – again, they have to have something in common, even if it is through contrast. The themes also have to be linked with appropriate transitions. In songs, a transition is often called a *bridge*, and it is usually an instrumental.

Sequential structures may contain movement which has been developed using choreographic devices like motif development. These structures are set, but may be applied creatively to become organic wholes – for example, to become the framework for one section or for the entire dance. A dance may even involve a mixture of different choreographic structures, and this may lead to overall structures which again are more organic. The arrangements are freer in style, such as AABCDAD, and will respond to the dance idea. This is a more intuitive way of working, and is probably the one which you will use most. Trying new approaches and structures like the ones listed below may be difficult at first, but they will help you build greater skill in your choreography.

The AB structure – binary (two-part)

This is the simplest form, like a verse and a chorus of a song. It is typical of many folk dances and songs. A and B may repeat many times and in any order: ABBAB, ABAB, AABA, ABAAB etc.

The ABA structure – ternary (three-part)

This is a form which is very comfortable to watch because of its feeling of completeness. A is the unifying theme and the centre of interest, then B gives contrast. The original A returns either as an exact repetition or in an easily recognisable variation or development. It is important that A and B be linked by *transitions*, and these may become important in their own right as they mix together features from both A and B. This allows B to grow *out* of A and then to flow easily back *into* A. The sections are still independent, but also connected. This again gives balance and unity.

Many popular songs use this structure: the chorus A, a verse B, and a repetition of the chorus which is often augmented or elaborated in some way to give emphasis to the idea of the song.

TASK SIX

Listen to 'We got the beat' by The Go-Gos. Analyse the music using A B C etc. When you are satisfied with your analysis, compose motifs which fit with the music structure. The movement may, however, be of a contrasting and unexpected style – e.g. balletic vocabulary with a strong, fast, dynamic quality.

ABACADA structure – rondo

Here, the basic theme A returns after each contrasting theme. A must appear at least three times, but it can itself be varied. Indeed, the variations of A will maintain interest in the theme. The other sections should be individual and different, but should also be linked with appropriate transitions to provide continuity for the audience.

The rondo structure was popular in Europe in the eighteenth and nineteenth centuries as a lively round dance. A would be danced by everyone, and the B, C and D sections by individual soloists.

The Martha Graham solo *Frontier (*1935) is in rondo form. In a series of scenes from her life on the frontier of the Wild West, Graham is first seen against the fence looking out across the vast plains. After each exploration away from the homestead, she returns to the fence in a clear rondo.

Ghost Dances (Bruce, 1981) is in rondo form. The ghosts start the dance, enter at the end of each section and end the piece. The different sections feature differing groupings and relationships. The last movement of Kenneth MacMillan's *Concerto* (1966) is a rondo. Section A is a lively solo gradually involving the other soloists and the *corps de ballet*, developing the turning and travelling around the stage and followed finally by the whole cast in an energised final section.

Theme and variation – A1, A2, A3, A4 etc.

Varying a motif is a real test of compositional skill. A must be sufficiently interesting to keep the attention of the audience. Unlike developing a motif, varying it involves keeping the original order of the movements the same. The variations then take the form of subtle adjustments in dynamics, space, style, mood and tempo.

The variation of the motif of a hopscotch stepping pattern in *Four Scenes* (Christopher Bruce, 1998) is a link throughout the dance. It reappears with variations of dynamics and spacing and glues the whole together. Another good example is the *Fairy Variations* in *The Prologue* of Petipa's *The Sleeping Beauty* (1890). Petipa wrote detailed notes so that each Fairy had a different variation, such as *Fleur de Farine*, flowing and *Violante*, animated.

TASK SEVEN

Listen carefully to *Theme & Variations* by Fernando Sor on *Romantic Guitar* and distinguish the four variations on the opening theme. The fourth variation is preceded by a bridge in the music and at the end runs into a call/response form.

Using the idea of 'A Garden Party' compose a dance with five others to show the various garden inhabitants: birds; insects and spiders; reptiles; humans and their interactions. The opening theme in the music may suggest some basic motifs which are varied in time and space to the music's variations.

CONTRAPUNTAL STRUCTURES

The above structures give forms which are sequential, but there are also structures in which the main theme appears *throughout*. Again, these are musical forms also. Here, the main theme is seen/heard against itself, or against one or more *other* themes. This leads to a weaving of material, through which the main theme must be clear and strong enough to stand out from the complex structure. These structures are called *contrapuntal*, and in music, they create *polyphony*, that is a playing of two or more independent melodies heard together. The final effect is more complex and richer than each of the sequential forms. There are three different kinds of contrapuntal structure:

1 ground bass
2 round (or canon)
3 fugue.

Ground bass

Here, a single theme starts the dance and is repeated over and over all the way through the dance. This would be monotonous on its own, but other themes are danced at the same time. This structure offers good opportunities for groups to work either in contrast to each other or against a soloist. In addition, the content should be one appropriate to this structure – say, for example, a dance entitled 'The inevitable is difficult to avoid'.

TASK EIGHT

Working with four dancers:

1 Choreograph a simple motif e.g. 6 walks, turn, jump to the side and repeat on the other side;
2 Teach more complex versions to soloists;
3 Organise dancers to move in and out of the group paying attention to the transitional phrases/counts for this so that the bass theme can be left and rejoined easily.

Round (canon)

This is like a song sung in a round, for example 'London's burning'. The first dancer states the theme, the second enters at the end of the first half-phrase, the third enters at the start of the second phrase, and the fourth enters on the last half of the second phrase. The round ends in the same order as the last dancer finishes off the theme or movement.

The theme motif is often developed or varied as it is played off against itself. In this way, a simple type of *counterpoint* is involved here as one movement is seen simultaneously with another.

Counterpoint is the juxtaposing of the main theme to something that enhances it without distracting from it. Too much contrast between the theme and the other movement may make things messy for the audience's eyes.

Fugue

> Four abstract themes, all moving equally and harmoniously together like a fugue would convey the significance of democracy far better than would one woman dressed in red, white and blue, with stars in her hair.
>
> (*Doris Humphrey in* The Shapes of Change, *1979*)

Here, the original theme appears and disappears in various developed forms throughout the dance. This makes for an irregular and complex structure, but one full of surprise and intricate interest. In music, the theme melody can be reversed, inverted, augmented or diminished, and movement motifs in dance can be treated in the same way. Sometimes, *counter-themes* appear with the main motif, and these may take over.

A fugue builds to a clear climax, then gradually winds down and may return, in a *coda*, to a softer repetition of the original motif. This can be useful for carrying dramatic ideas. *Fugue* (1988) by Ian Spink (and directed for television by Caryl Churchill) uses the formal pre-set structure to create dramatic tension. The accompaniment in part uses Bach's *The Art of Fugue*, mixed with text. The story is about a man's death and his family's way of coming to terms with it. The interest lies in Spink's use of formal structure to draw the audience's attention to the everyday. The dance uses the contrapuntal repetition of the main theme in numerous variations. Although it could appear to be yet another soap opera, the use of the fugue structure allows it to rise above that. In fact, there is an atmosphere of unreality because the audience is *equally* aware both of the narrative and of the structure. In a way, this makes the story even more moving, because the repetition here emphasises the strength of feelings as the family grieve. This is a typical post-modern approach to choreography insofar as it avoids cliché and provokes audiences into responding on a deeper, more thoughtful level.

Episodic Structures

Unlike the above, these are not musical forms. They are instead found in literature, as a story gradually unfolds. The narrative is told in connected and progressive sections, chapters, or – as in all good soap operas – episodes. Each section reveals more of the plot: A, B, C, D, E, F, G. Classical ballet often uses this form. *The Sleeping Beauty* (Petipa, 1890) and *Swan Lake* (Petipa, Ivanov, 1877) are such story-type dances. Each individual section must have its own interest, variation and contrast.

In *The Nutcracker* (Petipa, Ivanov, 1892) the Tchaikovsky music was written to the requirements of Petipa's scenario so the episodes are well ordered. One example is the start of the ballet. Petipa wrote:

> The President and his wife and guests decorate the tree
> (delicate, mysterious music 64 bars) . . .
> The fir tree is burning brightly, as if it were magic (modulated music 8 bars)
> The door is thrown open (noisy happy music for the children's entrance 24 bars)
> The children stop, full of amazement and delight
> (a few bars for the children Tremolo)
>
> (*As translated by Joan Lawson, 1960*)

The music for this ballet blends the story, magic and its darker elements into a fluid connected series of episodes which move along and reveal the narrative and its characters to the audience.

Kenneth MacMillan was a prolific choreographer of full-length narrative ballets. *Romeo and Juliet* (1965), *Anastasia* (1967) and *The Invitation* (1960) are some of the more famous. The dramatic story and structure of *The Invitation* were stimulated from two books: *The House of the Angel* by Beatriz Guido and *Le Blé en Herbe* by Colette. MacMillan devised the main characters from these books and developed the plot on from there. Sexual tensions between wife, husband and children drive the narrative from episode to episode. Even a seeming divertissement of an acrobatic act performing for the guests conceals deeper images from the story because it features two cocks fighting in rivalry over a hen. Later one of the male acrobats becomes the attention for one of the other male characters when he has been rejected by the girl. Detail like the motif of the boy trying to lay his head on the girl's breast adds intensity and unity to the episodes when it is repeated later with the wife.

Any fan of *EastEnders* or *Coronation Street* will recognise the addictive nature of this structure.

> The dancers here are playing real people. It's like rehearsing with actors: we argue about their motives when I suppose we should be designing movements. But my skill is as a director of stories, not movement for its own sake.
>
> (*Matthew Bourne, interview with Peter Conrad, 2000*)

In a narrative form the episodes must reveal the story, otherwise they are more of a mere collage of scenes with a unifying theme. This latter type of structure is seen in Christopher Bruce's *Sergeant Early's Dream* (1984). The different episodes in this work do not tell a story but present different scenes from one community. The scenes are linked via entrances and exits so that each flows easily into the next.

The episodic structure is not only a storytelling tool, it can have a range of subtle meanings. In some dances, where there is no intended story, viewers may make up one of their own. There is a belief that *all* dances contain some sort of story no matter how minimal.

> Dance, says Shobana Jeyasingh, runs the risk of being considered 'non-articulate unless anchored to an external narrative provided by a story or music score'. She makes an articulate case for considering her choreography as abstract calligraphy . . . Audiences for dance interpret non-verbal 'language' in different ways . . . [and] . . . can always find stories, whether or not the programme provides a scenario. The problem is that dance is non-specific: it does not necessarily deliver precisely what the creator intended.
>
> (*Jann Parry in* Guardian Unlimited, *March 1999*)

Siobhan Davies's dances contain human emotions as in *Wanting to Tell Stories* (1993) where she explores how to bring out feelings that are deep-seated in dance movement e.g. jumping for joy. Often her dances seem to explore people in relationship to each other as well as her own personal movement style. She may not be the teller of stories like Matthew Bourne, or the interrogator of issues and relationships like Lloyd Newson, and she may insist that dance can communicate on its own terms but perhaps its terms are inevitably, unavoidably human. The form may be intended to be pure dance for its own sake but gestures often suggest emotions, characters, communities and the associated 'stories'.

> Dance is essentially an art of metaphor. Plots, if they exist at all, are communicated not through words but through movement. Gestures tend not to have encoded meanings, as nervous new dance audiences sometimes worry. But gestures often do suggest emotions. Unlike incorporeal music, dance is tantalizingly close to recognisable narrative.
>
> (*Jennifer Dunning in* Gimmicks, Games and Explanation to Create Dancegoers, The New York Times, *July 2001*)

OTHER COMPOSITIONAL STRUCTURES

Natural structures

As mentioned at the start of this chapter, form is all around us in the natural world. The seasons, life cycles and so on offer rich material for organic dance structures. The passing of a day from waking to sleeping is used as a structure along with the four ages of life in *Four Scenes* by Christopher Bruce (1998).

Collage

Sometimes, juxtaposing the unexpected can create a unity of its own. This is an approach used greatly in visual art. In the paintings of surrealists like Dali and Magritte, fantastic and absurd images are created which often result in surprises for an audience. The overall form remains a whole even though the content may be illogical.

Lloyd Newson's *Strange Fish* (1992) has this structure. Almost dreamlike, perhaps more nightmarish, it throws things together that may surprise and shock us. A woman as a Christ figure on the cross is one such image.

> I think I am saying the same things about loneliness, about desire, need, feelings of emptiness ... we divert it and we go somewhere else, and there is much absurdism and surrealism.
>
> (*Lloyd Newson in interview with Nadine Meisner in* Dance & Dancers, *1992*)

The collage structure is a difficult structure, requiring careful and sensitive handling if it is not to fragment into an unconnected, discordant jumble.

Chance

The pioneers, in the early 1950s, of this type of structure were Merce Cunningham and the composer John Cage. They made detailed charts showing timings, spatial designs, sounds and movements. Then they would toss coins to decide on choices and the order of performance. This was how the dance *Suite by Chance* (1953) was composed. In 1969, different movements were matched to playing cards, and *Canfield* was the result. This method involves a detailed and careful choreography of the dance movements involved, in order that these be secure in the dancers' minds: then, and only then, can they be performed in different orders and spatial placings.

The chance structure was the beginning of a post-modern approach which highlighted an interest in the creative process for its own sake. The idea of the content of a dance having a specific meaning was rejected in favour of *movement* being important for its own sake. This innovation was taken up in the UK in the early 1970s by choreographers such as Richard Alston. (Up until then, modern dance had been very much based within the technique and expressionist style of Martha Graham.) Cunningham himself visited the UK, as did others who had worked with him - like dancer Viola Farber. They visited The Place, in London, which offered a staple diet of Graham tuition, but at the same time a great deal of experimental work was happening. In 1972 the new experimental company 'Strider' was founded by Richard Alston. The founder and benefactor of The Place, Robin Howard, encouraged all such experimental work.

Siobhan Davies became acclaimed as one of the UK's foremost choreographers in the 1980s and 1990s. Davies was trained at the London School of Contemporary Dance at The Place, and she went on to dance with the London Contemporary Dance Theatre, again based at The Place, under the direction of ex-Graham dancer, Robert Cohan. By the 1980s, she was making more independent work. One such work, which develops the chance-type structures, was *Plain Song* (1981). This is made up from seven complex phrases for seven dancers. Using a device introduced by Cunningham, she reshuffled the order of the parts of the motifs, changed their facing on stage, changed the dimension they were performed in, or developed them by adding lifts or falls. In this reordering, new phrases and motifs would also be created.

It would be fun for you to think up a system of your own that would enable you to create a dance-by-chance. You could use coins, dice, playing cards, or board games. Through the random use of the categories of action, space, dynamics and timing, movement phrases may be composed. Then, the order, place and time of their performance, on your own or in a group, may again be decided by a chance device.

TASK NINE

1 Read the following list of dance titles and decide which of the above compositional structures would give it the most supportive form. (Answers below.) Explain briefly why you have chosen that structure.

(a) A dance to 'Chocolate (Spanish dance)', from *The Nutcracker* music by Tchaikovsky, 1 minute 9 seconds.
(b) A dance entitled 'United we stand, divided we fall'.
(c) A dance entitled 'Mood swings'.
(d) A dance based on the story entitled *Amazon Sisters* which tells of a group of women in the Amazon who fought against a large electricity company building a dam because it would ruin the environment.
(e) A dance based on a collection of letters and images from a magazine.
(f) A dance entitled 'The planets'.
(g) A dance to 'Fishin' Blues' by Taj Mahal from *The Collection.*
(h) A dance entitled 'Random dance'.

2 Choose one of the above, and if not already stated find a suitable accompaniment for a composition for three, four or five dancers. Choreograph a group dance

COMPOSITIONAL STRUCTURES – A CONCLUSION

Choosing and using these pre-set structures for your dances can be a helpful way to put your ideas in order. Again, try to use them in ways that are appropriate to what a particular dance is trying to convey. This may have a dramatic emphasis, or may be more involved with the movement content for its own sake.

ANSWERS TO TASK 9, QUESTION 1

(a) AB.
(b) Ground bass.
(c) Fugue.
(d) Episodic narrative.
(e) Collage.
(f) Natural forms.
(g) Rondo.
(h) Chance procedures.

The relationship of dance to the accompaniment

When more is meant than meets the ear.

(*John Milton*, L'Allegro *and* Il Penseroso, *circa 1632*)

In the preceding sections of this chapter, the devices and structures which give a dance its overall form were examined, and by now you should have tried out many new ideas from which to start your choreography, or new ways to *organise* your ideas. You may have also read earlier about choosing from a variety of possibilities for accompaniments for your dances, and you now realise the wide variety of choices available to you. The most commonly chosen accompaniment (aural setting) is that of *music*, and so this next section of the book is going to look in some depth at this aspect. As well as an enormous range of choices for the style of music itself, there are also choices to be made about how the movement will interrelate with the sound. An understanding of these choices will help to make choreography *interrelate* with the music in more appropriate, varied and skilled ways.

Dancers and choreographers need an awareness of the structural elements in music. As we saw in the previous section, musical structure is rich and varied. This is similarly so for the elements which go to make up these structures. In dance, we manipulate the elements of action, space, time, dynamics and relationships. In music, composers are faced with similar factors.

This section will focus on:

- musical terms
- different possible relationships between music and dance.

MUSICAL TERMS

> In the Schoenberg score there aren't any long phrases. He states his theme concisely. He uses little repetition, but there are extremes of sudden, fast tempos, and there are slow tempos that happen quickly, and then that rhythm's broken too. Another score like 'Voluntaries' ... one of Poulenc's best ... takes me to the opposite extreme. That's an inward score with a beautiful ... lyricism and a deep religious feeling.
>
> (*Glen Tetley in* The Dance Makers, *1980*)

Could *you* be so specific in describing a piece of music? The description above shows a real understanding of music and its terms. Before we can consider how dance and music interrelate, we too need an understanding of various musical terms that will help us in our dance compositions:

Rhythm

Rhythm is the basic pattern of sound and silence. It can be a steady pulse or beat, or it can be made up of regular repeated groupings.

> All Musick, Feasts, Delights and Pleasures, Games, Dancing, Arts, consist in govern'd measures.
>
> (*Thomas Traherne*, 1657)

During the classic and romantic ballet periods, most music was written in even rhythms: in 2, 4 and 8, or 3, 6 and 9. Rhythms can, however, be both even and uneven. An example of an even rhythm is 4/4 because there are always 4 units in one *bar* (or *measure*):

= 2 bars of 4/4, containing *crotchets* (or *quarter notes*)

After about 500 years of even rhythm in music, modern Western composers began to write in uneven rhythms – 5/4 or 7/4, for example. They also began to vary rhythms within one piece of music. This trend reflected the *social context* of the twentieth century, and of course affected modern dance choreographers like Martha Graham. Life in society was no longer so predictable or balanced. The pulse of society was reflected in the phrasing of sound and actions.

> One of the earmarks of the restlessness of our age is shown in our rhythmic groupings.
>
> (*Marion Bauer, in* Twentieth Century Music, *1993*)

An uneven rhythm combines notes of *different* values in one bar:

(a) (b)

= 2 bars of 4/4 containing (a) 2 crotchets + 1 *minim* (or *half note*), and (b) 2 *quavers* (or *eighth notes*) + 1 crotchet + 2 quavers + 1 crotchet

Accumulative rhythm is where each new bar adds one extra count:

| 1 | 1 2 | 1 2 3 | 1 2 3 4 ||

Subtractive rhythm is where one count is lost from each new bar:

| 1 2 3 4 | 1 2 3 | 1 2 | 1 ||

Musical notation – the time value of the notes

As you saw above, musical notes have different *time values*. In the score example shown:

=4 counts (a *semibreve* or *whole note*)

=2 counts (a minim)

The time value of 8 quavers is the same as the time value of one semibreve.

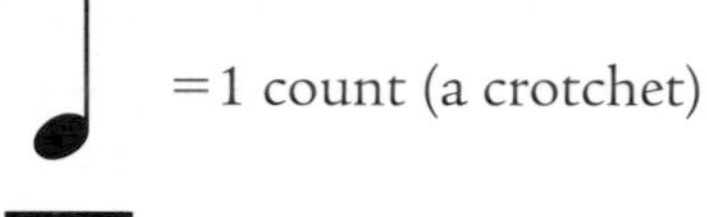

=1 count (a crotchet)

=half a count (a quaver)

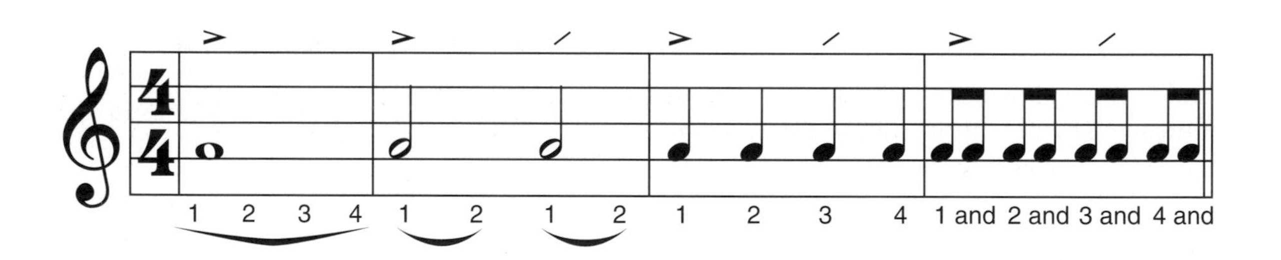

It is possible to divide a single note into *three*. So, one crotchet is equal to a *triplet*:

= 3

Accent

An *accent* is an increase in the stress on a beat, and is shown here by the sign '>'. A less heavy accent is shown by '/'. This is seen in the score example shown. Shifting the accent away from the first beat in a bar creates a more irregular feeling in the rhythm. When this shift is set in a regular measured rhythm, it produces *syncopation*. Syncopated movement can be very exciting to watch because the accents fall in unexpected places and give an element of surprise. Here are some examples of syncopation.

(a) The accent is usually on beat 1, but now is on beat 3.

(b) Missing beat 1 shifts the accent to count 2

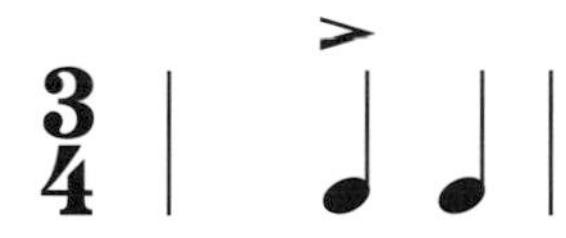

(c) Usually

becomes

(d) This is a *progressive* accent:

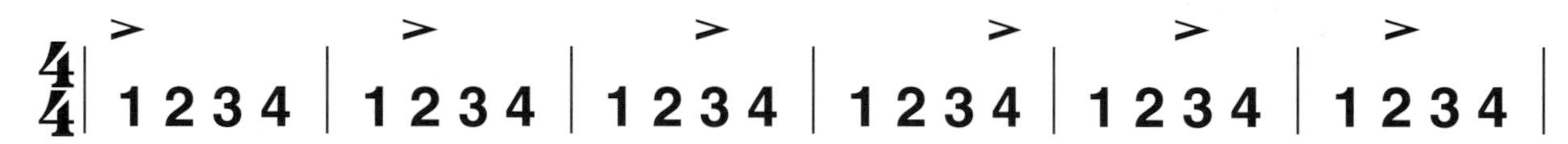

TASK TEN

1. Syncopation can be easily felt by walking in regular 3/4, 2/4 and 4/4 rhythms and then changing to any of the above variations. As you move, feel where the *up-beats* (the weaker beats) and where the *down-beats* (the stronger beats) are.
2. Take any technique exercise that you know well and alter the accents so that it becomes syncopated.

Dancers do not have to stress the same beats as those stressed in the music. Indeed, the choreography can be richer and more interesting if the dancer's movement uses the *off-beat*. In this way, a feeling of increase in speed results, and this is called *double time*:

Clap this repeatedly:

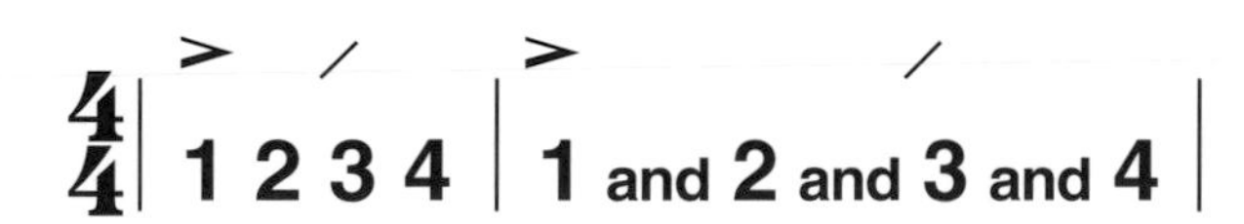

Time signature

The *time signature* is a number which tells you the number of beats which make up a repeated group (i.e. a bar or measure). It is always shown at the start of every piece of music, and usually at the start of a dance notation score too. The time here is divided up by a regular accent or emphasis, and this gives the *metre*.

The number of beats in a bar (measure) gives the time signature. For example:

The top number shows how many beats are in one bar. The lower number shows what kind of note receives one count.

There are many common time signatures in music: 2/2, 2/4, 4/4, 3/4, 5/4, 7/4, 3/8, 6/8, 12/8. Each one has its own distinctive feel. For example, 2/2 can feel military and march-like, where 6/8 has a lively steppy feel. 3/4, in turn, is more lyrical and swing-like. The asymmetrical rhythms – like 5/4 – favoured by modern composers and choreographers may feel distorted and unstable for an audience. Actors using an uneven walk to enter into a scene know that the audience will respond by feeling an emotional disruption. Clearly, emotional responses of the dancer, the choreographer and the audience can all be influenced by the use of different rhythms.

When two metres of unequal length and accent are combined, a *resultant rhythm* is produced. Combining 2/4 and 3/4 makes 6/4, 3/4 and 4/4 combined result in 12/4 as in the example shown.

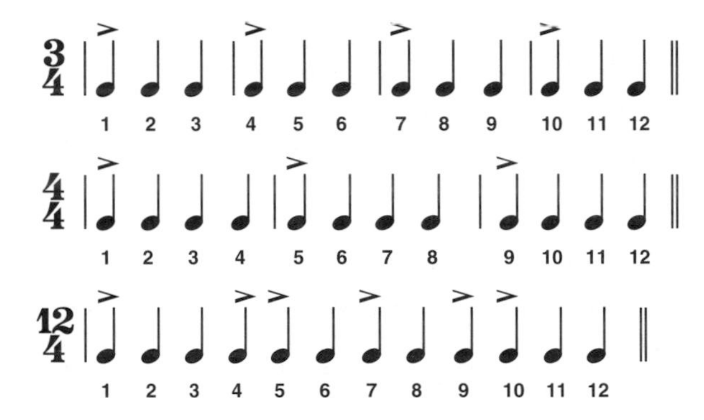

TASK ELEVEN

1. Clap the 12/4 resultant rhythms in the example shown. Then, *walk* the rhythm clearly, showing the accents by stamping. Then, walk the rhythm *and* use other movements to show the accent – e.g. a jump, arm gestures, clapping or a change of level.

2. In trios, let one person move to the 3/4, another person to the 4/4, and the third person to the resultant 12/4, simultaneously.

A *mixed metre* is the result of mixing two time signatures which have different underlying beats. This results in bars with different time values – for example, combining 3/8 with 2/4, or – as shown below – 2/4 and 3/4:

Or, combining 4/4, 1/4 and 2/4:

Some metres mix more satisfactorily than others.

TASK TWELVE

Find two or three metres which mix comfortably.

Tempo

The *tempo* is the *speed* of the beat. This may get faster or slow down. The tempo is usually shown at the start of the music score. Doing triplets travelling with clear changes of tempo is an easy way to experience this. As you increase tempo, there are clear changes in mood from the lyrical to a sense of urgency and directness. The *intensity* and the *dynamics* of the music is changed by changing the tempo.

The Italian terms that music uses to describe tempo are (from fast to slow): *presto, vivace, allegro, moderato, andante, adagio, lento, largo* 'Allegro' means briskly and brightly, whereas 'largo' means very slow. The speed is measured by a metronome, so:

- Presto = approximately 180 beats per minute.
- Adagio = approximately 100 beats per minute.

If a tempo gradually increases, it is *acceleration*, and if it is gradually slowed down, it is *deceleration*.

The intensity of the music can also change if the *force* with which it is played alters. If the volume and force of the playing is increased, the music will rise to a *crescendo*. By *decreasing* the same, a *diminuendo* results, as the dynamics softens.

Ostinato

An ostinato is a musical idea (phrase) which repeats itself throughout a piece or a section of a piece.

As in dance motifs, musical motifs can be varied and developed. They may be:

- played faster;
- played at a higher pitch – i.e. *transposed*;
- inverted – i.e. played upside down;
- played backwards – i.e. retrograde;
- played with longer notes – *augmented* – or shorter notes – *diminished*;

or any combination of these.

Melody
Melody is a succession of notes, of differing pitch and with a rhythm, that results in a recognisable and repeated tune.

Polyphony
Polyphony is music consisting of two or more independent melodic lines which sound together and which counterpoint each other. This technique was first used in fourteenth-century Europe, and it produced a new element, harmony. Counterpoint is produced when two phrases, or themes, are played *against* one another. This can look effective if used in choreography.

Harmony
Harmony results when a *succession* of chords is played. Chords are three or more notes that are played at the same time. In the romantic period, harmonies, like rhythm, were evened out so as always to be pleasing to the ear. This approach was challenged by modern composers, and the richness of dissonance gave music a new raw edge. Impressionist composers like Debussy and Satie worked in this way, as did Stravinsky later on to an even more extreme extent. Painters of the time like the impressionists Monet and Seurat experimented in similar ways in their use of paint: they broke up the colour rather than mixing it in the palette, and the viewer now had to make the mix for themselves. This too developed further in the shocking colours of Matisse.

So too in modern dance:

> . . . the modern dancer has infused movement with that vibrant restless texture and that inner concentration typical of our psychologically oriented age.
>
> (*In* Modern Dance Forms, *by Louis Horst and Carroll Russell, 1961*)

The inward searchings of the works of Martha Graham into the new psychologies of Freud and Jung were the dissonance and discord of the modern dance world.

Different possible relationships between music and dance

Different choreographers use music very differently. Some stay very close to the score, while others may not even hear the music until the première. These are clear extremes of approach, but both of them have one thing in common: the *dance* is the most important element, and it is not a servant to the music.

> The new ballet, refusing to be the slave either of music or of scenic decoration, and recognising the alliance of the arts only on the condition of complete equality, allows perfect freedom to scenic artist and to the musician.
>
> (*Michel Fokine in his letter to* The Times, *6 July 1914*)

It is common to think that the perfect relationship is one where dance and music support and enhance each other, whether through their similarities or through their differences.

The relationship can involve any one of the following:

- a direct correlation;
- a music visualisation;
- the showing or emphasising of character and narrative;
- a call and response;
- a mutual co-existence;
- a disassociation.

DIRECT CORRELATION

Here, dance and music work *together*, so that, for example, in quieter moments in the music, the dance also uses a softer dynamic. This may be the result of dance and music having been composed together. Marius Petipa, the ballet master of St Petersburg, Russia, worked with the composer Tchaikovsky on *The Sleeping Beauty*, 1890. This was a fine score, and it won over audiences. Petipa gave very clear instructions to Tchaikovsky in the form of a *libretto* (a text written for and set to music in an opera etc.). In this scenario, the full story is told and broken down in fine detail showing when each section requires musical changes. The final result was music which directly correlated with the action, mime and movement – as, for example, in the celebration waltz for the birthday party. The opening prologue serves wonderfully to introduce the characters. It involves variations for each of the fairies at Aurora's christening.

This tradition was continued in the Diaghilev work of The Ballets Russes. Diaghilev was a catalyst in the close collaborations of choreographers, composers and artists. For the ballet *Petrushka* by Fokine (1911), the score by composer Stravinsky was met measure for measure by the movement. The solos for the sad puppet who comes to life are movingly contrasted with the crowd scenes at the fairground. His failure in love is made to look even sadder by its juxtaposition against the contrasting gaiety of the carnival.

The work of Sir Frederick Ashton was also famous for its closeness to the music. The critic Alistair Macaulay reported about Ashton's *La Fille Mal Gardée*:

> . . . never before had they seen ballet with the harmony, structure and fluency of music – that watching it was like reading a score.
>
> (*Alistair Macaulay, the* Financial Times, *1994*)

It may be worth finding a music student to collaborate with. There are no rules about how to start. It may be your idea or it may be the musician's. You may talk about what the starting point, images, structure, instruments and so on may be, and so arrive at the overall direction together. It is worth, indeed, trying to work as closely together as possible throughout the rehearsal period.

In the genre of modern dance, Martha Graham would usually commission the music for her choreography. Graham would supply the scenario of action, mood and timings of each section. She and the composer would then collaborate during the writing of the score, and the composer would be free to add detail. Once the music was written, she would start to choreograph. Often, the music was inseparable from the dance: she would work on the dramatic idea *during* the composing of the music, and so she did not then need to interpret the music because this already correlated directly with her choreography. In *Primitive Mysteries* (1931), the rhythms, cadences and silences in the music are used to great effect. All the processions take place during the silences, conveying the ritualistic, spiritual feel of the religious event. At one point, a 5-count melody which had captured the dancers in a repeated back and forth motion changes to a 6, and the now even rhythm releases them into a jumping section. Their energy rises up towards heaven. Often the cadences draw attention to the main figure of the virgin. In one, she rises as the other dancers sink and fold in, bowing to her. In another, two women fall and she quickly stands up in a crucifix-like pose. The titles of two of the sections, 'Hymn to the Virgin' and 'Crucifixus', show of her intent to portray intense religious feeling, probably a result of her encounters with American Native Indians who had been converted to Catholicism. The music seems to drive the spiritual forces at work in the women. As dancers and characters, they seem possessed by the dance idea and the music simultaneously.

Music Visualisation

> In my choreographic creations I have always been dependent on the music. I feel a choreographer can't invent rhythms, he only reflects them in movement.
>
> (*George Balanchine in* Dance From Magic to Art, *1976*)

The way of composing dance that Balanchine describes here results in dance and music appearing as one statement. Balanchine and Stravinsky – as already noted – once described their way of working as being able to *hear* the dance and *see* the music. Balanchine once wrote that everything the composer Stravinsky wrote could be choreographed, 'every note of it'. The final result is movement which has a life of its own and yet which subtly relates to the musical structure. Balanchine's earliest ballet *Apollo* (1928) is a fine example of this. Stravinsky's music was finely interpreted by putting the movement in syncopation with it and shifting the accents into unexpected places. The story in the music shows the god Apollo with the muses of poetry, mime and dance. In a series of solos, duets, trios and quartets, Apollo gives each one creative energy before returning to the heavens. The typical clean, sharp lines of Balanchine's style are distinctive of his neo-classical style. Through the influences of society at that time, the modern and the traditional are brought together: the mix of the fashionable Art Deco sculptural shapes with the percussive hip isolations of jazz are blended with the classical technique. Together, they illustrate and visualise the music sensitively.

> When I listen to a score by him (Stravinsky) ... I am moved ... to try and make visible not only the rhythm, melody and harmony, but even the timbres of the instruments. ... You hear a physical sound humanly organised, performed by people.
>
> (*Balanchine,* Dance Index, *vol. 6, nos 10, 11 & 12*)

Kenneth Macmillan also used this approach. In his *Concerto* (1966) the movement reveals both the structure and moods of the music (Shostakovich, *Piano Concerto No. 2*). The music has a refreshing youthful mood which is emphasised through the dance but the clever interchange of solos and groups ensures that the dance stands strongly in its own right.

In the genre of modern dance, the work of Robert North is a good example of music visualisation. This is seen in his dance *Death and the Maiden* (1984). The dance takes the Schubert score of the same name, which is based on a story. In the Ballet Rambert video which features the dance, North states his belief that dance should fit the music exactly. North was artistic director of the Ballet Rambert company at that time. Following this style, present Rambert Dance Company Director Christopher Bruce relates the dance to the music in this way. In the same video, *Different Steps,* his *Sergeant Early's Dream* (1984) shows the dancers performing movements which illustrate the lyrics almost word for word sometimes.

SHOWING OR EMPHASISING CHARACTER AND NARRATIVE

This is commonly used in the genre of ballet. In Adam's score for *Giselle* (1841), it is clearly seen. It uses *leitmotiv* to identify the main characters. This approach usually involves a mixture of music visualisation and direct correlation.

In John Lanchbery's score for Frederick Ashton's *La Fille Mal Gardée* (*The Unchaperoned Daughter*) (1960), the actions of the characters are clearly supported by the music. In the section entitled 'Lisa and Colas', Act 1, scene 1, the two lovers are involved in a flirtation. There is a romantic melody theme in the music which opens the scene over five bars as Colas approaches Lisa. Then, nine bars of butter-churning music play as she ignores him and tries to look busy. The two themes are interwoven as he in turn tries to catch her attention, giving counterpoint. The music then changes to a polka as they play together.

We see a clever use of the music to show a range of character and story in the disco scene of Bourne's *Swan Lake*. The original libretto (1877) is followed closely at the end of Act 1 as the Prince becomes drunk and dances with the 'peasants' who are a range of characters; sailors, strippers, Teddy Boys, gangsters and molls. The story moves quickly as the characters interact in fights and in social dancing.

In the modern genre, Robert Cohan describes how Maderna's music for *Hunter of Angels* (1967) just happened to be absolutely right for the narrative of the bible story of the twins Jacob and Esau, conveying the conflicts of the twins and the angel's fight with Jacob. The final ascent to heaven in the epilogue was also suitably enhanced by the music.

In some instances, the narrative may not involve something as obvious as story-telling. Siobhan Davies is a case in point here. In her *Something to Tell* (1980, music by Britten: Cello Suite No. 3), the source is a text by Chekhov. A woman, lonely and isolated, is depicted in the various sections of the dance at different stages of her life. These show a number of her troubles and comprise less of a story and more of a description of her personality as she goes through a troubled and unsatisfying relationship. This was one of the pieces where Davies fitted the dance rhythms to the music. At the start of the dance, the music has phrases which alternate between a high and a low pitch, and this gives the dance an opportunity to explore the idea of a *conversation* in a duet between Davies and Robert North. Davies' style is less likely to respond to melody or rhythm. It will rather syncopate and counterpoint phrasings. This allows greater breadth and freedom of movement, but it still also supports the narrative in its broadest sense.

TASK THIRTEEN

Use *L'allegro, Il Penseroso ed Il Moderato* by Handel, Part 1: 'Hence vain deluding joys' (53 seconds), 'Haste thee nymph' (solo and chorus, 2 minutes, 26 seconds).

1. Listen very closely several times until the structure and elements of the music become clear. You should have a pencil and paper handy to write down notes on the rhythms, phrasing, motifs/ostinato, repetition, variation and developments, metres, accents and lyrics (it would help to have a copy of the score).
2. Consider the context of the music (consult the sleeve notes or information at the library), particularly how the poetry of Milton contrasts 'cheerful' and 'pensive' attitudes, and how this is reflected in the soprano, tenor and bass voices.
   There are many images in the poetry which can give ideas for a group dance.
3. Compose such a dance for four, five or six dancers which works either by directly correlating with, or by visualising, the music. You may choose to use the characters as depicted in the poem.

CALL AND RESPONSE

Indian and African genres often use this relationship between music and dance. The master drummer in African ensembles signals to the dancers when to change steps by calls on the drum. In Indian dance, the musicians watch the dancer and change when the movement does. In *Bharatha Natyam*, the dancer is the choreographer. The dances tell classical stories, and there are abstract sequences. The dancer and drummer play off each other in improvisation, rather like in jazz. The dancer wears bells on the ankles, and the stamps weave with the beat of the drum. The final effect looks and sounds exciting. The work of Shobana Jeyasingh is a fine example of this approach. In one section of *Duets with Automobiles* (1994) the dancers echo and answer the intricate counts of the chanting.

Call and response, as in much African music, can become a complex relationship when different rhythms are played simultaneously. Often we see this device used by Siobhan Davies. In *White Man Sleeps* (1988) a motif is developed by fragmenting it into smaller parts and sharing it between different dancers. The notes and instruments in the Kevin Volan's score have the same structural relationship.

The modern dance choreographer Richard Alston (as already quoted earlier) describes his use of music as one involving timing in a 'conversational rhythm'.

In *Strong Language* (1987) by Richard Alston, the movement often has its own logic and independence, loosely working in response to the music. In the section named 'Strumming', the musical count is in 8, but the movement is counted 3-3-2. The effect is a resultant rhythm of shifting accents and metres which gives a look of music and movement being fresh and complementary. The mixed metre of the dance would also help to give an energised appearance, full of rhythmical delights for the audience. It would further help to avoid predictability, and yet still provide a very strong overall structure.

MUTUAL CO-EXISTENCE

The innovative choreography of Vaslav Nijinsky for Diaghilev's Ballets Russes was difficult for the audiences of the day who had been used to a direct correlation between dance and music. Nijinsky's ballets such as *L'Apres-midi d'un Faune* (1912) and *Le Sacre du Printemps* (1913) broke many rules. In *Faune*, the score by Debussy contained clear rhythms, but Nijinsky did not follow these. Instead, he used them almost as a background to give atmosphere.

Stravinsky's music for *The Rite of Spring* was in itself demanding enough for an audience unused to the discords that it contained. Faced with a combination of layers of counterpoint in the movement and a defiance of the rules of classical ballet in the *style* of the movement, the audience was unable to cope, and so it started a riot. The dance here holds its own identity strongly against a monumental piece of music capable of swamping the efforts of lesser choreographers. Indeed, it has done so on many occasions of attempted revivals. This is what *mutual co-existence* is about.

> It is the rhythmic life of the dance and the music, their strengths as independents holding their own, as they merge then separate away, that gets under your skin.
>
> (*Shobana Jeyasingh* in interview with *Christopher Thompson in* The Stage *1992*)

Siobhan Davies and Richard Alston often work in this type of relationship with the music. Davies uses the device of canon to create cross-rhythms between dancers, thus enriching further the interrelation with the music.

Lea Anderson treats the music in a similar way, working closely with the composer on the overall structure. In her collaboration with Steve Blake, *Flesh and Blood* (1989), the *tempo* of the music rather than the phrases is her main point of focus for the movement. The dance and the music run alongside each other, sharing the interpretation of the mood, but they are not so concerned with sharing devices and structures. One critic wrote about *Flesh and Blood*:

> Everything this community of women do is authoritatively fitted to a live chamber systems-jazz score by Steve Blake, whose irony, fragmented, recycled melody and impersonal urgency catch Anderson's tone perfectly. The piece keeps changing, and achieves a sense of ritual and ceremony.
>
> (*Alistair Macaulay, the* Financial Times, *21 November 1989*)

DISASSOCIATION

Allowing both music/sound and dance to develop totally *independently* of each other was the innovation of Merce Cunningham and John Cage, and many others have since followed this approach. The strategy of bringing dance and accompaniment together for the first time only on the opening night itself gives both of these aspects its own separate value.

> It is hard for many people to accept that dancing has nothing in common with music other than the element of time and the division of time...
>
> (*Merce Cunningham in* The Vision of Modern Dance, *1980*)

Balanchine and Cunningham are thus almost opposites in this regard. For Cunningham, the only way to make the dance is to scrutinise the phrases of movement. It is from these phrases that the rhythms of the dance emerge. The Balanchine belief that a choreographer does not invent rhythm but only reflects that of the music has no place here. In his performances, the dance and the music live together, but their effects on the audience are *disassociated* from each other. For Cunningham, time is not beats to the bar. For him, 'Dancing is propelled by dancing.'

The early work of Siobhan Davies used commissioned music scores that were also created *separately* from the dance, with little direct relationship between the two. Often, the music served merely to set the mood or atmosphere – as in *Relay* (1972) where the musician improvised jazz piano. In her later work, Davies developed movement which responded more to the structure of the music in mutual co-existence.

TASK FOURTEEN

1 Use the group dance which you composed to *L'Allegro, Il Penseroso ed Il Moderato*. Dance it to the following pieces of music:

- *Purple Haze*, by the Kronos Quartet, 3 minutes;
- *Speaking in Tongues II*, by Sheila Chandra, 3 minutes 8 seconds.

The dancers will need assistance in making alterations in timing (perhaps in the transitions) to compensate for the very slight different lengths of the pieces of music.

2 Assess the effects of the mutual-coexistence and disassociation approaches on the look of the dance. Did the contrast of the music with the dance emphasise and enhance features of the choreography? Was the disassociation uncomfortable but of interest for you as the viewer? Are you prepared to allow discord to be both interesting and challenging to the way you see things?

THE RELATIONSHIP OF MUSIC TO DANCE – CONCLUSION

It is a good idea to try to listen to as many different types and styles of music as possible and see if you can hear and analyse what the composer is doing with the sounds.

It is probably clear to you by now that the elements and structures of dance and music have a great deal in common. When the two come together in choreography, a whole Pandora's box of surprises, delights and troubles pops open! The relationship between the two aspects opens up many choices for the choreographer, and many skills are in turn demanded of the dancer. If appropriate choices are made, and if accurate performances are given, there may be many surprises for the audience.

The devices and structures presented so far are mostly involved with arranging movement for groups in time. However, the concern with design in *space* also requires attention, and this will form the final part of this chapter.

Organising groups in space

As seen in Chapter 2, the choice of dancers and the numbers of them are an important part of the choreographic process. In giving a dance a coherent form, organising their placement in *space* is another crucial factor.

A radical approach to this may be seen in the work of post-modern choreographer Trisha Brown. In her own words:

> *Walking on the Wall*, 1971, gave the illusion that the audience was overhead, looking down on the tops of the heads of the performers walking and standing below. It also showed what it was, the performance of a simple activity against the principles of gravity. The rigging and technical business of getting up there was in clear view.
>
> (*Trisha Brown in* The Vision of Modern Dance, *1980*)

This approach was extreme but effective in arranging the spatial relationship not only of dancer to dancer, but also of dance to location (i.e. the walls of the Whitney Museum), and of audience to dance. As Sally Banes describes it, the whole orientation of the audience was turned upside down, sideways, every which way:

> . . . one has the distinct sensation that one is on a tall building, watching people walking back and forth on the sidewalk below. When they turn the corner on the walls, suddenly one feels as though one were positioned sideways, sticking one's head out of a window, perhaps, and seeing a sideways image of an upright person below.
>
> (*Sally Banes, in* Terpsichore in Sneakers, *1980*)

Brighton and Hove Youth dance

Of course, this was a highly unusual way of designing groups in space, and the usual scenario which you will be presented with is that of making movement for the *proscenium stage*. Placement on stages is described in Chapter 3. The concern here is with *arrangements* of groups of dancers, and this includes:

- group shapes/formations and their stage placement;
- spaces between the dancers;
- relationships between the dancers.

GROUP SHAPES/FORMATIONS

The overall shape of the group involves a careful arrangement of the dancers that is appropriate to the content of the dance idea. There are many arrangements to choose from. Traditional lines and circles, as seen in folk dances, are often used to convey ideas like community, ritual, courtship, war, celebration and procession. These formations are often symmetrical, and if interest needs to be added, they may be placed off-centre in the stage space. Contrasting formations placed next to them will also add interest.

Formal lines like those of a corps de ballet – for example, in Fokine's *Les Sylphides* (1909) – are very different from the less regular formations of a dance like Alston's *Wildlife* (1984) where the concern is for the energy of zigzags and for the angularity of shape.

Close masses and scattered groups convey contrasting expressions to an audience. Close masses include clusters of loosely arranged dancers and arrangements of dancers in more geometric shapes like triangles, wedges, squares and circles.

In the entrance to the Ball in Bourne's *Swan Lake* (1995) a tightly clustered group is used for the press and autograph hunters, whereas the celebrities promenade formally in pairs.

TASK FIFTEEN

Look at paintings from different periods of history – e.g. primitive, mediaeval, Renaissance, cubist, surrealist etc. Find figurative paintings, i.e. paintings with people in them. Notice *how* the people are placed in relationship to one another – i.e. the groupings and poses. Choose one of the paintings and develop from it a series of group shapes that follow on logically from the ones in the paintings. Link the stillness with appropriate movements. Pay attention to the placement of the shapes in the space.

Pay attention to other details in the chosen picture, such as other objects or the scenery. Allow these to feature through the motifs when choosing actions, dynamics, the use of space, relationships.

Use the style of the painting to influence the corresponding style of movement you use. For example, a primitive-style painting may lead to a dance with a tribal feel.

Find an appropriate accompaniment for the dance.

SPACES BETWEEN THE DANCERS

If the dancers are placed close together, they will create a very different set of feelings in the audience than they will if they are scattered about. *Decentralising* the space and scattering the dancers is a characteristic of Cunningham work, and a similar aspect of the work of Sir Frederick Ashton was noted in the following critique:

> ... his use of space, especially in his purest dance works, *Symphonic Variations* and *Scènes de Ballet* and *Monotones*, was as unconventional as Merce Cunningham. Of *Scènes de Ballet* he said, 'I ... wanted to do a ballet that could be seen from any angle – anywhere could be the front, so to speak.'
>
> (*David Vaughan in* Dance Now, *Summer 1995*)

This is quite an unexpected use of the stage space in the context of classical ballet, which is usually designed for the proscenium stage.

Care must be taken, however, not to allow the dancers to be so far apart that the audience is unable to see the whole group. The most common fault of all is placing one dancer on one side of the stage and the other so far over to the other side that the audience is left looking at a hole in the centre, or moving their heads from side to side as if watching a tennis match without a ball!

The use of contrasting levels, and of the spaces that are created between these levels, is often an effective device. Similarly, if the body shapes of the dancers *overlap*, the spaces *in between* can be of as much interest as the overlapping shapes themselves. Using the space between dancers to create dramatic tension or simply to connect one dancer to another is also a possibility worth exploring. This can serve to *isolate*, to put the dancers in *conflict* with each other, or it can bring about feelings of *harmony* or *uniformity* between the dancers.

RELATIONSHIPS BETWEEN THE DANCERS

This follows on quite simply from the use of spaces between the dancers. The dancers' body shapes may be deliberately chosen to copy, complement or contrast with one another.

TASK SIXTEEN

Draw the shape shown in Figure 5.2 (page 164) on a piece of paper three times. Add a shape to the first drawing which copies it. Add shapes to the second which complement it, and add shapes to the third which contrast with it.

Figure 5.2 *Body shapes*

The interest of group shapes, placements and timings are enhanced by using *contact* between the dancers. There are special skills involved here, as well as a need to build trust between the dancers. A whole technique was created around this concept by Steve Paxton in the 1960s as part of the Judson Church post- modern group in New York. Paxton was a gymnast who later studied dance and who combined his experiences to produce a style based on giving and taking weight. Trust between partners, if you decide to fall or lean on them, was the priority. Paxton tried to create a Western type of martial art that did not contain any combat. There was an emphasis on equality of partners, between genders, races and abilities.

It is worth experimenting in duets and larger groups with simple handholds and counter-balances, feeling exactly how much or how little energy is appropriate to maintain a counterbalance and to lose it. Similarly, other contact situations, such as lifting, lowering, supporting, catching and throwing, initiating turns or assisting jumps, can all have exciting results.

In *The House of Bones* (1991) dance company Motionhouse use contact work to great effect. Choreographers Kevin Finnan and Louise Richards depict how a town laid to siege in mediaeval times became infected by the plague. Instead of the dead and dying being looked after with compassion, their bodies were catapulted over the city walls at the enemy! This is used as a metaphor for the present-day treatment of AIDS victims, and as a reminder of the need for compassion. Similar concerns for the humane treatment of our fellow human beings come through in the work of the company VTOL, and in the work of the company DV8 (director Lloyd Newson), whose *Dead Dreams of Monochrome Men* (1988) is set in a desperate world of gay bars. In this latter piece, the desire and loneliness of desperate men in need of company is portrayed. There is frantic, frenetic contact work as desire turns to demand:

> Newson transforms emotion into movement via several big physical set pieces where the dancers fling themselves full tilt at one another like combatants in a war dive-bombing one another's bodies.
>
> (*Allen Robertson in* Dance Now, *1996*)

Newson explores issues of how people hurt and love each other in a hard-hitting, highly emotionally charged atmosphere. His work here is similar to the work of the German choreographer Pina Bausch:

> Her ... performers seem to use their innermost secrets of their lives as a springboard into these performances. They spew out their guts both physically and emotionally with an honesty that has become a byword for all of the Bausch imitators. ... [in *Café Muller*, (1978):] ... A woman repeatedly throws herself into a man's arms, but he does not bother to catch her. ... she simply grows more frantic ... clambering and

> tossing herself down again as fast as she can...
>
> (*Allen Robertson, Donald Hutera, in* The Dance Handbook, *1988*)

Concerns such as these are important in post-modern work, which regards the creation of a truly human world as a priority. Here is an extract from the information which accompanies the video *Different Dancers, Similar Motion* (1989) by Motionhouse.

> This video is designed to encourage you to change the way you think about dance. It shows ... how people can learn to overcome ignorance, anxieties, prejudices and inexperience through constructively led workshops.
>
> (*Information from Different Dancers, Similar Motion, Motionhouse, 1989*)

The video shows an integrated group, i.e. a group comprising those with and without disabilities, working during a fortnight with Motionhouse. Contact improvisation is used a great deal, and there are some enchanting moments as the participants talk about their discoveries both about dance and about themselves.

V-TOL Dance Company 'And Nothing but the Truth' 1998. Dancers James Hewison, Marcia Pook. Photo by Chris Nash

TASK SEVENTEEN

1 In threes, let two people dance while the other person reads the following instructions slowly enough so that the dancers have time to feel the movements.

'Sit back to back and gently let your backs rub together as if you are mapping out the surface of your partner's back. ... Let this movement enlarge until you begin to roll around each other ... feel the circular movement. ... As you move, find a couple of stillnesses which are resting points. They are comfortable for both of you. Pause in them before continuing the movement. Try to share supporting and being supported equally.'

2 Dancer No. 1: go on all fours, holding a strong flat back. Dancer No. 2: hang over. ... Ensure that your centre of gravity is over the supports'. ... Relax as you hang ... feel balanced. Breathe, melt down to the floor softly and roll off your partner.'

3 'Stand close to your partner. ... Slowly melt down to the floor, giving way together in contact all the way. ... Roll apart and return to standing easily.'

4 'Take a walk together, not allowing your partner to fall. ... Support your partner all the way down, going down to the floor yourself if it is necessary. ... Speed this up so that the falls are followed by rapid rebounds, and so that the recoveries are seamless with the falling and walking.
When you are more confident, add jumps.'

5 See photos (a), (b), (c) and (d) below for the illustrations to this task. Practise making the five shapes shown in the photographs. Connect them, in any order of your choice, with suitable movement which emphasises contact and loss of the same. Try to make the whole phrase as fluid as possible, but with some clear changes of tempo. Make sure that you share roles equally.

Brighton and Hove Youth Dance (a)

(b)

(c)

(d)

Other simple dancer-to-dancer relationships may include the use of *unison*, and here, the more dancers who are doing the same movement, the more forceful the impact of that movement. Any of the following are also worthy of exploration:

meet and part	complement/contrast
action/reaction	different facings
match/mirror	passing
side-by-side	back-to-back
alone, together	conversation
lead, follow	one behind the other

Having come thus far in the book, we now have a reasonable overview of many aspects of the constituent features of dances, the form in dances and the dancer in training. After the studio technique class and rehearsal, the inevitable happens: lights, curtains, ACTION! The next chapter will present important matters for dancers and choreographers to consider before, during and after the actual performance.

TASK EIGHTEEN

Creating a Group Dance for Performance

(This task can be adapted to suit tasks 3, 4, 5, and 8 in Chapter 6)

 **Problem Solving. Working with Others.** 

You should record your own progress in this task. Your teacher may assess you on this evidence.

You will work in a group of between three and six, but can be assessed as an individual on:

- Working with others – in rehearsal and project management.
- Choreography – contribute movement and ideas to the dance.

Working as a group:

1. Choose one of the tasks from this chapter. *Select* from Task numbers 4, 5, 7, 8, 9, 13 and 14 (together), 15.
2. Outline the project schedules. Each individual should contribute two or three ideas/suggestions/tasks and should take responsibility for putting them into action.
3. Research the idea to find: accompaniment, movement or equipment as appropriate.
4. Rehearse to produce the dance: each individual is responsible for selecting and developing movement for the dance.
5. Perform the dance according to the agreed schedule.

You should evaluate your personal work and progress using the grid on page 169. Back up with further records and evidence in your portfolio e.g. a record of schedule, research data you found.

In Chapter 6, Task 8 you will find an evaluation grid to assess your performance skills. This could be used for the group dance.

Self-evaluation grid

DANCE/PROJECT TITLE ______________________ NAME ______________

START DATE ______________________ FINISH DATE ______________________

How well did you. . .?	Strategy	Needs improvement	Mostly effectively	Consistently/ imaginatively achieved
1 Work with others Example: Communicate and listen Copy this table into your own portfolio. Select and enter three target areas. Take direction from others . . . Support others' ideas/ suggestions . . . Contribute two or three ideas . . . Respect the ideas of others . . . Make clear and put your ideas into action* . . . Keep to schedules Punctuality . . . *See Chapter 6 for more detail on rehearsal strategies	✓ Ask teacher to help me find a way to improve my listening skills. She has suggested the 10-second rule.	✓ 2nd Sept. Once I start talking I have a habit of going on and not letting others speak. Sometimes I make it worse by dancing about to make my point. My friend has suggested that I should find a way to stop this.	✓ 9th Sept. I am counting to 10 before I speak and find that the others have good ideas. Also my friend has a secret sign which he uses when he thinks I am going on and it's working quite well.	✓ 2nd Oct. We have nearly finished the dance and the group are much friendlier to me now. Also our dance is looking very good and we are ahead of our schedule because we work so well together. When we pool our ideas we end up with better dance. I'm not so anxious about having to listen to others.

How well did you. . .?	Strategy	Needs improvement	Mostly effectively	Consistently/ imaginatively achieved
2 Contribute to choreography Research ideas . . . Example: Improvise to find movement Keep a written record of your movement . . . Select as appropriate: motifs/devices . . . structure/form/style . . . Use appreciation process in rehearsal to refine ideas* . . . *See Chapter 6 for more detail on rehearsal strategies	✓ I need to organise my time to include experiment with movement for the group dance. One of the things I forget is to book time in the studio.	✓ 2nd Sept. I tend to use the same movements all the time. Usually they are the ones that a teacher has taught me. But they don't express lots of things and so I have to try and think for myself more. In the past I always forget what I improvise, so I'm going to try to write down movements as I find them.	✓ 9th Sept. I booked an hour in the studio to find some motifs for our group dance. I had done research and found some music but it wasn't right so I worked in silence. Funny really but even though I didn't find much I have a couple of phrases which seem very expressive. The rest of the group like them.	✓ 16th Sept. Success is patchy but I wrote down a couple of things that aren't good for this dance but I like them and maybe one day . . . My ideas are now in the dance and we have developed them as they feature a fair amount and help to express the content.

References and resources

BOOKS

Balanchine, G., *Balanchine's Complete Stories of the Great Ballet*, New York: Doubleday & Co., 1954

Banes, S., *Terpsichore in Sneakers: Post-Modern Dance*, Boston: Houghton Mifflin Company, 1980

Horst, L. and Carroll, R., *Modern Dance Forms*, New York: Dance Horizons, 1961

Lawson, J., *A History of Ballet and Its Makers*, London: Dance Books, 1964

Robertson, A. and Hutera, D. *The Dance Handbook*, Harlow: Longman, 1988

Siegel, M.B., *The Shapes of Change*, New York: Avon Books, 1979

Teck, K., *Ear Training: a Dancer's Guide to Music*, USA: Princeton Book Co., 1994

VIDEOS

available from NRCD www.surrey.ac.uk

Motionhouse, *Different Dancers, Similar Motion*, 1989, and *The House of Bones*, 1991

available from www.dancebooks.co.uk

Essential Alston (1998)

Romeo and Juliet – K. MacMillan (1984)

Sleeping Beauty – The Australian Ballet (2000); Petipa choreography reproduced from the Sergeyev notation by Monica Parker

Sleeping Beauty – The Bolshoi Ballet, Yuri Grigorovich production

White Man Sleeps, Wyoming – Siobhan Davies Dance Company

MUSIC

The Chieftains, *Strike the Gay Harp*, 3 Claddagh Records, 4CC10, PCO 1984, recommended for Task 1

Penguin Café Orchestra, *Broadcasting from Home*, EGDC 38, recommended for Task 4

The Go-Gos, *We Got the Beat*, IRS 7243 8 31756 2 8, 1994, recommended for Task 6

Tchaikovsky, *The Nutcracker*, recording by the Royal Opera House Orchestra, Conifer Records, ROH 002 (or similar recording), recommended for Task 7

Handel, *L'allegro, Il Penseroso ed Il Moderato*, Soli Monteverdi Choir, English Baroque soloists, Erato, 2292-45377-2, 1980 recommended for Task 13

Kronos Quartet, *Purple Haze*, Nonesuch, 75559-79111-2 1986, recommended for Task 14

Sheila Chandra, *Speaking in Tongues II*, RW24 07777 7 867227, recommended for Task 14

Taj Mahal, *Fishin' Blues* on *The Collection*, Castles Communication, CCSCD180 1987

Theme and Variations by Fernando Sor on *Romantic Guitar*, 450 146-2 10, 1994 Karussell UK Ltd

SIX

DANCE APPRECIATION

The significance of dance

Appreciating the significance of a dance of your own, of other students or of professionals, is a complex process. You need to be able to recognise the constituent features and understand how they relate to: each other; the content of the dance; the context. It is not enough for you to say, 'I liked it. It was good.' If you understand more about what makes a successful dance your own work will improve.

> Initial response to a painting should be a starting point and not a finish line. It should lead not only to more prolonged scrutiny but also to the posing of questions. Just what is it in this picture that seems so pleasing? Is it the colour? the light? the conveying of the artist's emotion? ... the forms themselves? ... Above all how has the artist gone about achieving (the) effects?
>
> (*Helen M. Franc in* An Invitation to See 125 Paintings from the Museum of Modern Art, *New York, 1973*)

Often dance students may think that analysis is a dry and rather unnecessary process. Indeed if overdone it can kill the impact and enjoyment of a dance. However, if it is done with passion, and uses imagination, it can enhance the enjoyment. Try to write creatively about what you see. Read the following passage and notice its rich descriptive use of words.

> Against a heavenly blue backdrop, the dancers are dressed in bright, often primary colours, twelve soloists co-existing as only in one of Cunningham's comradely democracies ... a tonic to the dance-goer's eye. Its setting of steps to Charles Amirkhanian's brilliant collage of words or phrases of speech trains us to look more intensely at movement – its components, the steps and phrases. Alston in 'Rainbow Ripples' draws wit and beauty from the dancer's achievement of balance; we constantly notice a dancer at the peak of a wave before falling – as in the multi-refracted figure on the backdrop. Or in reverse: we watch dancers dive deep without dropping. Alston builds this daring into pouring lyric lines which have a silken flow that I, chauvinistically no doubt, like to label as a sign of English classic dancing.
>
> (*Alastair Macaulay in* Dance Theatre Journal, *1983*)

This critic writes artistically and leaves us feeling almost as if we have seen the dance ourselves. Finding the words that a dance is worthy of requires great powers of description, interpretation and evaluation. In the review above we see clearly all three stages of the appreciation process:

- He *describes* the dancers, the movement, the set, costumes and accompaniment.

- He *interprets* the content (this dance is *about movement*) and identifies certain styles.
- He *evaluates*; key phrases such as '... *a tonic to the dance-goer's eye*' confirm its success for the reader.

As you watch dance whether in rehearsal or performance you respond to and appraise what you see. As a student of dance you are trying to make your response more of an *informed* one, not based only on personal taste.

The preceding chapters should have increased your understanding of the first stage of the process of dance appreciation – *description*. For instance you may be able to describe how a dance uses space or motif development in certain ways and how it relates to the accompaniment. The next stage is to interpret what the selected constituent features may be expressing.

Interpretation

Interpretation involves understanding the content and style of a dance as expressed in the constituent features. It involves asking questions like: What is the theme? Why were certain movement constituents chosen? Or why are dancers moving in particular ways? A choreographer's choice of content and movement technique is part of their personal style.

Content

Content is the subject matter, theme or ideas chosen by the choreographer or being expressed to a viewer. Content is expressed by the appropriate selection and structuring of constituent features. This process of choosing and transforming content into a dance is described by American post-modern choreographer, Anna Halprin:

> ... as an artist ... essentially your job is to be a vehicle for other people. ... when you take responsibility for an audience, you are then accepting the fact that you must go through some sort of distilling process in which the personal experience has become so zeroed and so heightened by a clarity that you know exactly what you're dealing with ... Then you find the movement ... essence of that idea inherent not only in how your body moves, but in ... an awareness of the total thing.
>
> (*In* The Vision of Modern Dance, *1980*)

TASK ONE

Try to do this exercise as quickly as possible.

Allow 15 minutes maximum. In groups of three or four brainstorm content that would translate into movement. It could include poetry, sculpture, current events in the news, movement itself. Keep the list handy because this task continues in Tasks 3, 4, and 5.

If we scan various well-known choreographers we may see that they have themes of content running through their work. Indeed some say that all choreographers spend their lifetime working on only one or two dances in essence.

The content of the work of Kenneth MacMillan often focused on sexual conflict and violence. In a similar way the works of Lloyd Newson address how people relate to each other and the problems that this may create. Content involved with movement for its own sake, 'pure dance', is a concern in the works of Merce Cunningham, Siobhan Davies and Richard Alston. Christopher Bruce seems interested in themes of social conscience such as political conflict and aging. Shobana Jeyasingh combines concern for the traditional Indian with that of life in society of today. *Badejo* aim to develop African dance and performing arts creatively as a contemporary phenomenon relevant to the lives of people (especially black people) in Britain.

The content itself may indicate certain styles in which it may be treated most successfully. This may bring about a certain 'look' or style in the movement. For example, a dance entitled *Gravity and Impulse* is likely to be post-modern genre, where movement for its own sake is the content and a Release style of technique is performed.

STYLE

In the world of fashion, clothes by the famous designers Katherine Hamnett, Christian Dior and Calvin Klein each have their own distinctive style. When worn, they give the wearer a certain look. Similarly, in the music world, Enigma sounds unmistak-

Les Patineurs *(1937) by Frederick Ashton and* Birthday *(1992)*

ably different to The Beatles. *Style* is the key here. Style in dance is seen in the technique that a dancer performs. Look at the photographs on page 175 and you will see contrasts in the styles of the two genres – the classical ballet of Frederick Ashton and Lea Anderson's post-modern dance.

So genres appear different in style. However there are different *named* styles within genres:

> What is classical anyway? That of New York City Ballet and Balanchine? Or Bournonville? Or Petipa? Or Ashton? They are so different.
>
> (*Mark Baldwin in* 'Dance Bites', *Ismene Brown, The Electronic Telegraph, 27 February 1999*)

Similarly in the genre of modern dance, you would not mistake Martha Graham technique for Merce Cunningham. Or in post-modern genre Lloyd Newson's movement style is noticeably different to that of Siobhan Davies.

TASK TWO

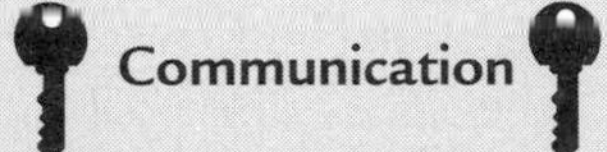

Communication

1. In groups of three or four compare two works from different genres e.g. *The Sleeping Beauty* (Petipa, 1890) and *Strange Fish* (Newson, 1992). List how they differ or are similar in content and style.
2. Make a presentation of your findings to another group.

In music, literature and the visual arts there is a tradition of studying the 'greats'. This should be so in dance too. You may find that a style other than your own actually has similarities to yours as well as containing elements which are very different. Therefore it can reinforce your personal style as well as offer up new ideas to be explored. It may well reveal things which really do not fit your body and mind. It is useful to know what they are too. Matthew Bourne's parody of modern dance in his *Car Man* (2000) grew out of his dislike of Martha Graham technique, which he thinks wrecked his back during training. It didn't stop him from making effective use of it in his choreography.

TASK THREE

Communication, Problem Solving and Information Technology

1. From the list which you prepared as a group in Task 1, individually choose one of the ideas, research it and find an example which you can use as a starting point for a dance. Explore movements that would be appropriate for a solo dance.
2. From the images which you have abstracted choose the work of a choreographer who has a recognisable style and choreograph the short solo in that style. You should use photographs and videos of your chosen choreographer for reference. Allow several hours for this work, including library, video and Internet research.
   This task continues in Tasks 4 and 5.

Your personal movement and choreographic style is something which will develop over time. As you analyse your own and others' dances use your findings to inform your personal dance development This process of development is seen in the work of many artists. In the work of Martha Graham we see times when America was the main focus of content and other times when Greek dramas or the Bible were important. In the early twentieth century she totally rejected ballet and would not allow her dancers to attend ballet classes, but later she accepted the different genre as complementary to her own in training dancers. Her personal development used the torso in new ways in the stylised contraction, release and spirals. Its harsh, angular appearance, with flexed feet and hands, suited the expression of the content she chose. This too was new at that time and so in order to express it she needed a new style of moving. Nowadays her style is part of modern dance tradition but it came from her invention. Similar developments of style can be traced in most choreographers.

Experience of a range of genres such as South Asian and Pan-African, can broaden the scope of your personal style. The key is to explore and not to be afraid of mixing genres and styles. Working with other art forms can also enrich and enhance your work. Your personal style is not a limitation but a beginning.

So now the first two stages of the dance appreciation process have been explained. You should understand more about how the chosen constituent features, structures and styles can be described and how they express content in the process of *interpretation*. The third and final stage of the process of appreciation is *evaluation*.

Evaluation

Evaluation is judging the success, or lack of it, of a performance taking into consideration how effectively the constituent features and style have been used to portray the content and the quality of the actual performance of the dancers.

> Evaluation is creation … is itself the value and jewel of all valued things. Only through evaluation is there value.
>
> (*Freidrich Nietzsche, philosopher in* Thus Spoke Zarathustra)

As Nietzsche describes above, the process of evaluation (and appreciation) gives value to the performance. Also it is useful in the rehearsal process of making and refining dances. Although in rehearsal and performance you are looking at the same features, the evaluation of a dance may be from differing points of view.

Evaluation brings into play the concept of *context* of the dance because this will tell how successful a dance is for a specific viewer. In working with students the word context sometimes seems to cause great anxieties.

CONTEXT

In your dance studies your choreography may be in the context of some sort of assessment. Therefore it functions as a means to gain marks to pass the exam! Probably you will be working in your community with your peers. Can you see how this is the context of *your* work? We will now apply this to the wider field of professional dance work.

Dance is always created at a certain time and in a specific place. When we analyse and evaluate dance these contexts must be considered. In particular we may look at the contexts of:

- the development of an artist, genre or style over time;
- history and social conditions;
- the function and role of the dance;

THE DEVELOPMENT OF AN ARTIST, GENRE OR STYLE OVER TIME

As you saw earlier in the section on style a choreographer's work, like that of other artists, develops over time. Their choice of content, structure and style may well vary over the years. Similarly genres such as ballet change in style over time. The 2000 Kirov reconstruction of Petipa's original 1890 *The Sleeping Beauty,* from the Stepanov notation, presented the problem of recreating the correct style. Even though the notation gave detail about the steps it did not supply descriptions of *how* they danced at that time. The Kirov ballet master Sergei Vikharev, who was responsible for this reconstruction, reported that the original tempi was faster than the versions of the late twentieth century.

Post-modern dance too, from its early experiments in the 1960s, has continued to develop and now has many different styles within it.

Richard Alston is a good example of the development of a choreographer. Originally trained in Graham technique at the newly formed London Contemporary Dance School, his *Nowhere Slowly* (1970) showed Graham influences of fall/recovery. He then went on to become one of the first British choreographers of note to work with a Merce Cunningham influence which suited his style. There are balletic influences too, of the Cecchetti style, but moulded into his personal language. Nowadays his style also incorporates the *Release* techniques of post-modernism. He maintains strong links with visual art, from his art background. His experimental nature has meant that he used a wide variety of accompaniments, from silence to complex word-sound collages. But later work seems more set to classical music such as that of Stravinsky in *Movements from Petrushka* (1994), or the romantic Brahms in *Waltzes in Disorder* (1998).

He prefers to use formal structures, although as he admits on the video version of *Soda Lake*, sometimes the 'pure' movement and the figurative images become mixed together. For a while his work was very intellectual, 'pure' dance, like *Rainbow Bandit* (1974) and *Zansa* (1986), but there were pieces where human emotion did feature more, like *Pulcinella* (1987).

> ... its characters are very broadly drawn – almost like cartoon characters.
>
> (*Richard Alston in interview with Justine Reeves*, Sussex Dance web site, *2000*)

Recently semi-narrative structures have featured more, although he still hankers to the Cunningham legacy in structure, such as *Sophisticated Curiosities* (1998) which presented excerpts from such early works as *Rainbow Ripples* (1980) and *Strong Language* (1987).

> My work now is primarily about the relationship between movement and music and the relation of the phrasing is very exact and for that I need a very exact language. The language that has evolved is a flowing, fluid form, I guess the clearest influence ... is Cunningham. And that's because his movement language was so objective.
>
> Alston describes his own choreography in four words: musical ... fluid ... detailed ... humane
>
> (*Sussex Dance web site, 2000*)

His working methods have stayed much the same throughout, preferring a collaborative style of relationship with dancers. This may reflect his beginnings in the early 1970s with *Strider*, *X6 Dance Collective* and *Second Stride* – all these companies worked in communal collaborations, breaking away from traditional ballet company hierarchies.

TASK FOUR

(This Task may be associated with Tasks 3 and 5)

Communication and Information Technology

Research a well-known choreographer of your choice. Write a summary of the key features of their development. These may include: training; different techniques; preferred movement genres/styles; choice of content, choreographic structures, dancers, accompaniment; relationship to other art forms.

Prepare your summary for presentation to your group. This may make use of some of your original resource material from text, photos, video, and Internet images.

HISTORY AND SOCIAL CONDITIONS

If viewers of a dance have knowledge of the time and place when it was made it will help them to understand, interpret and evaluate the performance.

> Why is it . . . that a young choreographer is still more likely than a young painter or composer or playwright to regard an intimate knowledge of tradition as something that inhibits originality – rather than something that feeds and nourishes it?
>
> (*Roger Copeland in* Dance Theatre Journal, *1994*)

The historical and social context may include any or a combination of:

- dominant social values
- changing social structures/values
- philosophies and psychologies
- technological developments.

Dominant social values

The world of Renaissance ballet was dominated by the rulers of European Royal courts. Manners and rules of everyday behaviour were reflected in the ballets where everyone knew 'their place'. So the ballets were successful if they glorified the Kings and Queens and maintained that social order.

If dominant values are questioned in an artist's work it can affect the public reaction to a dance. Nijinsky provoked a riot in Paris because his audience expected to see 'ballet'. Isadora Duncan outraged people by her disregard for the rules of being a woman in society of the twentieth century. Similarly works of Kenneth MacMillan like *Manon* (1974) were not a success in his lifetime (died 1992). It is thought that, because in the 1970s ballerinas were still regarded socially as little princesses, to give them roles of seductress and calculating whore was totally unsuitable. Nowadays *Manon* is a much sought-after role of the ballet world even though it is far removed from the notion of romantic love.

Dominant social values were the context for the classical dances of the Indian sub-continent. Although there are many different styles they came from one set of religious and spiritual beliefs which ordered people's lives. Teaching of such dance is a sacred task and its performances were dedicated to the gods.

In some African dance the dominant culture of white mine owners deeply affected the dance of the black peoples. We see this noticeably in the Gumboot dance which used the stamps, chants and slapping sounds as accompaniment because they were not allowed drums or other musical instruments.

Changing social structures/values

When we watch romantic ballet today, we must consider the time when it was first choreographed in order to understand its significance. We could never really experience romantic ballet as audiences did in the 1800s, because we live in a very different age from them. We can appreciate it for what it is and enjoy it, but not relate to it as new and fashionable in the way that the original audiences would have done. The changing social order which resulted from the French Revolution turned society upside down and is difficult for us to grasp. The aristocracy and their classicism in the arts were no longer to be worshipped as perfect. Now was the turn of the peasants to be glorified and idealised. This directly affected the choice of content in the romantic ballet. The types of characters, roles, settings and stories are all a result of the social context of the late nineteenth century when fairies, spirits, exotic foreign places and peasants became ultra cool.

Today dance may use the same stories but the treatment of the content will differ to reflect a different social order. The choreography of Matthew Bourne in *Highland Fling . . . a romantic wee ballet* (1994) shows post-modern treatment of a classical ballet story. It is based on *La Sylphide* (1832), the classic Romantic ballet but twists the story to tell of James, an unemployed welder, who is lured from his nuptial bed by a rather grungy-looking fairy temptress. So the romantic vision of a classic style hero becomes the ramblings of a drug addict. The movement style mixes techniques of modern with social dance and some ballet.

Similarly in Matthew Bourne's *Swan Lake* (1995) we note the romantic references in the use of a comical classical ballet divertissement. Being in the post-modern genre, it is most appropriate that he should parody a dance style from the past and the romantic one is highly suited to the original subject matter of *Swan Lake*. But Bourne's treatment of content is not romantic because it echoes the context of people's lives today. Similarly Mats Ek's version of *The Sleeping Beauty* (1996) varies the original story by making the sleep representative of drug-dependency. Aurora is a heroin addict who is attracted to Carabosse, the traditional villain. The Prince helps her but it has to be Aurora's own power of mind that causes her own awakening. Ek says:

> When something is part of a culture, like a fairy-tale, it has a value of its own, you expect something from it. But only by keeping what people recognise can you deal deeply with it . . .
>
> (*Mats Ek, interview with Ismene Brown,* The Electronic Telegraph, *August 1999*)

The 1960s was a time of great social change in value systems. 'Free love' and 'Flower Power' were signs of a changing society and dancers responded to this by experimenting with new methods of working. In 2000 an event called *PastForward: The influence of the Post-Moderns* happened in California. It presented some of the key innovations of the post-modern work of the 1960s of the Judson Church Dance Theatre. Works from David Gordon, Yvonne Rainer and Lucinda Childs to name a few were on show:

> … strategies that once sent dance audiences and critics fleeing into the night reign again, newly revived and still as provocative as ever. Minimalism. Structuralism. Endless Repetition. Everyday Movement … And you know what? The simple honesty of this work looks awfully appealing compared to the desperate narcissism … emotional grandstands and empty virtuosity of … these days. And that, of course, is why it came into being in the first place: as a rejection of corruption in the dance world, a way of starting over.
>
> (*Lewis Segal in* Los Angeles Times, *2000*)

For post-modern dancers in North America in the 1960s the success and significance of the work may only, indeed, be truly understood when looking back in time:

> It may be true that neither critics nor audiences absorbed what happened in the sixties but I don't think I'd be doing what I'm doing now if that hadn't happened.
>
> (*Douglas Dunn in* The Vision of Modern Dance, *1980*)

Experimental work by its very nature pushes the boundaries of understanding for the audience. It is easy to dismiss what has been presented as obscure and pointless if you're missing the point! Sometimes to evaluate success new strategies may have to be adopted by the onlooker. When this fails evaluation may be achieved later only from a *retrospective* view. Hindsight may allow us to understand the impact which a dance made in its original context. The criteria by which we evaluate success must consider the whole artistic, social and historical conditions of its time.

Philosophies and psychologies

When modern art burst into existence at the start of the twentieth century it rejected all the accepted values which had dominated art and society. In so doing it reflected a society in turmoil from war as well as the discovery of new psychologies and philosophies.

Martha Graham presented psychodramas, stark movement and hard-edged truths springing from the new psychologies of Freud. She demanded that her audiences *contribute* to the final performance by putting their own interpretation on her dances. Dance was no longer just entertainment, as it had been in the previous years of vaudeville and rather stale ballet: the audience had a greater role to play in the success of the final product.

Merce Cunningham took this approach even further. Eastern philosophies, such as Zen Buddhism, influence his personal style: of using *chance procedures* to make dances; of the mind set which keeps the constituent features of dances totally separate; in his expectation that individuals will all view his dances from their own perspectives.

Recent developments in Release Techniques also draw on Eastern philosophies of meditation to internalise movement, acknowledging the holistic nature of dance.

Technological developments

The development of the pointe shoe and the stage light of ether as used in *La Sylphide* (1832) enhanced the ethereal presence of ballet in performance, which was such a vital part of the romantic palette.

In more recent times the explosion in computer technology has opened up the use of more film and mixed media work in dance performance. Dance can now be viewed on and is made specially for small screens via the Internet or in the new form of videodance.

THE FUNCTION AND ROLE OF DANCE

This book concentrates on Western classical ballet and twentieth-century modern and post-modern genres so the dances which we are concerned with have mainly artistic function. Most of Western theatre dance has significance as *art*. Its role is to be watched by an audience, and functions as a way of improving the quality and depth of experience for the onlooker. The audience is the final judge of whether a dance has been successful in enriching and energising their lives. Each one of them will have their own thoughts, preferences and interpretations from any single performance.

Other genres such as South Asian or African dance had different functions for the societies that they originally came from. The dances may have been a part of religious or social life, keeping people in touch with their origins and beliefs. This does not mean that they are not artistic as well, but they may contain meanings which carry important messages for the culture in which they were made. They may tell stories of important gods and goddesses, or be a part of social rituals which are important celebrations connected with successful growing and harvesting of crops.

In multi-cultural Britain today dances of Asia and Africa are performed more and more for their artistic function rather than for the social role. However some companies such as *Adzido* aim to preserve traditional African culture in what they perceive to be its clash with Western contemporary social values.

PUTTING APPRECIATION INTO PRACTICE

The process of appreciation involves a set of sensitive comparisons of how effectively the constituent features are combined with the content, style, context and function in determining how successful a dance is. The three-stage process is useful in different ways depending on the situation:

- **Choreographers** will evaluate as an ongoing process of developing a dance in rehearsal and performance.
- **Dancers** will evaluate according to the specific demands that the choreographer's style and performance places on them.
- **Audiences** will evaluate the significance and success of a dance in performance. The remainder of this chapter will look at how you may find the process of appreciation useful in making and watching dances.

TASK FIVE

(continues from Tasks 3 and 4)

 **Communication and Improving Own Learning and Performance** 

Prepare a brief programme note for the audience which includes information on content and style.

Share the final short solos with your group. Use the sheet on page 183 to evaluate each other's solos noting how successful they are in:

- Putting across the original content.
- Compositional form and structure.
- Showing the style of the chosen choreographer.

In Task 8 an evaluation sheet is provided to evaluate your performance skills.

Name ______ Title of dance ______

In the style of ______

Evaluation of solo dances – composition and style

✓ the columns

	Needs improvement	Mostly effectively	Consistently / imaginatively achieved
1 Expresses the content			
2 Shows the chosen style			
3 Chooses interesting and appropriate ▮ actions ▮ use of space ▮ use of time ▮ use of dynamics			
4 Choice of accompaniment			
5 Relationship to accompaniment			
6 Uses appropriate choreographic devices			
7 Uses appropriate choreographic structure			

Comments and suggestions based on the above:

______

______

______

Set targets for improvement:

______

______

______

OR TASK FIVE PART 2

Test your understanding of a specific dance genre.
Choose a dance genre. Name it and complete the questions below:

- When the genre was first developed.
- The context of the genre.
- The purpose and function of the genre.
- Any influences on it from other dance traditions or art forms.
- Significant characteristics of the style of the chosen genre. This may include choice of: physical constituents; structure and form; accompaniment and relation of dance to it; physical setting; dancers; content.

Over time there may have been changes in the genre. Select a specific context, time and place, and describe:

- How any of the following changed: social conditions; function/role.
- Any resulting changes in significant characteristics of the style (as listed above).

Applying the appreciation process in making and rehearsing dances

Once you, as choreographer, have decided on your content and you know a bit about constituent features you had better head for the studio. You are ready to make a dance so where do you start? Perhaps with a warning:

> Making a ballet takes an unbounded patience from everybody concerned.
>
> (*Edward Denby in* Dancers, Buildings and People in the Street, *1965*)

Strategies which can help avoid mental blocks

- Remember your improvisations and be alert to when something feels right or when it requires further refinement.
- Accept that there is often little apparent logic in the order in which movements are discovered. You may find the end first!
- Be open to possibilities. Mistakes are often useful. You don't have to follow a fixed plan – if a better idea appears go with the flow!
- Think how movement may look to an audience.
- Work in small manageable sections e.g. with one section of music.
- Allow form and structure to develop gradually.
- Sometimes work without the music to clarify certain moments and movements.
- Remember choreography takes time. The process of trial and error can be frustrating but it is usually necessary. Infuriatingly sometimes you select the thing that you threw away first!
- Manage your time so that you work your schedule backwards from a performance deadline. Block in time slots for rehearsal and don't forget to book studio space.
- Keep a working log or diary of all your work whether alone or with dancers. A video record is great, if you happen to have a camera.

THE REHEARSAL PROCESS

In composing and rehearsing dances the appreciation process is ongoing and in constant use as you make improvements to the dance. This is called *formative assessment* and it occurs in all the different phases of rehearsal:

- preparation: research and improvisation.
- selection: abstraction and organisation.
- refining and polishing: working with dancers

Preparation will involve research on content, gathering resources such as accompaniment, experimenting with and selecting constituent features through improvisation. *Improvisation* is a crucial part of this process. Although you may not be intending to go into the first rehearsal with dancers with every single movement sorted, neither should you go in empty-handed. Therefore your exploration of movement in private experiment is precious time to find some key material. It is a time when you need to be sensitive to your inner thoughts and to your nonverbal instincts so that you can assess which constituent features best interpret your chosen content.

At this stage a working log or diary is recommended so that you can keep a track on progress. The research that Lloyd Newson and DV8 do for a new piece can take months. The research period for *Enter Achilles* (1995) went on for almost two years. Your working diary may include things which you decide to throw away, but you never know when they might be useful so the golden rule is 'Write It All Down!'.

Selection may involve working alone or with dancers and trying out some movements. In selecting the constituent features, and in forming the dance, you will have to *interpret* and *evaluate* what is most appropriate to express your chosen content.

Abstraction is a key to crack these physical puzzles. You have been abstracting in many of the tasks that you have done so far in the book. The choreographer takes ideas from any aspect of life – other art forms, emotions, stories – and selects what may be the most powerful images. The selection process of abstraction reduces an idea to its essence.

> Of this deep responsiveness between body and mind the art of dance is formed ... It is built of symbols abstracted from daily living and intimately associated in the memory of experience with action and emotion.
>
> (*Lois Horst in* Modern Dance Forms, *1961*)

This process will further engage your intellect, imagination and intuition in making creative and sensitive choices as to what movements will be most successful in expressing the content to the audience. The artistic decisions involved in transforming idea to final image are closely linked to a sense of personal interpretation:

> Until the artist is satisfied in perception with what he is doing, he continues shaping and reshaping. The making comes to an end when its result is experienced as good.
>
> (*John Dewey in* Having an Experience, *1934*)

Organisation of devices, form and structure may have been decided in the research stage but will be part of a continual selection and refinement process as you work with the dancers and begin to evaluate what works best where, when, how and with whom.

Refining and polishing are ongoing up to the moment of performance. Ongoing *evaluation* of constituent features, form and structure should occur so that eventually movement is refined to express the content in the best way. As you see the dance, motif or section over and over again you will evaluate and make fine adjustments and improvements. For the dancer the repetition is an opportunity to increase accuracy and to pinpoint any problems or queries. It is rather like cooking a fine meal: starting with all the separate, recognisable ingredients and selecting the right amounts of everything, timing to perfection to make something which has a flavour all of its own.

> The hard thing is … dropping the keystone in, so it completes itself in its language, without destroying what's gone before. So that you go: 'Oh, of course. The inevitable solution!'
>
> (*Mark Morris in* The Electronic Telegraph, *September 1999*)

Remember: 'If you haven't anything worth throwing away then you probably haven't anything worth keeping.' Evaluation involves making decisions on what is successful and what is not. Sometimes this may come incredibly late in the rehearsal process:

> I feel that within this form (of classic ballet) every day I will set something and then say 'You can't do that'. With *Rite of Spring* I worked for three weeks and produced fiendishly difficult choreography and then had to scrub the whole thing because I felt it was wrong.
>
> (*Kenneth MacMillan in* Making a Ballet, *1974*)

In Chapter 2 choosing dancers appropriate to the choreography was explained. Making these choices involves making evaluations which arise from the process of appreciation. For example if your dance has lots of jumps and explosive energy (*descriptive*) then you would choose dancers who have strength and stamina. As choreographer you need to guide and work with the dancers, making clear what expression you require. You need to 'listen' to and answer their questions both verbal and nonverbal. This means sharpening your powers of observation, description and interpretation. Questions such as 'Is that gesture appropriate to express the content or not?', 'Is it the step or the dancer's style which needs adjustment?' are vital in formative evaluation. Choreographers will need to make clear to dancers what the dance requires from them, working on details like phrasing, timing, transitions and physical setting. You will need to *describe* movement and other constituent features to yourself and to the dancers in order to remember, repeat, change and write them down. Sometimes you may need to give physical support and adjustments in alignment, facings and line. Dancers too need skills of description, interpretation and evaluation. They may need to describe a problem or offer relevant suggestions to overcome physical or expressive difficulties in the polishing process.

As dancer or choreographer great perseverance and resilience of mind may be called for in the rehearsal process. In rehearsal, dancing with others demands that you maintain a pleasant, professional and responsible attitude to each other. The disciplines of warming up before rehearsal, punctuality, approaching problems such as timing and spacing efficiently and sensitively with others are all vital if the work is going to succeed.

Strategies for working in rehearsals for dancers and choreographers:

- building rapport
- making movement clear
- making content clear
- developing the dancer's interpretive skills.

Building rapport

In dance companies this is done over a long period of time, and it is unlikely that you will have such a luxury. Your task is to achieve as much rapport as possible, between dancers and choreographer, in the short time you will have available. But the basic approach is the same: one of communication between dancers and choreographer – sharing information, questions and problems, and gradually building common ground and the understanding necessary for the dance to be shaped. Richard Alston was observed in rehearsal:

> ... constantly feeding the dancers he works with ... you see someone who isn't just telling the dancers what to do, he's advising them how to do it and explaining why it's best, easiest or most efficient to do it that way.
>
> (*In* Dance Now, *1995*)

There are instances of choreographers in ballet and modern dance who have struck up special relationships with individual dancers. Ballerina Lynn Seymour had a long working relationship with Kenneth MacMillan. She describes how they rehearsed together at the start of a new dance.

> He will perhaps just say ... 'I had this sort of idea', and you will listen to a piece of music and he will show something and say 'Like this' or 'Why don't you start over there and dash over here?' And you try it. He doesn't name the steps but he gives examples. And the problem usually becomes to translate this idea into rhythmic form that the music has, and make it possible. This seems to be the thing that I have been best at and I do it for MacMillan.
>
> (*Lynn Seymour in* Making a Ballet, *1974*)

But what works on one occasion may not always work. Arguments, such as the ones heard all around the Royal Opera House between Kenneth MacMillan and Sylvie Guillem, are probably best avoided. As a dancer she claims to need to be convinced and explained to:

> He never said anything nice to me. He said to me after a rehearsal of *Manon*, 'You are just a boring French star.' ... I just said, 'I'm sorry but what you just said is completely stupid. If you want to talk to me about the rehearsal, the work we did, please try to find something else to say...'
>
> (*Sylvie Guillem talking to Ismene Brown in* The Electronic Telegraph, *1999*)

Although this was a tempestuous working relationship it produced brilliant performances from Guillem, whose rendition of Manon is claimed to be the finest. Even so it is not to be recommended as a working strategy generally! Finding constructive and informative comments and questions to improve expression and performance is probably a better approach.

Making movement clear

> A choreographer, though possessing the same emotions as other creative artists, has no way of expressing himself but through movements which he must implant in the muscles of other dancers.
>
> (*David Lichine in* Ballet, *1947*)

The working methods in the traditional classical ballet world of Marius Petipa are well documented.

> The most fascinating moments of all were those when Petipa composed his

> mimic scenes. Showing each participant in turn he would get quite carried away.
>
> (*Nicolai Legat in* Ballet for All, *1970*)

What he was showing them was in enormous detail, as revealed in his note to the composer Tchaikovsky concerning the knitting women mime between the King and Catalabutte in *The Sleeping Beauty*:

> Four beats for the questions and four for the answers: ... Question: 'Where are you taking the women?' Four Beats. Answer: 'To the prison'. Four beats. Question: 'What have they done?' Four beats.
>
> (*As translated by Joan Lawson in* The Dancing Times, *1942*)

It is interesting to note that the mime skills possessed by nineteenth-century dancers are not needed in modern versions of *The Sleeping Beauty*. In the 2000 Kirov reconstruction of the 1890 version, one of the problems for the dancers was to study and acquire the lost skills of mime, so that the pantomime and masque scenes, usually cut from the ballet as we know it, could be replaced.

This need to prepare dancers and develop their skills when tackling new content, style or technique is illustrated again here:

> In company training ... DV8 ... bring in different people to develop new skills: in *My Body, Your Body* they did aerobics and long-distance running to build up stamina ... and voice teachers are brought in at times ... When we were looking at football, (we) ... considered why is it acceptable for men to do footwork around a football, but not to do footwork around Irish dancing or ballet? So we brought in an Irish dancing teacher because I wanted to explore ... what is acceptable and unacceptable male movement?
>
> (*Jo Butterworth interview with Lloyd Newson, 1998*)

In the world of 1960s post-modern dance and British New Dance a more collective way of working represented a shift of concern away from traditional rehearsal strategies to those which held more holistic principles. The concern for the dancer as a whole human being is a priority, and dialogue between choreographer and dancer in making and choosing movement for dances is a preferred strategy.

> From Ballet all the way to Cunningham technique, the dancer's body has been at the disposal of the choreographer to produce the desired effect. A technique equal to that was, and is, required ... The dancer was becoming more responsible; their direct contribution as themselves was more pertinent.
>
> (*Claire Hayes in* New Dance, *1987*)

> Improvisation is used as an exploration into movement possibilities focusing on specific problems, which form the central point of the choreography. The dancers have the responsibility of discovering their own movement and energy level within the outer structure of the dance.
>
> (*Rosemary Butcher in* New Dance, *1977*)

Artists such as Siobhan Davies are typical of this type of approach in rehearsal. It requires use of the three stages of appreciation. There are some fine descriptions of her approach in Catherine Quinn's dancer's log. Here is an example:

> I've made up seven or eight phrases so far using poetry, architecture and geometry as starting points to set the body in motion. (*Later in the log, Quinn describes*

> *how this material was refined by Davies.*) ... My material was pulled and pushed into a new shape and feel, and is certainly more hectic than I had in mind. Still one trusts her judgment ... and already the few phrases ... are looking more like part of an emotional journey than exercises in dance making.
>
> (*Catherine Quinn in* Dancer's log, *1999*)

Gradually you will find whether 'teaching steps', or giving dancers structures to improvise around and select from their movement discoveries, or a combination of these two approaches suits you best.

Making content clear

The choreographer gives the essence of the dance to the dancers by making content clear to them. Different choreographers do this in different ways. We may note the way that Lea Anderson emphasises the use of *inner narrative* for her dancers. She is concerned that the dancers are aware of the reason behind each of the tiny gestures which they perform.

> The inner narrative is something that the audience doesn't know and is nothing to do with them ... I'm very interested in the physical attitude of the performer. For example the traditional way of ... holding your body and relating to the audience. I'm not much impressed with those ways of being ... not how you remember the movement but thinking of the given image. The dancer must go through the same thought process every time.
>
> (*Lea Anderson in interview in* Flesh and Blood, *Cholmondeley's education pack*)

Discussion with the dancers is another method of making the content clear:

> The dancers here are playing real people. It's like rehearsing with actors: we argue about their motives when I suppose we should be designing movements.
>
> (*Matthew Bourne in interview with Peter Conrad in* The Guardian, *September 2000*)

Here the German post-modern choreographer Pina Bausch describes how she does it.

> Well of course, I have asked them hundreds of questions. The dancers have answered them, tried something out ... Every one has a think about it and gives an answer. Sometimes we'll be trying to put things into words ... Gradually we build up short dance sequences and memorise them. I used to get scared and panic and so I would start with movement and avoid the questions. Nowadays I start off with the questions.
>
> (*In* Ballet & Modern Dance, *1992*)

Preparing a dancer for the role is crucial for a successful performance. Similarly a dancer describes how the choreographer Alvin Ailey helped her to understand a role. She describes how she needs personal images in order to find the right dynamic in her movement.

> In *Streams*, I'm a woman who, perhaps, is in the stream of water trying to move with it, or trying to move through it. Or I can take the idea that it's like life and then you try to move as smoothly as you can through everything.
>
> (*In* The Dance Makers, *1980*)

Sometimes you may find difficulty in giving the right information to dancers. The dancer may need more detail concerning content and you are giving movement information. Perhaps this relates to the earlier example of the Guillem-MacMillan working relationship. From his point of view, and in his words, this is how he may have seen things:

I am inspired by the dancers' bodies ... I have to find the right thing for their bodies. I tell my cast little in the beginning therefore I like to get the whole shape of the music planned first; then I elaborate on the characterisation ... I think I do this purposely because I like my artists to find themselves in their roles ... so I allow the dancers to improvise within the limitations imposed by the steps ...

(*Kenneth MacMillan in* Making a Ballet, *1974*)

The quality of audience experience can be directly affected by the standard of performance by the dancers. A dance can be evaluated by how well the dancers have performed. A part of the art of choreography is making sure that it shows off the dancers to their best advantage. Finding movement which is not only successful in terms of compositional form but sits on the dancers like well-fitting clothes is essential. It should suit their abilities, being not too difficult for them, using their strengths but also challenging them. Dancers who achieve greatness in performance have at some point taken into their body and mind what the choreographer has intended.

An idea is transformed and stylised into a coherent dance form using the skills and ideas that dancers and choreographer have available. During the rehearsals the choreographer should be aware of how best to draw out those skills from the dancers in order to give a dance the most expressive performance possible. Once the choreographer hands over the dance to the dancers he or she then relies on their skills to perform it and recreate it for an audience. So the choreographer *and* dancers must be aware of what these skills are.

DEVELOPING THE DANCER'S INTERPRETATIVE SKILLS

As well as the technical necessities of the physical skills of dance training, a dancer in performance also needs other important skills. A dancer must be able to communicate and express the overall intention of the dance. In order to do this, certain skills of interpretation and expression are a necessity. The great romantic ballerina Marie Taglioni was greatly admired for such performance charisma. In this description of her by an actress of the time, we have a feel for that inspirational quality that she had, dancing the lead in *La Sylphide*, (1832), the first romantic ballet.

What was it then? It was, once again, the ideal Beauty that radiated from depths of the soul into this body, animated it, lifted it with such power that something marvellous took place before our eyes as we saw the invisible made visible.

(*Maxine Shulman in* Ballet and Modern Dance, *1992*)

As a natural presence on stage, the ballerina Taglioni is well known, but there must also be *training* beforehand. We know that the physicalities of training are rigorous, and virtuosity alone is not enough. In the end, it is the expressiveness of a performer which must be right for a particular dance. Jean Georges Noverre, the great reformer of ballet in the eighteenth century, remarked that the corps de ballet should harmonise their feelings with their movement. He believed that only then would they be able to express the emotions of the dance and give life to the dance.

> A true dancer has a temperament which directs him to express feelings and ideas through moving the body in space. This instinct must be greatly enhanced by training so that he not only has a strong and co-ordinated instrument, but an immediate impulse to translate his comments and reactions into rhythms, muscular dynamics and spatial arrangements.
>
> (*Louis Horst in* Modern Dance Forms, *1961*)

The nuances of the dance content are likely to be a part of the exchange between dancer and choreographer in rehearsal. The dancer must be capable of tricky technical adjustments and yet keep the flow and expression of the movement.

The choreographer should be aware of how to make the most of a dancer's *interpretative* skills so that the appropriate ones are prompted.

Interpretative skills include:

- projection
- emphasis
- group awareness
- musicality
- involvement of the whole self.

Projection

Projection involves throwing the energy out from the body so as to give a quality of life to the movement. When a dance is performed technically correctly but lacks projection, it is unlikely to reach an audience in a significant way. Projection enables the dancer's movement and energies to reach out beyond the body and 'touch' the audience's feelings. In this way, it makes dancing come alive. There should be an inner awareness in the dancer that is part of each movement and that sparks off various corresponding tensions and muscular reactions in observers.

An efficient and correct use of energy contributes to projection. Isadora Duncan was one of the first to talk about energy flowing from and to the centre of the body and the extremities. She believed that this enabled the feel of the movement to travel across space.

Irek Mukhamedov is a dancer highly praised for his projection:

> But there was more to Mukhamedov than muscles ... as Kenneth MacMillan ... suspected ... he proved to have an unexpected dancing soul, and he became a powerful stimulant for MacMillan's complex ballets in his last years.
>
> (*Ismene Brown in* The Electronic Telegraph, *May 1998*)

Choreographer Kim Brandstrup describes Mukhamedov's skill as:

> Like Sinatra he can whisper into 2,000 ears at once. He works from the inside out. He finds out why he does things. If you know what the feeling is you can enhance the feelings rather than the gesture.
>
> (*In interview with Louise Levin*, The Telegraph, *1999*)

Correct breathing also aids projection. The technique of breathing through the movement should be practised first of all in class.

An appropriate use of facial expressions is also important. A calm, pleasant, open face will help to animate a performance. Cheesy grins, however, are not often appropriate, and likewise, downcast or stressful expressions can kill a dance stone dead for an audience. This was observed as a problem when executing the very difficult *fouettes* of classical ballet. The great choreographer Mikhail Fokine did not favour dancers showing virtuosity for its own sake. He believed that the movement should serve as part of the expression of the dance, and that 'tricks' like the fouette undermined the projection of feeling:

> The fouette ... is the most hateful invention of the ballet. The dancer expresses ecstasy and joy, but her face – what does that express? Quite the opposite. She seeks for balance and her whole face proclaims it. The face betrays her losing her balance. ... unity of pose and movement is a law which, to my regret is not felt by everybody.
>
> (*Mikhail Fokine in* Mikhail Fokine and his Ballets, *1945*)

Hanya Holm has this to add:

> The face is of course the mirror of all that goes on, but it should not be more prominent than is intended and it should not be a substitute for all that isn't going on in the body. The face should have a relationship to the whole attitude and complement it. ... I very often see absolutely dead eyes inside a multiple moving body.
>
> (*Hanya Holm in* The Vision of Modern Dance, *1980*)

Focus is also an important element of projection. Traditionally, this should be thrown out to the back part of the auditorium. This is particularly necessary when the audience is seated above the stage looking down. A dancer who continually looks down is not delivering a real performance, and this has the effect of cutting the audience out of the action. This approach is not, necessarily, accepted in post-modern dance. For example, the choreographer Yvonne Rainer describes the performer as a 'neutral doer'. She believes performance to be something artificial, and an unnecessary display of technical virtuosity. This 'problem' of artificiality is addressed by:

To show face in use in performance, in DV8

> ... never permitting the performers to confront the audience. Either the gaze was averted or the head was engaged in movement. The desired effect was a work-like rather than exhibitionlike presentation.
>
> (*Yvonne Rainer in* Trio A, The Vision of Modern Dance, *1980*)

In addition, the dancer should correctly *orientate* the dance to the audience, ensuring that body facings are accurate, and that the audience sees movements and body shapes at their most expressive angle. These facings and angles will have been determined by the choreographer, but the dancer must make sure that their reproduction is accurate.

Similarly, the dancer must realise the need for a high *energy* level throughout the performance – in the quieter moments, indeed, as well as in the faster, stronger sections of the dance.

Being generous with your gestures and movements when dancing will also help an audience to enjoy the performance more. These serve to engage them in the dance and make them feel that they are interested to know more about what they are looking at. This is particularly so in classical ballet, whereas in modern dance, the choreographer's intent may involve a more closed feeling. Either way, the dancer must use the appropriate focus and projection. The choreographer should know what type of projection is appropriate and, in rehearsal, cue the dancer to make the right choices.

Emphasis

Emphasis involves knowing what aspects of energy, space and time to accent at different moments throughout the dance. The dancer is responsible for giving a clear performance to the audience. This involves colouring the movement with the right kind of expressions, namely those which the choreographer intended. The dancer must be able to direct energy impulses, and to make use of space and time in the way laid down by the choreographer. Energy impulses may be directed between dancers, or to a certain fixed point on stage. They may sometimes have an inward, thoughtful feel, directed in at the dancers themselves. The shading of the dynamics and qualities by the dancer is vital to the expression of the dance.

> You must master the physical experience so that it becomes a kinesthetic experience. ... You will find out that movement can contain only a certain amount of emotion before emotion outdoes the physical experience. ... Emotion is only a stimulus not an end result. ... It is arrived at but not emphasised.
>
> (*Hanya Holm in* The Vision of Modern Dance, *1980*)

This process of understanding the physical emphasis begins in rehearsal, and it can be a tiring affair. It is important, however, for the dancer to keep energy levels up throughout for two reasons. First, the choreographer often needs to see the dance performed fully to decide if it really works. Second, the dancers themselves need to repeat the movement over and over again so that they too know intimately what is required. This may involve discovering what kind of quality a particular role or character needs, or it may involve acquiring a feel for where the movement phrases begin and end. There may be a particular highlight in the dance which requires a certain dynamic emphasis. In rehearsal Shobana Jeyasingh often turns off the music so that dancers can hold the dynamic of the movement independently and not be too controlled by the musical phrasing. Or the climax of the piece may need a very specific timing or position on stage which is crucial to the expression. Many small subtle details thus need close examination and practice.

When a role is danced by different dancers the emphasis of phrasing, timing and dynamics may change. This would alter the expression so that varied interpretations may be seen between performances over time. In Kenneth MacMillan's *Manon* (1974) this has been the case. It is a role well known for its difficulty in expressing a character who has many different sides. In 1998 the Royal Ballet's *Manon* was danced by three different ballerinas:

> ... the incomparable Sylvie Guillem ... has all the answers to this complicated heroine. In the brothel, she is a witch and yet she is also a vulnerble girl ... Viviana Durante was more calculating, sensual but with a nasty edge ... Darcey Bussell is

> pretty and complacent, oblivious to hunger, indecision or fear.
>
> (*Ismene Brown in* The Electronic Telegraph, *August 1998*)

Over time as a dancer repeats a role many times, emphasis may change. A critic noted in the 1996 performance of *Winter Dreams* (1991) that:

> Darcey Bussell's poignant Masha, touchingly matured since she created the role five years ago.
>
> (*Ismene Brown in* The Electronic Telegraph, *November 1996*)

Through rehearsal and practice, the dancer will build a secure knowledge of the emphases that occur in a dance. This will provide support and will help the dancer to remain calm during those last few moments before the performance begins when stage fright may be a problem. Being able to focus clearly on the movements and expression, marking these through calmly, will take your mind away from yourself, and your nerves, and put it exactly where it should be: on the dance for the audience, not on your ego.

Group awareness

When dancing in groups, the dancer has to think not only about the content of the dance but also about movement cues which may come from others. *Peripheral vision*, i.e. what you see from the corners of your eyes, is useful here. Some dancers have a 'sixth sense' or a 'third eye' which helps them to feel where others are in relation to themselves even if they cannot actually see the others. Of course, these responses also have to do with good timing in relation to others, and they make for accurate unison, canon or action–reaction relationships.

Brighton and Hove Youth Group

> My company is fortunate; it's not very large, but it is nonetheless filled with people who are willing to take responsibility, not just for themselves, but for every other member of the company, which means that a dancer doing one of our pieces not only knows her own part, but knows everyone else's part who is working at the same time, and knows how that fits into the whole work ... it's something few dancers seem to take seriously. Musicians are much better about it because harmony is easier to hear than it is to see.
>
> (*Twyla Tharp in* The Dance Makers, *1980*)

When the dancer is learning the choreography, *sensitivity* to the other dancers is vitally important for cues given both for others and for themselves. The dance requires a group rapport if it is to be presented as a whole, unified item. If one of the group is having an 'off' day, you can guarantee that they will be the one the audience notices most. This will ruin the dance for the audience, and so is not to be tolerated. Each individual dancer is responsible to their own self, to the group, to the choreographer and to the audience.

TASK SIX

Work in groups of at least five dancers. Using a short phrase learnt in technique class, dance it:

- in unison, facing the same way as each other;
- in unison, facing different ways from each other;
- in canon, facing different ways;
- dance the phrase, starting at different points within it. So some may start at the end and others in the middle and so on.

If possible, take turns to watch to check the dancer's accuracy and sensitivity to the group timings.

Musicality

Musicality is the sense of rhythm and musical structure in a dancer's movement.

> At my feet, my dancing-mad feet, you threw a glance, a laughing, questioning, melting tossing glance.
>
> My heels raised themselves, my toes listened for what you should propose: for the dancer wears his ears in his toes!
>
> (*Friedrich Nietzsche*, Thus Spoke Zarathustra)

As a dancer learns a new dance, information is received from the choreographer, and various body images and engrams become related to the music and to the content of the dance. Gradually, the kinesthetic memory stores these, and the dance communicates, through performance, the various sensations and feelings that arise from inside the dancer.

Kenneth MacMillan was a choreographer who looked for:

> musicality and expressiveness of the body rather than great technique ...
>
> (*Kenneth MacMillan in* Making a Ballet, *1974*)

So the dancer has ears in the feet, and they listen carefully for cues and shadings in the music. This may involve picking out certain instrumentation in the music or particular changes in tempo, metre. The basic ability to count within the music helps dancers to fix certain phrases of movement in their minds within the rhythms of the music. Large ballet and dance companies often have musical directors who may assist dancers to do this.

Of course, in the choreography of Merce Cunningham – as we have seen – the dancers may not hear the music until the first performance. The music can often be very loud, and the dancer's role then is to dance with total accuracy in spite of sound crashing around them. One of the Cunningham Company dancers remarked once in the video *Travelogue* (1987) that the audiences often remarked on the ear-splitting sound, but that he didn't even hear it! This is musicality almost in reverse, and it needs just as much discipline and skill in order to be true to the rhythms set in the movement.

TASK SEVEN

Using the same phrase as in Task 6, dance it to different pieces of music. Let the music affect your phrasing, emphasis, dynamics. Add to the phrase in improvisation, exploring the different possibilities for each piece of music. (Suggested music: The Chieftains; Sounds of the Dolphin; The Orb.)

Involvement of the whole self

> You can do the steps with muscle memory, but once you get up on the stage, it's not about steps at all. You really have to reason why you're doing it. You can't just go through the motions; it has to involve your whole self.
>
> (*Alvin Ailey in* The Dance Makers, *1980*)

Moving from the centre of the body is an important physical sensation necessary for the correct execution of movements. However, the involvement of the *mind* is just as crucial: without this, the performance would be uninteresting and dull for the audience. The dancer needs an inner focus which relates to the content of the dance, to the movement and to how the latter engages them in giving an expressive performance. This inner focus is well described by Hanya Holm:

> The same moment you discover that focus you will burst forth in your outward appearance. Your audience will recognise it immediately. The people won't have to look inside of you for emotional overtones. Your chest will be right, your hip will be right, you will have a carriage that is supported and that is right for that which is intended.
>
> (*Hanya Holm, in* The Vision of Modern Dance, *1980*)

This involvement of the *whole* dancer in performance has to involve a response to the *style* of the dance.

Irek Mukhamedov describes how he approaches this:

> You know somebody made up that fairy story from real life ... Maybe it's the schooling I've had. To put your emotions through your body, through your fingers. Not just to go, 'I-Love-You', (and he

> mimed the three classic gestures), but to finish the phrase through … the whole body, eyes, even lips. Then it's not just signs – the audience will understand what I'm saying.
>
> (*Interview with Ismene Brown in* The Electronic Telegraph, *May 1998*)

Training in *Bharatha Natyam* has similar challenges. Learning the expressive skills of *abhinaya* is demanding and only possible by the dancer's belief in and identification with characters and situations. The subtleties of expressing love and loss must come from deep within if they are to convince an audience.

The whole person, body, mind and spirit, must be totally involved in the moment of performance. In the following description, Isadora Duncan reveals what she believes dance could be. You may be struck by the *total involvement* of the dancing child being the thing that captivated and transfixed Duncan's attention. It is a strong memory recalled with great impact.

> I gazed across the vast expanse of surging water, wave after wave streaming past. … And in front of it all, the dainty figure … dancing on the edge of the measureless sea. And I felt as though the heartbeat of her little life were sounding in unison with the mighty life of the water … she dances because she can feel the rhythm of the dance throughout the whole of nature. To her it is a joy to dance; to me it is a joy to watch her.
>
> (*Isadora Duncan in* The Dancing Times, *April 1926*)

TASK EIGHT

(continues from Tasks 3, 4 and 5)
Communication and Improving Own Learning and Performance

Perform a solo for your group. Use the sheet below to help you evaluate each others' solos in how successful they are in their interpretative performance skills.

This sheet can also be used to evaluate performance in group dances by adding a category for group awareness skills.

Name ______________________________

Title of dance ______________________________

Evaluation of solo dances – Interpretative and performance skills
✓ the columns

Evaluate success in:	**Needs improvement**	**Mostly effectively**	**Consistently / imaginatively achieved**
1 Projection – appropriate: energy/extension breath control, facial expression, focus facings			
2 Appropriate expressive emphasis use of dynamics style			
3 Movement memory			
4 Musicality			
5 Involvement of whole self			
6 Accuracy in emphasis of actions/body use of space use of time			

Comments and suggestions based on the above:

____

____

Set targets for improvement:

____

____

Applying the appreciation process in performance

> The art object . . . is a first presentation of a possibility truly felt and imagined.
>
> (*Arturo B. Fallico in* Dance from Magic to Art, *1976*)

The dance is choreographed. In rehearsal the formative evaluations have now resulted in a finished dance. Now the dance meets its audience. The choreographer, audience and critics are looking on and evaluating the overall impact of the dance. The dancers are nervously anticipating their appearance and they have a large amount of responsibility for the dance from now on. This is what they have been training for. This section will examine aspects of this special moment when the process becomes the product - live and direct!

> It only demands the dance be a moment of passionate, completely disciplined action, that it communicate participation to the nerves, the skin, the structure of the spectator.
>
> (*Martha Graham in* The Vision of Modern Dance, *1980*)

During and after performance choreographer, dancer, audience and critic will engage with the process of appreciation. We perceive dances through the senses. We see the movement and perhaps feel it kinaesthetically. We hear the accompaniment. We see the costumes and set. The process now is one of *summative* evaluation. If you are a student maybe it is a course assessment or examination. At this stage each viewer will have differing opinions ranging from a less informed/more personal taste 'I thought it was good' or 'It did nothing for me!', to an informed and articulate response such as one may read from a newspaper critic, or expressed by a dance student!

> . . . art is vision or intuition. The artist produces an image. The person who enjoys art turns his eyes in the direction which the artist has pointed out to him, peers through the hole which has been opened for him.
>
> (*Benedetto Croce in* Dance from Magic to Art, *1976*)

We will examine how the process of appreciation *may* differ depending on the point of view of dancer, choreographer, audience or critic.

APPRECIATION OF A PERFORMANCE AS DANCER

A dancer's concern is to evaluate their accuracy and expressivity of performance. During the performance a dancer may encounter unforeseen problems of execution of movement or interpretative skills. The usual process is to feed these back to the choreographer, who may have noticed them too, and proceed with correction in the studio. This can be an ongoing process.

> The dancers felt that it had gone well, but know that they could have made better choices with some of the phrases and spacing . . .
>
> (*Catherine Quinn in* Dancer's log, *1999*)

Similarly, if the choreographer has refinements to make post-performance it is back to the studio to put the new improvements into practice.

APPRECIATION OF A PERFORMANCE AS CHOREOGRAPHER

During a performance the choreographer has a job to do. On stage a dancer may show weakness in some type of interpretative skill and the choreographer should note this and give positive criticism after the show so that over time the performance improves.

Many dances are changed after initial and subsequent performances. The choreographer may detect something that could be improved upon in the choreography itself. This is a continuation of the formative evaluations and consequent refinements that took place in rehearsal. It may take into consideration comments from dancers, audience or critical reviews in the media. Generally speaking it is unusual for a choreographer to perform in their own work because they need to be the outside eye in rehearsal and in performance.

> ... now I sit through almost every performance ... giving notes and making changes ... it never stops. For example, when *Bound To Please* first showed ... it was a totally different piece to what was presented in London three months later ... Without constant change and development, a work becomes dead for performers and audience.
>
> (*Lloyd Newson in interview with Jo Butterworth, 1998*)

Recognising work which is not perhaps felt by the choreographer to be 'the best' is another way that the appreciation process is used. When questioned about his reaction to *Pulcinella* (1987) being selected for the A Level examination Richard Alston's evaluation of his piece was that:

> Well, there aren't many dances on video available are there? So I understand why they've chosen it. I don't think that it's a very good piece myself ... (It's) ... about someone else's work ... an interpretation of a score ... looking back I find that quite weak.
>
> (*Richard Alston in interview with Justine Reeves on* Sussex Dance web site, *2000*)

Equally, recognising *why* something is a success is just as important. Once Matthew Bourne saw the large audiences that were attracted to *Swan Lake* he realised that his work was a success. He figured out that many audiences were used to seeing films and theatre, but were perhaps new to dance, and that the attraction was seeing a story without words for the first time.

> Bourne: ... some (audience members) have said to me, 'After a bit we realised that nobody had said anything.'
>
> Interviewer: Which kept them there transfixed?
>
> Bourne: Yes ... the formula is as simple as that.
>
> (*Matthew Bourne interviewed by Simon Blow* in The Telegraph *September 1997*)

Another interesting development from this is that many people have described Bourne's work as quite avant-garde and as we know, experimental work can tend to put off audiences. So if Bourne's work is radical, why does it attract such large audiences? In the same interview his reasoning is that the work is not shaking up the dance world because it is old-fashioned:

> It's telling a story. There are laughs, there are tears – big emotions, old-fashioned values, you could say.

Then in the same breath he states that his

work is '*revolutionary*'. So it seems that choreographers can have it every way!

There may also be technical and production problems, like sound or light cues, or a badly fitting costume that need correction. So choreographers employ the procedures of appreciation to evaluate degrees of success and respond appropriately.

APPRECIATION OF A PERFORMANCE AS AUDIENCE

When the choreographer starts to work on the dance the target audience should have been a consideration. A dance for an audience of young children will be different to one for temple worship, or for a group of dance students.

Dances which have significance as art, and function to impact on an audience, are judged by specific criteria. Is the content of the dance presented to the audience in a form which they can understand? Or is there little to interest or stimulate an audience? Is there a flaw in structure or form which makes it difficult for the audience to interpret the content? Sometimes the audience and critic may perceive a weakness in a dance, however it is more likely to be the critic who can pinpoint what it is. As one critic put it when writing about Kenneth MacMillan's *The Judas Tree* (1992, as performed by the Royal Ballet in 1997):

> We become accustomed to the ballet's structure with repeated viewing. MacMillan's intentions become clearer. Since the majority of people do not get a chance to see ballet more than once, this is a serious handicap, and an unusual failure in MacMillan's narrative skill.
>
> (*Nicholas Dromgoole in* The Electronic Telegraph, *1997*)

A dance is an intense and potentially confusing experience for an audience. So why not go and see a dance more than once, like you would listen to music or read a book or look at a painting? Unfortunately cost is the problem. Maybe there should be a discount scheme for repeated viewings of a dance! As a dance student this would be good, wouldn't it? Meanwhile, however, video observation for study purposes will have to do, fraught with problems though it is (see next chapter). So we are stuck with the 'See it once and hope' scenario. This being so, choreographers have a duty to create dances with clarity of expression and form.

Some may say that dance audiences need educating. This is a thought because if they were informed they may understand and perhaps enjoy dance more. Many companies have outreach work such as post-performance talks by choreographers, lecture-demonstrations/showing extracts from dances with explanation and opportunity for questions. One scheme being run in New York, called *New Faces/New Voices/New Visions* was founded in 1990 by Laura Greer, at the Aaron Davis Hall, home to Alvin Ailey Dance Theatre. The aim was to nurture audiences in a predominantly black neighbourhood. The scheme included chances for beginners to do a class with famous choreographer Bill T. Jones as well as attend open rehearsals and discussions:

> The series gave our audiences a quality opportunity to experience the artists who live in their community as well as some art forms they may be unfamiliar with. Bill is a good example of that. When he first came ... he was on every cover of every magazine in the country ... Our audiences didn't know who he was, so the questions that were thrown at him initially shocked him ... Admission

> to each of the first two of the three rehearsals was $5 and both were sold out ... Those who came back for a third rehearsal got in free ...
>
> (*Patricia Cruz, executive director of Aaron Davis Hall in* The New York Times. *Interviewed by Jennifer Dunning, 2000*)

At last a discount scheme! Indeed the theory that audiences might *like* to think about what they see on stage is refreshing. Others disagree:

> I feel exactly the opposite. Most dance people need to be educated in the ways of normal living and learn what body movements mean to other people, both consciously and unconsciously. When the average person in the street watches a dance in which women fling their legs wide open, for the dancer it's just a technical event, but for the person watching it, it can have immense emotional, sexual and psychological implications ... we should understand what we do and what that difference in perception means.
>
> (*Lloyd Newson in* Enter Achilles programme note, *1995*)

Is it enough to entertain an audience as the work of Matthew Bourne does so well? Some would say that is insufficient, as Lloyd Newson states:

> I have felt over the last few years that many dance companies, including ourselves, have been coerced into doing easier pieces for audiences ... As the company plays to larger audiences, you are forced to consider mass appeal. ... DV8's values and politics will never be mainstream ... even if it means foregoing large amounts of money ... and perhaps results in smaller audiences.
>
> (*In an interview with Mary Luckhurst, 1997*)

Audiences of innovatory dance or sometimes the 'pure dance' style may struggle to find ways of appreciating it. Consequently audiences for these works may be smaller in number. Some may go once but never again feeling that they did not enjoy themselves because they did not find 'a meaning'. So how can audiences find a way to appreciate this less mainstream style of dance? Perhaps a clue lies in the process of making such works. Catherine Quinn in *Dancer's log* and Richard Alston in the video of *Soda Lake* comment on the wide variety of images, from animal to emotional, that they worked with during the creative process. Therefore if viewers see many different meanings, they can all be correct.

> ... audiences need to be reassured that gestures do not have encoded, unfathomable individual meanings and that dance is one particular thing.
>
> (*Jennifer Dunning in* 'Gimmicks, Games and Explanation to Dance Goers, The New York Times, *July 2001*)

The difficulty is encouraging audiences to have the courage of their own convictions and enjoy the dances on that level. As Merce Cunningham said the audience complete the dance by being there.

In the ballet world audiences may have different concerns. According to Irek Mukhamedov they evaluate quality of performance in dancers. He states that when the British public recognise his abilities of emphasis, musicality and involvement of whole self they:

> understand ballet much more than the Russian public ...
>
> (*Interview with Ismene Brown in* The Electronic Telegraph, *1998*)

But whether they are quite so understanding when seeing some seemingly less significant revived works is another matter. According to Richard Alston, they are not, and it irritates him when they complain about seeing *Les Patineurs* (1937, Frederick Ashton) again:

> Well my answer is 'Lucky old you.' ... to be seeing his earlier pieces and realising where the later things come from – that's important.
>
> (*Interview with Allen Robertson in* Dance Now, *1995*)

APPRECIATION OF A PERFORMANCE AS CRITIC

And so to those who everyone loves to hate – the critics.

> A critic is a bundle of biases held loosely together by a sense of taste.
>
> (*Whitney Balliett in* Dinosaurs in the Morning, *1962*)

The job of the critic *is* the process of appreciation and, many consider, to be publicly accountable. Their professional concerns are to be able to *describe, interpret and evaluate* accurately, and for this they must have thorough knowledge of *context.*

> I try to contextualise in terms of history and whatever else seems relevant. Literature, current events. I also might try to find things in a dance to look for, as guideposts rather than interpretation.
>
> (*Suzanne Carbonneau, quoted in* 'Gimmicks, Games and Explanation to Dance Goers, *Jennifer Dunning,* The New York Times, *July 2001*)

Presenting dances in context of their development of a particular artist's work is something that could inform audiences. Nurturing audiences is important and not least in being able to offer them contextual information both past and present. Especially if, as many think, the Internet is the opportunity to share opinions on dance and take criticism out of the small élite circles of critics and into the public arena. Many forums abound now and it would be good to be able to think that the opinions shared are based on some sort of informed appreciation and not on personal taste alone.

They themselves do not have to have been a dancer. They do need to be able to write well, be knowledgeable about arts generally and dance in particular. Perhaps what critics should be trying to do is distil:

> The visceral aspect of dance (which) precedes conscious thought ...
>
> (*Lloyd Newson in* Enter Achilles programme note, *1995*)

Just as the choreographer is distilling content into a dance for the audience's gut reaction, the critic is attempting to represent it in another physical act – writing!

Critics' styles can differ from the poetic to the documentary, advisory or informative. It is hoped that they give sufficient detailed analysis so that in its way the review can provide a document for history (see next chapter). Perhaps we can expect some information on principles like genre, context, content and style in dance and reasons for opinions expressed in reviews. All this would increase understanding generally of the elusive art of dance. Dancers, choreographers and audiences alike *may* read the reviews, whether they admit it or not, and find useful information within.

TASK NINE

The next time you go to see a dance performance, imagine that you are the dance critic for a newspaper. Write not more than 200 words about the show, trying to inform someone who has not seen the performance. Remember that the article is not only about your personal taste but should be written from an *informed* viewpoint; describing constituent features and physical setting; interpreting content and style; evaluating in context.

OR

The next time you go to a professional performance find two reviews in the newspapers or research them online (see Resources list at end of chapter). Compare the two critics' viewpoints to find differences and similarities in their writing styles and opinions.

At the very start of this chapter there was an example of informative criticism. Here are two others about Kenneth MacMillan's *Winter Dreams* (1991):

> Go and enjoy Kenneth MacMillan's *Winter Dreams* in which a man who usually took a sledgehammer to matters of the flesh applied, late in life, a butterfly net to the bursting hearts of Chekhov's 'The Three Sisters', and created a miniature ballet of such sadness as to make you weep.
>
> Enjoy ... Irek Mukhamedov's ardent Vasha, faintly more cynical than in 1991. Leanne Benjamin doesn't carry young Irina's restless world-weariness but she certainly registers the frissons of budding sexuality ...
>
> This ballet demands ensemble acting of great delicacy that is now the Royal Ballet's greatest strength.
>
> (*Ismene Brown in* The Electronic Telegraph, *November 1996*)

> ... it is more of a mood piece than a literal narrative ... It contains many character sketches which give the dancers opportunity to shine ... Bussell's dancing is as impeccable as ever ... The farewell pas de deux is very fine, but though it was beautifully danced, the audience was dry-eyed. The music (solo piano pieces from Tchaikovsky and Russian folk melodies on guitar and mandolin) was suitably melancholy and very well played.
>
> (*Lynette Halewood in* Ballet Magazine, *December 1996*)

Both reviews reveal the critics' main concern to evaluate a performance, giving reasons for their summative evaluations which are built out of their descriptions, interpretations and analysis.

TASK TEN

Read the reviews above and match quotations from them to the stages of the process of appreciation; description, interpretation and evaluation.

Next to each quote write which of the following features of appreciation are involved:

- constituent features
- form and structure
- style
- content
- interpretative skills
- context.

Some sample answers are given on page 206.

So if one review has completely annihilated a dance and then another declared it as a masterpiece, how are we to know why? Perhaps the most disliked is in fact so avant-garde that the audience and critic reject it out of hand, like Nijinsky's *Le Sacre du Printemps* (1913) which was, arguably, the first 'modern' dance ever made. Maybe the greatest accolades go to works which pander, entertain and amuse but with little depth and substance. So when is a 'masterpiece' not? When is a breakthrough mere gimmickry? How does the critic reason these evaluations and then write about such matters? Often the decisions come with hindsight. The post-modern work of the 1960s is a good example here. Perhaps the most difficult to judge is 'new' work which holds unfamiliarity within it, and a critic just has to present their own gut reaction (within their experience and knowledge) then wait to see if they are right or wrong!

> A good drama critic is one who perceives what is happening in the theatre of his time. A great drama critic also perceives what is not happening.
>
> (*Kenneth Tynan in* Tynan Right and Left, *1967*)

The key deciding factor is likely the context. If a dance confronts the dominant social values in its own time those experiencing it *at that time* may be unable to see or accept what the significance is. For example, is Matthew Bourne a hack or a Messiah? His work is generally well thought of but for critics to disagree is not uncommon:

> In his *Swan Lake* ... the mockery jarred with Tchaikovsky's imaginative and poetic score – at times he seemed to be cocking a snook at artistic creations considerably grander than anything he could come up with himself ... Bourne cannot find anything like the equivalent in contemporary dance for the exhilarating bravura dance at the heart of Bournonville.
>
> (*Nicholas Dromgoole in* The Electronic Telegraph, *March 1997*)

Even with excellent contextual knowledge and a degree of objectivity, a professional dance critic's review is only one person's opinion. A good review, however, will be able to give the reader a sense of a performance that they have not seen. The reader then decides whether or not to go. Clearly if the review is bad the audience may not go, so critics bear a great responsibility and power.

Task Ten – Sample Answers

1. Description – 'it is more of a mood piece than a literal narrative' – structure.
   'The music (solo piano pieces from Tchaikovsky and Russian folk melodies on guitar and mandolin) was suitably melancholy and very well played' – constituent feature, accompaniment.
2. Interpretation – 'applied a butterfly net to the bursting hearts of Chekhov's 'The Three Sisters' – content.
3. Evaluation – 'This ballet demands ensemble acting of great delicacy that is now the Royal Ballet's greatest strength' – context/interpretative skills.
   'The farewell pas de deux is very fine, but though it was beautifully danced, the audience was dry-eyed' – interpretative skills.
4. Interpretation/Evaluation – 'Leanne Benjamin doesn't carry young Irina's restless world-weariness but she certainly registers the frissons of budding sexuality …' – content/interpretative skills.

Below is an example of a list of headings under which a dance may be described, interpreted and evaluated:

Title of dance
Choreographer
Date of first performance
Genre/style
Content
Accompaniment
Dancers/company
Any specific demands placed on the dancers in performance
Movement and form
Set
Costume/prop
Lighting
Designer name(s)
Context and significance
Evaluation

An example of a specific dance analysis and evaluation is now given below:

'Brahms Waltz' (1925): Five Brahms Waltzes in the Manner of Isadora Duncan (1976).

Choreographer: Sir Frederick Ashton.

Date: 1975–76.

Genre/style: modern dance.

Content: Isadora Duncan's style.

Accompaniment: originally Brahms's Waltz Opus 35, number 15. In the 1976 version, four more waltzes were added (Nos. 2, 8, 10 and 13) and the first waltz (No. 15) was played as a prelude as in the original Isadora Duncan performance. The piano was played live on stage, again as in the original Isadora Duncan version.

Dancers/company: solo female. Originally, Lynn Seymour for The Royal Ballet, and later Lucy Burge for the Ballet Rambert (1984).

Specific demands placed on the dancers in performance: a very wide range of dynamics was required.

Movement and form: Ashton had strong memories of Duncan in performance – in particular, a lasting impression of the freedom of her movement – and this influenced his choice of movements, which included:

- subtle, light shifts of weight;
- movements relating the body to a universal space and not just to the stage space;
- plastic, fluid, expressive head, body and upper-torso movements;
- movements conveying a range of emotions. The choreographic form of each waltz was wide-ranging, and so were the dynamics.

Set: a bare stage except for a piano.

Costume/prop: a long piece of floaty fabric was used to enhance the spatial patterns of the movements. The costume was a tunic made of flimsy fabric very similar to the original worn by Duncan. This emphasised the flowing, rippling movements.

Designer name: David Dean.

Context and significance: it was originally choreographed for the 1975 Hamburg Gala night to celebrate the 50th anniversary of the Ballet Rambert and entitled *Homage to Isadora*. The later version (1976) was entitled *Five Brahms Waltzes in the Manner of Isadora Duncan*, danced by Lynn Seymour and dedicated to Dame Marie Rambert who, like Ashton, had been inspired by Duncan.

In 1921, Ashton had seen Isadora dance in London. He went back many times, fascinated by her grace, intensity and use of arms. He later stated that he used these influences in his own ballet.

The original Duncan waltzes were choreographed in 1902 and performed with great success in North and South America, Europe and Russia until 1924.

Evaluation: As a piece of modern dance it has historical, retrospective value. Ashton's memories of Duncan's work go some way to record what otherwise would be lost to dance history as there is little remaining of her legacy. As a piece in its own right its revival recognises its worth. The dancers were recognised as having the high degree of technical control required for the wide range of dynamics and the authentic Duncan expressive style.

Ashton's gala piece was so successful that, unusually for a gala piece, it was placed in the Royal Ballet repertoire in a fuller version. Later still, it was revived for the Rambert repertoire.

TASK ELEVEN

Communication and Information Technology

Apply the list of headings to a dance of one of the choreographers which you are studying.

Present your findings to a group on overhead projections in text, images and the spoken word.

APPRECIATION – A SUMMARY

By considering the many dimensions of a dance in appreciation its value and worth are enhanced. It may be treasured as a precious jewel in the lives of all who come into contact with it. A written record, analysis and evaluation of it are vital ways of preserving the history of dance. Whether in writing, on film or in a notation score the description, interpretation and evaluations are the life blood for progress in the art of the dance.

References and resources

BOOKS

Anderson, J., *Ballet and Modern Dance: a Concise History*, New Jersey: Princeton, 1992

Binney, E., *Glories of the Romantic Ballet*, London: Dance Books, 1985

Bland, A., *Observer of the Dance 1958–1982*, London: Dance Books, 1985

Bremser, M., *Fifty Contemporary Choreographers*, London: Routledge, 1999

Denby, E., *Dancers, Buildings and People in the Streets*, New York: Horizon Press 1965

Dewey, J., *Having an Experience*, New York: Minton, Bach & Co, 1934

Guest, I., *The Dancer's Heritage: A Short History of the Ballet*, Dancing Times, 1988

Jordan, S. and Allen, D., *Parallel Lines*, London: Libbey & Co., 1993

Kurth, P. 'Isadora: a sensational life', New York: Little Brown, 2001.

Mackrell, J., *Out of Line*, London: Dance Books, 1992

Patsch-Bergsohn, I., *Modern Dance in Germany and the United States: Cross-currents and Influences*, Harwood Academic Publishers, 1996

Preston-Dunlop, V., *Dance Words*, a review of words used by the dance world, London: Routledge, 1995

Spencer, P., *Society and the Dance*, Cambridge University Press, 1985

Stearns, M. and Stearns, A., *Jazz Dance: the Story of American Vernacular Dance*, New York: Da Capo, 1993

ARTICLES/REVIEWS

In Dance Theatre Journal:

Copeland, R., *Revival and Reconstruction*, no. 3, vol. 11, 1994.

Macaulay, A., *Process, Bloodlines, Connections*. no. 1, vol. 3, 1983.

Lloyd Newson in interview with Jo Butterworth, published by The Centre for Dance and Theatre Studies, University of Bretton 1998.

Other interviews with Lloyd Newson on: www.dv8.co.uk

The Electronic Telegraph: www.telegraph.co.uk

Other useful sources of newspaper reviews on line:

The *Independent:*
www.enjoyment. independent.co.uk

The *Guardian:*
www.guardianunlimited.uk/Archive

www.artsworld.com/dance

www.sussexdance.co.uk

Sources for Lewis Segal and J. Dunning articles and many others available on: www.artsjournal.com

MUSIC

The following music is recommended for Task 7:

The Chieftains, *Strike the Gay Harp*, 3 Claddagh Records, 4CC10

SEVEN

Recording Dance: walking boldly backwards into the future

The issues in question

> Ballets are the most transitory of things – once a step has been danced it is dead.
>
> (*In* Making a Ballet, *1974*)

This chapter will question the truth of this statement, and offer alternative options which may allow us to *record* dances so that they may be a part of the future:

> The future is made of the same stuff as the present.
>
> (*Simone Weil, philosopher*)

As we saw in the previous chapter a review, if it provides enough detail, can be a way of documenting dance history. The writings of dancers and choreographers themselves are another form of recording dance history. There are many examples: Petipa's scenarios; Jean-Georges Noverre's *Letters on Dancing and Ballet* (1760); Fokine's reforms in 1914; Catherine Quinn's online *Dancer's log*; the many books, newspaper and magazine articles; web sites documenting choreographers' working methods. It is important to understand that in appreciating a dance we may also record it for dance history.

As a part of your dance course you should acquire skill in recording dances. For instance you may be improvising in your research for a solo and record the movements as you find them (even if later you throw them away!). A written record will make it easier to remember them, to teach them to other dancers and to build a logical form and structure. Some of you will have to present an analysis of a solo dance for examination. You will have to identify and record the movements, devices which you used, floor patterns, actions, locations and so on. You may use words, diagrams, numbers of a prescribed notation such as Labanotation or Benesh Notation. These are all written records for your own personal diary of work.

Recording dance in picture form is another way of preserving it. Archaeologists have found possible evidence of dancing dating back as far as from 5,000 to 9,000 years ago. Recent finds of carved stone and painted scenes from sites in the Balkans and the Middle East depict figures in lines or circles, hands linked. Of course nowadays we have much more sophisticated technology to record dances.

Videotape is a fairly accurate way of making a record of a dance which can be used for study or for a choreographer's/dancer's own development.

> For all of its obvious limitations, the technology is here to stay and it does perform some vital functions; dancing moves forever into history on a practical note, important decisions are being made today on the basis of viewing videotapes.
>
> (*Daniel Nagrin in* Dance Theatre Journal, *1988*)

Many dancers are using video to tape their rehearsals and improvisations as a way of finding new material for choreography. This medium can also be used for making archives to monitor their own growth and development. A simple camera set-up may be adequate for these purposes, but is it able to deal with the complexities of teaching *large-group* choreography to new dancers? This may be made more difficult if the original dancers are not present at a reconstruction, or if the original dancers remember it differently. Is video adequate to record complete and accurate versions? What if a video recording of a particular performance contained mistakes, and this then becomes the archive? What if the camera could not cover the whole stage area? Questions and problems arise if video is the only record. What, then, are the alternative options?

Certainly, it is worrying to think of how much of our dance heritage has been lost forever. In comparison to music, visual art and literature, we have little record of the past. These days, most large dance companies employ *choreologists*. Their job is to notate during rehearsals when new dances are being choreographed. They give advice to the choreographer about what was done in previous rehearsals, how much music is left in a section, and so on. Choreologists also are responsible for reconstructing old repertoires. This means that a dance can be reconstructed and performed centuries after it was created, just like a Mozart symphony. Many dances, however, are revived without scores, and one has to wonder how accurately they are remembered.

> Perhaps more than any art form ballets develop over time, especially those created before there was a universal language of notation (or video) to record the movement. Steps and formations were handed down from dancer to dancer, so as with Chinese whispers the detail was bound to mutate, particularly with popular classics where choreographers and directors often want to reinterpret the action as well as the movement.
>
> (*Claire Wrathall in* The Sleeping Beauty awakens, The Independent, *June 2000*)

Although the legacies of dance may be passed on verbally between artists the real way ahead must be to document and record. From accurate records classics may be reconstructed, appreciated and reworked in updated forms for new audiences.

The innovative Mats Ek mad-house version of *Giselle* (1982) may never have come about if the original classic had not been kept for posterity throughout the centuries. Similarly, Matthew Bourne's works often contain references to other genres and styles from the past.

Sometimes fragments of a legacy are passed on between choreographers in reworks; for example the scenario of John Cranko's *Romeo and Juliet* (1958) which influenced Kenneth MacMillan's version in 1965. In turn MacMillan's version is seen as influential on the 1998 Deane version and is quoted in the Moricone ballet (1991 for Northern Ballet Theatre) in moments like Juliet's skips in the Balcony (scene 1) and her frozen misery (act 3).

Sometimes reworks are intended by the choreographer to explore dances that were created earlier in their career. Siobhan Davies reworked *Sphinx* (1977) in 1995 in view of how her style had changed. Working from memory and video, she incorporated new material which used Release style and fluid energy, these being more typical of her later work and superseded concerns with body shape and design.

Whether for the purpose of reconstruction, reworking or study two main ways of recording dance are:

- notation;
- film and video.

So let us now first look more closely at *dance notation* as a means for revival, reconstruction and study.

TASK ONE

Improving own Learning and Performance, Communication and Information Technology

Begin keeping your own log/diary of all your work. This should be an ongoing activity to which you add daily or weekly.

You could record any of the following:

- movement (taught, improvised and composed);
- ideas and thoughts on content/style;
- deadlines and how you managed your time to meet them;
- ideas for dances which you might like to make 'one day';
- notes on music, costume, lights, set props which may interest you;
- notes on diet, injury and health;
- feedback and comments from other people about your work or comments that you have made about the work of other students and professional work which you have seen.

To keep the diary you could use a mix of:

- your own writing, diagrams, number;
- Labanotation or Benesh;
- magazine/newspaper cuttings;
- photos, sound tapes and if you can access a video camera you could keep footage of your rehearsals;
- information found on the Internet.

Dance notation

A HISTORY

In the fifteenth century, dance steps were recorded on paper. In 1588, the l'*Orchésographie* by Thoinot Arbeau was published. This recorded well-known steps using abbreviations – e.g. s = single, d = double, R = reverencia – written next to the music score. The steps and dance terms themselves were explained in detail in the form of a lesson to a pupil.

A system called *Feuillet notation* was devised by Pierre Beauchamps and published in his *Chorégraphie* in 1700. This was adopted by French ballet master Raoul Feuillet at the time. In Kellon Tomlinson's English dance manual *The Art of Dancing*, published in London in 1735, an engraving shows a couple dancing the minuet. The steps are drawn in Feuillet notation at their feet, rather like a floor pattern for each dancer. It can still be read today, although it only gives information about footwork.

Later, in 1852, there was an attempt to show *whole* body movement, rhythm and timing when Arthur Saint Leon published *Stenochoregraphie*. Here, stick figures were drawn under the music score. A modified version of this by Albert Zorn in 1887 was used quite widely in the USA and Europe.

The classics of *Swan Lake* and *Sleeping Beauty* survived in Russia partly as a result of the notation of Vladimir Stepanov. He was a teacher and dancer with the Imperial Maryinsky Theatre in St Petersburg. In 1892, he published *Alphabet des Mouvements du Corps Humain*. This was used mainly in ballet, and tried to show whole body movements in *anatomical* terms. The continuity of training and performance in Russia also contributed to the survival of the above works. One wonders what their fate would have been without the notation.

In 1917 Nicolai Sergeyev brought the Stepanov notation from Russia to France and worked for Diaghilev on *The Sleeping Princess* (1921) and *Giselle* (1924). Later he recreated productions of *Swan Lake* (1934) and *Sleeping Beauty* (1939) for the Vic Wells Ballet. His physical knowledge combined with the scores laid down some of the classics for many later Western productions.

In this way, the classics had not only been preserved (an important enough achievement in itself) but had also been communicated across international borders. Astonishingly the 2000 revival of Petipa's original *The Sleeping Beauty* by the Kirov Ballet was only made possible by a chance remark of an American scholar to the company's artistic director in 1996. The ballet company had not known that the Stepanov scores were still in existence and housed in the USA at Harvard University. It took two years to decode the notation and reconstruct the work.

The Minuet: the conclusion, or presenting both arms. An illustration from The Art of Dancing, *Kellon Tomlinson, 1735*

Figure 7.1 *To show Benesh notation*

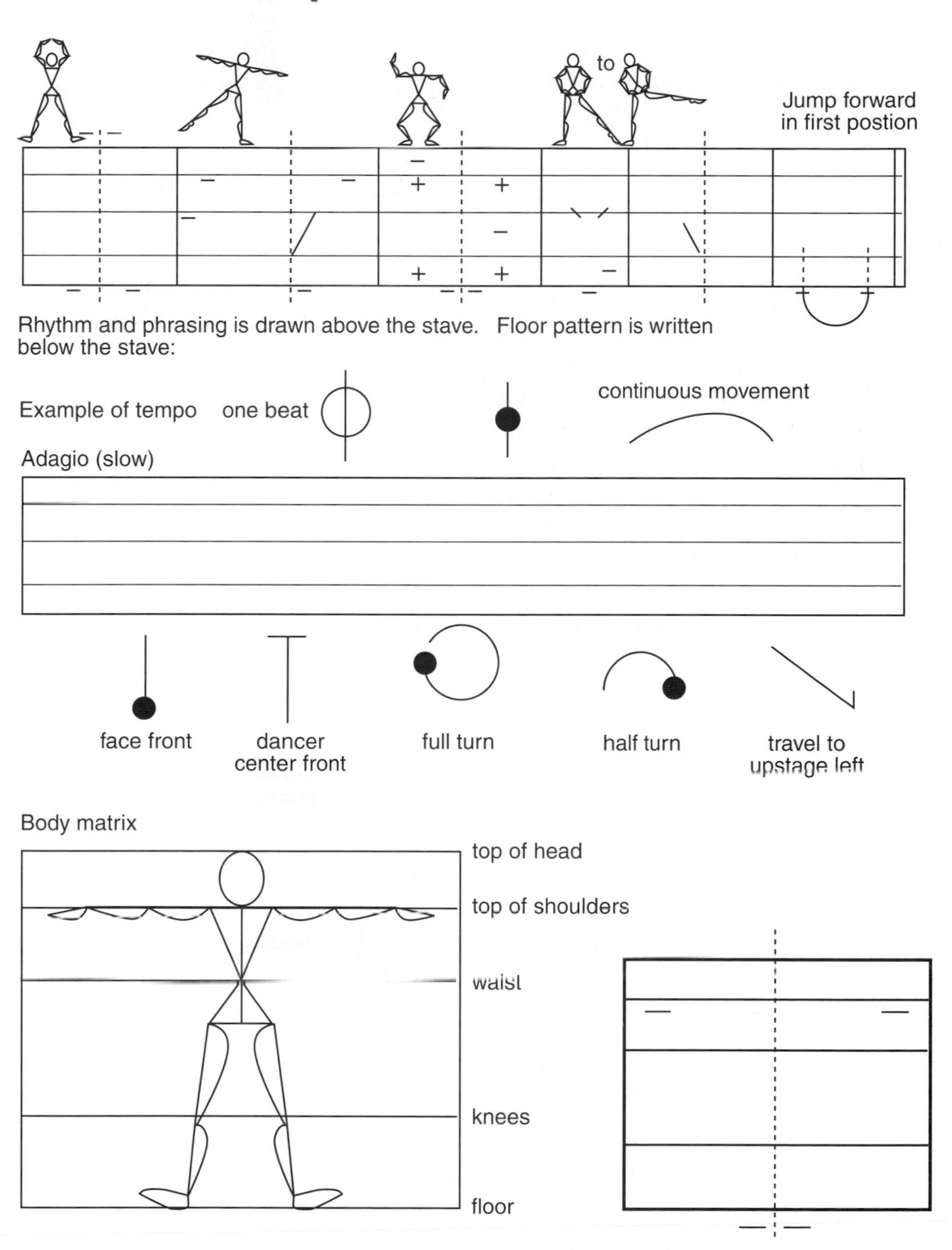
The movement reads from right to left along the stave. *Limb and body movements are drawn in the stave.* '+' is a bend sign
to
Jump forward in first postion
Rhythm and phrasing is drawn above the stave. Floor pattern is written below the stave:
Example of tempo
one beat
continuous movement
Adagio (slow)
face front
dancer center front
full turn
half turn
travel to upstage left
Body matrix
top of head
top of shoulders
waist
knees
floor

In ballet, the use of words to describe movement is very helpful. But the dance of today can be very complex in its use of gesture, space and lifting, so an adequately sophisticated system of notation is required to deliver precision. Two systems have been developed. *Benesh Notation* and *Labanotation* are both used extensively today. The two systems look very different, but their aims are the same.

Rudolf Benesh (1916–1975) was a mathematician who was married to a ballet dancer. They were concerned about the loss of dances, and after eight years' work they launched a system in 1955.

Benesh uses a musical stave (see Figure 7.1). It is read across the page from left to right, and each of the five lines represents a different area of the body. Benesh also uses the same Italian terms as found in music to show dynamic qualities – like *adagio*, for example. The timing of the movements corresponds to the bars of music. Symbols show both where body parts are placed and the direction of movement. There are also signs to show actions like jumps and turns. The movement is traced by the pathways that the body parts make as they change position.

Figure 7.2 *Labanotation signs to show extension and flexion of limbs*

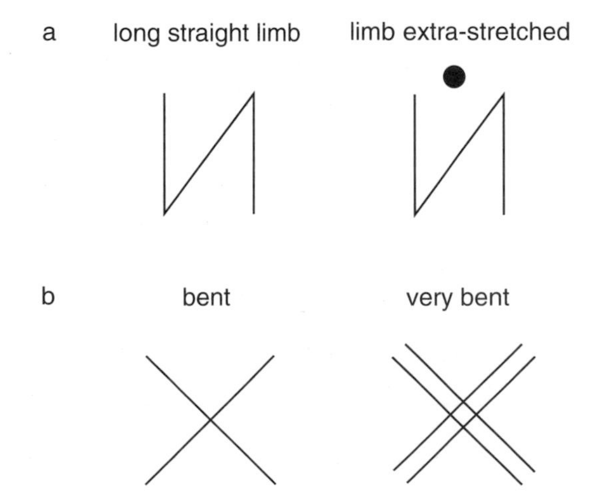

Figure 7.3 *Notation for (a) leg extension (b) arm extension*

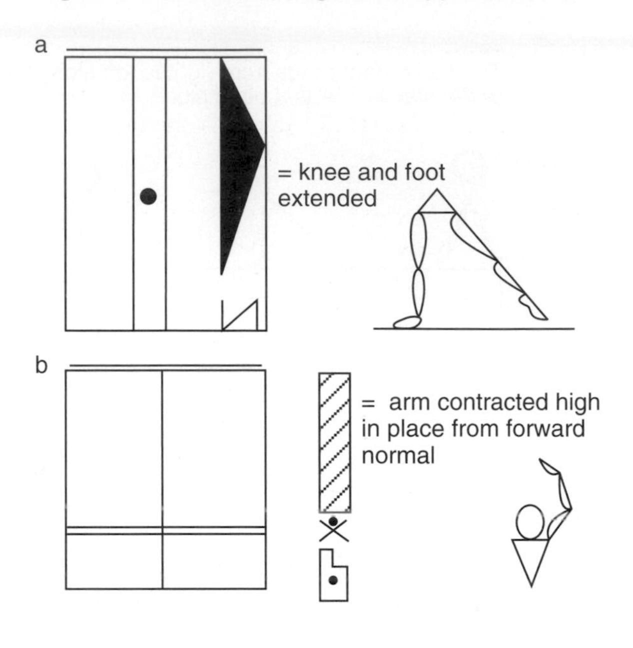

Figure 7.4 *Other Labanotation signs*

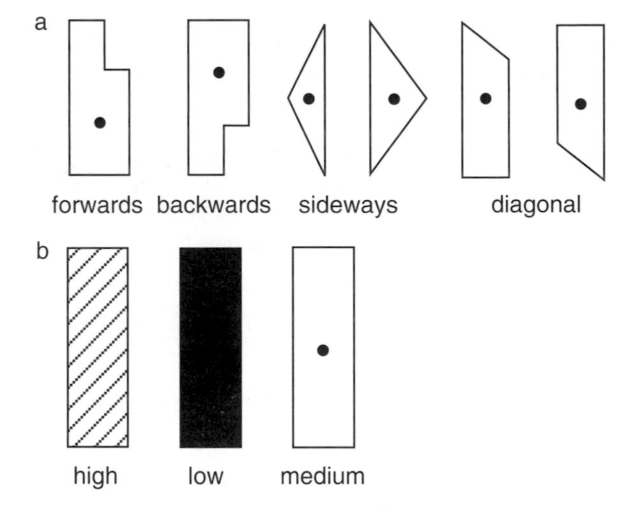

After Benesh had been taken up by the Royal Ballet, other ballet companies also used it to record their repertoires.

Rudolf Laban (1879–1958) (yes, it is odd that *both* are named after famous reindeer!) was one of the pioneers of modern dance.

German-born, he moved to the UK in 1938 to escape Nazi Germany. Laban's influence in the world of dance teaching, mainly within the world of women's physical education, is regarded as a crucial influence in the building of dance education in the UK today.

Laban's work centred on the analysis of human movement. He choreographed *movement choirs* from 1910 onwards, firstly in Germany and later in his own dance company. He was also ballet master of the State Theatre of Berlin during the 1930s. But his main work was in the analysis of dance and the training of dancers, which he worked on with his pupil and collaborator Kurt Jooss.

The analysis which he produced was called *eukinetics* and *choreutics*. This divided movement into two categories, 'outgoing' and 'incoming', and carefully broke movement down in terms of *dynamics* and *direction*. Laban also devised a complicated movement scale within an *icosahedron*, which is a 20-faced geometric form. This was used as a systematic base for dance training. His pupils Kurt Jooss and Mary Wigman in turn made huge contributions to the development of the Central European School of Modern Dance. Wigman also influenced modern dance in the USA through her pupil Hanya Holm, whose work often contained social criticism. Wigman's solos were milestones of German expressionist style.

Labanotation (see Figures 7.2, 7.3 and 7.4) is read from the bottom to the top of the page, in a three-line stave. The advantage of this strategy is that it gives the body movement continuity and shows the dancer's actual right and left as it is read. Symbols on the right of the column are for the right side of the body, and those on the left are for the left side. Basic symbols indicate the directions, levels, timings and duration of a movement. Bar lines indicate the music timings. The notation also allows for the recording of dynamics and quality changes.

Today, libraries of dance scores are available. In terms of the future, these libraries can form an invaluable source of study, for dance students and researchers. This makes dance history more accessible for all, and in valuing this history we strengthen the value of present-day works also.

A controversial issue arises from the 1978 changes in copyright law which do not favour the traditional passing down of works from dancer to dancer, backed up with notation and video. The idea that a dance may be owned is causing some problems. Who has or has not the right to revive a work? New technologies make illegally reproducing others' work easier and so the 'rights' to reconstruct dances (or teach techniques) for public consumption is seen as needing stricter legislation. So for example dances by Lester Horton, who died in 1953, were all left to Frank Eng. He created the Horton Foundation in 1999 and appointed a former Horton dancer to stage the works. Eng says that:

> My only interest at this point is to reconstruct and hand down the most accurate material possible.
>
> (*In*, 'Warning: Ephemeral but Private Property' *J. Dunning, The New York Times, 2000*)

The knock-on effect is that others, who consider themselves Horton trained, are left disenfranchised in their work, as dancers or teachers, to use what they know.

A dance is legally under copyright when it is first created but for actual damages to be claimed a score (notated and/or filmed) must be filed. Meanwhile some may feel that imitation is flattery and so not be bothered too much by plagiarism, especially if the cost of a camera or notator is the deciding factor. The ownership issue is a complex one and still being debated. For example if a dancer has made phrases for a choreographer who actually owns what?

New computer technologies are also involved in the future of dance notation. There is an Apple Macintosh software package for Benesh called MacBenesh and Labanotation programmes called Calaban and Labanwriter for AppleMac.

TASK TWO

Information Technology (if using notation software)

Choreograph a simple 4-bar phrase in 4/4 meter. Include a turn, a jump and some steps in different directions. Indicate that it is repeated on the other side of the body. Notate it in either Labanotation or Benesh, or your own note form which may include words, counts and diagrams.

Exchange scores with another student, and read each other's. Compare how accurately the phrase is reproduced. (Suggested music: the 'Aquarium' from Carnival of the Animals by Camille Saint-Saëns.)

NOTATION FOR RECORDING AND RECONSTRUCTION

Obviously, in dance, studying a notation score can give insight into the composition, structure and style of a dance. By noticing the variations and developments of motifs through an observation of the way in which they are repeated on a score, you can gain an understanding of how a choreography is structured. If the signs for toe and heel feature numerously in a score, the style may be quite folky. Or if there appears to be a great deal of stamping, a dance may be within South Asian or African genres. Or again, the Martha Graham style or modern dance genres may show through if there is lots of floorwork – i.e. where the knees, hips and torso make contact with the floor.

TASK THREE

Read the Labanotation in Figure 7.5, and suggest in what genres the styles of walking shown here are most likely to be. (Answers on page 222.)

OR

Communication and Information Technology (if using software)

Write two different types of document about a dance that you have choreographed:

- Document no. 1 describes in words the movement of two of the motifs;
- Document no. 2 describes in diagrams and number one other motif and the floor pattern of a section of your dance (you may use Labanotation or Benesh if you prefer).

As already mentioned, choreologists are responsible for the process of reconstructing and reviving past works. Where possible, it is best to use also a video record. Notating dances from rehearsals is a time-consuming business. As Monica Parker wrote in a Sadler's Wells Ballet programme: 'It is common for one minute of choreography to take two hours of rehearsal – and a further six hours for the full notation of that minute to be made.' This is certainly slower than making a video record! However, in other instances, reconstructing from a videotape alone may actually prove to be slower and less accurate, if the following example is anything to go by. In 1973, notator Anne Whitley notated Tippett's *The Ice Break*. Over 100 performers, multi-level staging, dry ice and other theatrical effects had to be recorded. The work was revived two years later, and she used the score to teach from. It was staged in four days! This would seem to be accurate, fast and cost-effective. In such cases, notation plays a vital part in conserving our dance heritage.

Figure 7.5 *Notation for Task 3*

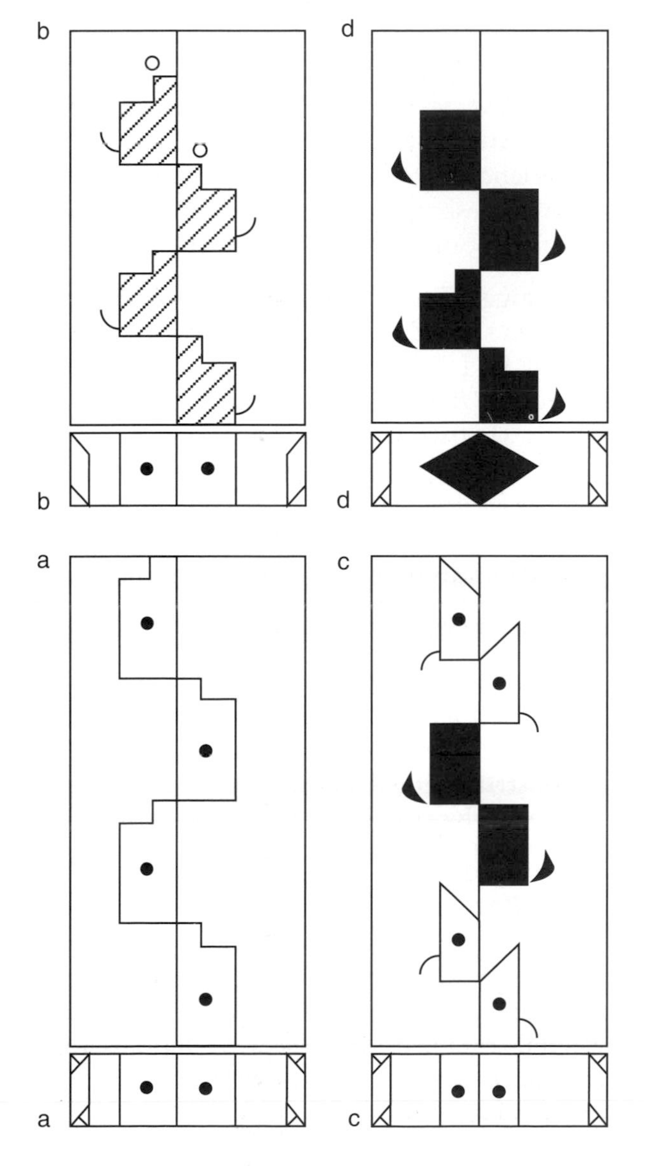

A description by Judith Mackrell (The *Guardian*, 1996) of rehearsals of the revival of MacMillan's *Anastasia* for the Royal Ballet reveals much of interest about the process of reconstruction. Choreologist Monica Parker (who notated the ballet when it was first created) read and showed the steps to the dancers whilst shadowed by Lynn Seymour (original creator of the leading role). Seymour offered information about interpretation, telling the new dancers what '*Kenneth wanted ... to help them find themselves in it.*'

Revivals and stagings of past ballets or modern dances, seen through the eyes of another era, may sometimes look dated, but they may still nonetheless have value as a 'dance antique'. However, as already mentioned, classic ballets are often reworked in a modern style, and this approach may also even be considered for those modern works which are already now a part of our dance past. As with new interpretations of Shakespeare, such reworkings can remain accurate to the basic form but convey new emotions and fresh dynamic colour, and this may bring to the surface new ideas which lay hidden in the original dance. Or, they may have different and possibly more up-to-date costumes, sets or lighting arrangements. A museum of dance reconstructions faithfully copying the originals is one possibility, but this alone may only have 'cobweb potential'. Reworking dances to live again in *new* times with *new* relevance for *new* audiences should also, therefore, be a possibility.

Some of choreographer Doris Humphrey's work from the 1930s only exists today because it was notated and filmed. It has been suggested by the Doris Humphrey Foundation that such reconstructions should be faithful to the original.

> ... the history of modern dance needs these living illustrations, particularly while the first 'generation' dancers can still provide them.
>
> (*Lesley Main, director of the UK Doris Humphrey Foundation, in Dance Theatre Journal, in Rubidge, S. 1995*)

In 1995 three works of Doris Humphrey, *Shakers* (1931), *Water Study* (1928) and *Air for the G String* (1928), were reconstructed with students from The Place (the London Contemporary Dance School) by one of the dancers from the original cast, Ernestine Stodelle. The reconstruction promised much, using not only the score as the base but also memories of the original performance. However, as observed by dance critic Sarah Rubidge (*Dance Theatre Journal*, 1995) the final performance of *Shakers* was not entirely successful owing to the failure on the part of the students to commit the level of energy which the work required. The new dancers were from another era, and did not seem to have the particular physical or mental outlook that was required for dances from the early twentieth century.

In 1998 a similar reconstruction from an original score and physical memory of the time took place at the University of Birmingham. Kurt Jooss's *Big City* (1932) was reconstructed with the score and Jooss's daughter, Anna Markard. The aim was to complete an accurate score, typeset it using CALABAN and publish it.

There is no doubt that live performances of authentic reconstructions contribute an immediacy of energy and a view of history that film and notation may not be capable of providing. But this is not the only option. An alternative view was also expressed in the same article by Sarah Rubidge, namely that experienced professional directors should be allowed responsibility to use the *scores* as a starting point for giving life to the work.

The suggestion that less experienced or able dancers should not be allowed access to these scores is, I find, questionable. The value of scores to dance students (and let's face it, that's what we *all* are in the end) is that they offer an insight into the past of a kind not otherwise available. The physical experience of a score or film is the most important thing a student can have. All the books in the world cannot recreate the intimate learning experience that a physical reconstruction can offer. Of course, we are not saying that these reconstructions *must* be performed, but only that they ought, at least, to be *experienced*. Such reconstruction will be vulnerable to inaccuracies, and the student should be aware of this.

As a student you may find software like CALABAN and Labanwriter helpful, even essential, in keeping records of your work. They are also important in current professional research, recording, analysis and digital storage of dance scores. Digitalisation of dance scores increases ease of recording, retrieval and storage.

There is much cutting edge research going on using Labanotation to push the boundaries of not just dance but areas of science and technology. Listed at the end of this chapter are several web sites which discuss such research.

So where does this leave us? Well, it would seem that the dance world needs to respect and cherish its heritage. Whether this should be done by notation, film or live reconstructions is debatable – from now on, maybe it should always be all three. What *is* certain is that the heritage can only serve to *enrich* the future of dance.

OTHER USES FOR DANCE NOTATION

Information provided by movement notation can be used for many different purposes.

Labanotation has been used to record the movements of workers in factories in order to find ways of increasing productivity. Once the relevant movements were notated, the analysis showed up which were productive and which were non-productive. In this way, machinery could be repositioned to make use of the most efficient order of movements.

Notation is also used in sport, physiotherapy, psychiatry, medicine and therapy. Benesh notation has been used in the treatment of cerebral palsy. When the patients' movements have been recorded over time, the results can be analysed to see how the patients are responding to different types of treatment. Labanotation has been applied to sufferers of schizophrenia, and again this has involved the observation, recording and analysing of body posture – for study by psychiatrists.

In scientific research, movement notation has been used to record motion in a weightless state, and it has contributed to the computerisation of instructions for movements for robots. There has also been some use in anthropological research: a study of the dances of different cultures in the Pacific Islands and South Africa has used notation to make comparisons between the roles of the male and the female in the community.

DANCE NOTATION – CONCLUSIONS

Being able to access our dance past is vital. For young choreographers, studying past originals in a systematic way brings them into line with students of other arts. The research and study of tradition is not as inhibiting as the dance world sometimes seems to think. It is a way of moving on and improving on the past, and this can only be done if we have an *accurate knowledge* of the past – it is not possible to develop on from nothing. Video, being such a relatively recent form of recording, is limited in terms of how far back into the past it can go. It also fails to give the kind of detail, depth and accuracy that a notation score can offer.

Important choreography like that for *The Sleeping Beauty* may have been lost forever if it had not been notated in Russia. We cannot afford to ignore our past; nor to neglect putting on record the present, as this will be the *past* for students of the future! So, for all dance students who feel that notation is the drudgery of your dance life, try to adjust and look at it in a new light. It is part of your own future, and may even be contributing to the future survival and growth of dance generally.

ANSWERS TO TASK 3

Figure 7.5:

(a) modern genre, because parallel and medium/natural level.

(b) classical ballet genre, because turned-out and high level on toes.

(c) folk dance, because uses heels and stamps.

(d) African or South Asian, because uses low level and stamps.

Filming dance

There has been a rapid rise in interest in television commissions for dance. There have been various dance series, including Channel 4's *Tights Camera Action!* (1993 and 1994), as hosted by Lea Anderson, and BBC2's *Dance for Camera* (1995). So why this growing interest in dance on screen rather than live at the theatre? The answer is connected to the availability of new technology and the breaking-down of barriers to 'what dance can be and do'. This is not a huge step away from creating *virtual realities*. Certainly, with the massive range of special effects now available, dancers on film can perform superhuman feats beyond their wildest dreams. For example, in the 3-minute 1994 video *Waiting*, directed and choreographed by Lea Anderson, with The Cholmondeleys dance group, the dancers are seen to be flying and floating around in a state of suspended animation as they simply wait around. Similarly, in *Mothers and Daughters* (1994), choreographed by Victoria Marks and directed by Margaret Williams, the dancers spin at unbelievable speed in a close embrace.

DANCE ON FILM – A SHORT HISTORY

To understand why this new art form within dance is developing so quickly, it would be worth looking at where and when it all started.

The first dance films to become widely seen were the Hollywood musicals like those of Fred Astaire and Gene Kelly of the 1930s. Some ballet and ballroom dances were also broadcast on television at the same time. In the late 1940s, ballet became popularised through such feature films as *The Red Shoes* (choreography Leonide Massine, 1946) and later in the 1950s several blockbuster musicals, like *Seven Brides for Seven Brothers*, were released. The combined effect of these films inspired many to take up dancing.

In the USA in the late 1960s, the concern shifted towards making dance films. For example, Merce Cunningham, who is often regarded as the pioneer of dance on video, collaborated with composer John Cage and CBS-TV on a version of *Field Dances*. Cameras panned everywhere, and there were out-of-focus shots, unexpected interruptions with fragments of interviews, and shots of Cage at the piano. Sometimes there was no sound or picture at all! Cunningham's usual strategy of *random composition* was clearly in place! As a result of this collaboration, Cunningham decided to research further into how the two art forms of dance and video may work together, and this led to a later collaboration between Cunningham and Charles Atlas in the early 1970s. This produced some innovative ideas. They experimented with making a new form of dance especially for the screen, called *videodance*. Here, the camera was located in amongst the dancers, moving with the action rather than relying on a zoomlens close-up. This gave a greater feel for the *energy* involved in dance, a factor which is often washed out in film/video productions. The camera strapped to the body of the operator – called a Steadicam – was found to give a smoother look. Cunningham and Atlas went on to make many more videodances, including *Walkaround Time* (1969–73) and *Locale* (1978–80).

Atlas went on in the early 1980s to work with other post-modern dance artists such as Karole Armitage and Douglas Dunn. He developed a very distinctive style which had the following characteristics:

- quick-moving, hand-held cameras to give a look of spontaneity;
- abrupt editing which looks almost amateur and experimental;
- documentaries that have a slight fictional, surreal feel.

These techniques, combined with very careful planning, created intense visual interest for the viewer. The film-biography on dancer Michael Clark, *Hail, The New Puritan* (1986), shows these characteristics very clearly. It portrays Clark's life in punk London combined with several dances. The opening section featuring many of his friends – including the late fashion designer Leigh Bowery – is full of surreal images. As the introductory titles then start to roll, Clark is filmed waking up (in Chisenhale Dance Studio, London, but you would be forgiven for thinking it was his flat), and you realise the opening was all his dream! It is full of humour and startlingly clear observations.

> I wanted a psychological element, not so much a mystery but to do with personalities. ... It's a sort of blurring of forms ... Fiction and reality.
>
> (*Charles Atlas in* Dance Theatre Journal, *1983*)

More and more television coverage in art-magazine-type programmes like *The South Bank Show* and *Arena* gave dance more exposure. These usually involved straightforward films of stage works. This type of dance film is generally regarded as limited in scope nowadays.

In the UK in the 1970s, the producers Bob Lockyer and Colin Nears led the field. Lockyer collaborated with the London Contemporary Dance Theatre, concentrating mainly on the works of choreographer Robert Cohan. From then on, dance-on-film series became more regular.

One such early series of *Dance on 4* (Channel 4, 1983) showed a range of genres and styles, including: a documentary of *Backstage at the Kirov* with excerpts from *Swan Lake*; *Plainsong and Carnival* by Siobhan Davies with Second Stride; Robert North's *Troy Games* for the London Contemporary Dance Theatre; and Twyla Tharp's *Dance Scrapbook*. There was a wide range of use of camera and approaches to the filming of dance across the whole series. The Twyla Tharp film was an autobiographical study of her experimental work with dance and film, and it had a raw, exciting energy. This work contrasted with a more conventional use of film in the stage performance of *Troy Games*, where the camera angles and some of the timings employed shut out some of the humour of the original. When cameras were used more freely, moving amongst the dancers, there were varying levels of success. In *Swan Lake*, there was an increase in the physical impact for the viewer, as the camera almost became one of the *corps de ballet*. However, in *Plainsong*, the same technique produced rather a mismatch. Here, the cameras seemed to intrude on the calm quality and clear structure of the choreography.

In 1986, television directors Terry Braun and Peter Mumford formed an independent production company called Dancelines. This aimed to research the different possibilities involved in making dance for television. Their first project, itself called *Dancelines,* involved a collaboration with Siobhan Davies, Ian Spink and a group of dancers/choreographers including Paul Clayden, Lucy Burge and Matthew Hawkins. The idea was to involve the *whole* team in the use of camera, editing and choreography. Dancers used the cameras, and camera operators joined in with the dancers' daily class. In this way, a close exchange of skills and understandings occurred. Everyone was on a very steep learning curve, and very valuable communication channels between the different art forms opened up. The final programme documented the whole process.

The Featherstonehaughs in Immaculate Conception. *To show the use of photographic effects similar to the use of video, to distort and create unusual images*

The *Dance on 4* series was repeated in 1988. All the featured work was made for film or television. *Dancelines 2* featured in this series, and it carried on, in a more sophisticated way, from where the earlier research had left off.

As a part of this series also, Richard Alston collaborated very closely with Peter Mumford on an adaptation of the stage work *Strong Language*. This was no simple adaptation. It is still very recognisable as *Strong Language*, but it shows off certain features of the original dance which were less emphasised in the live performance. For example, the music and overall form of the piece was reorganised to suit a 25-minute programme, and there was substantial re-choreographing: one whole section of the original was missed out. Furthermore, the use of sudden changes in images, angles and perspectives resulted in more highlights than the original dance had. In place of the original contrapuntal structure, a new concern with close-ups involved the audience more with each individual dancer, and the former could now relate to the whole piece by building relationships with individual dancers rather than with the broad compositional structure of the piece. This approach was far more suited to small-screen viewing than to a live stage work. It was a radical piece of dance filming.

From the 1980s into the 1990s, there were many more series of specially commissioned works, as well as showings of earlier works. A comprehensive view was given in the above-mentioned Channel 4 *Tights Camera Action* Series 1 and 2 in 1993 and 1994. Many superb and experimental works from Europe, the

USA, Canada and the UK were shown. The point was clearly being made that dance made for film had matured into a new genre. It enabled choreography to reach new heights of possibilities in terms of increasing movement vocabulary from the real to the superhuman. There were wonderful tricks, effects and fun to be had.

In 1995, a series broadcast on BBC2 called *Summer Dance* showed a wide mix of work: a full-length ballet of Kenneth Macmillan's *Mayerling*; a documentary on Martha Graham; a videodance by Merce Cunningham called *Beach Birds* (director Eliot Caplan); *Outside In*, a post-modern work by Candoco choreographed by Victoria Marks and directed by Margaret Williams; *White Bird Featherless* by Siobhan Davies; *Rooster*, *Ghost Dances* and *Moonshine* by Christopher Bruce; and a full helping of Balanchine as the grand finale to the series. All in all, a mixed bag of genres and intentions showing the whole spectrum of dance, from stage works on film to videodance in the twentieth century.

There are currently many interesting videos of dance available. Some which you may find helpful in your studies are listed in the Resources section at the end of chapters in this book. Nowadays the broadcasting of videodance and dance films on British television is fairly regular, and it is worth keeping your eyes open for them in the weekly listings.

The manipulation of video images in creating 'virtual' environments and performances is common these days. Often the video footage is mixed with light, sound and human movement in computer operated interactive mixed media performance. Such presentations are examined further in Chapter 8.

PROBLEMS OF FILMING DANCE

The future of dance on film is a complex one, needing a close regard for the *aim* behind the filming of any particular dance. Depending on *why* a dance is being filmed, various problems will appear. These problems arise from a certain amount of incompatibility between how the human eye works and how the eye of the *camera* – as controlled by the film director – works.

Problem: long shots versus alternative options

Long shots from one or several static cameras show the broad structure of a work but do not allow the viewer a clear image of the movements involved because the figures appear so small. The human eye, when watching dance at the theatre, will choose *what* to watch and *when* – from a broad overall scan, including exits and entrances, to a focus on a particular piece of detail or a particular soloist. Some stage works do not adapt to filming easily.

If we consider Mats Ek's Freudian interpretation of *Giselle* as an example of fine choreography which is difficult to film, we see the point. This director used cameras in a *conventional* format when transferring the stage work onto screen. The basic problem here is that if the usual number of cameras is employed, the field of view is insufficient to include large casts in one shot. And because the director is trying to be faithful to the choreographer, the result is a no-win situation. As an audience watches the dance on the stage, both their eyes and the choreography itself work mainly *side-to-side*. Television, by contrast, works mainly *foreground to background*, and so the two are not easily compat-

Figure 7.6 *Showing problems of filming dance caused by camera angles/field of vision*

a

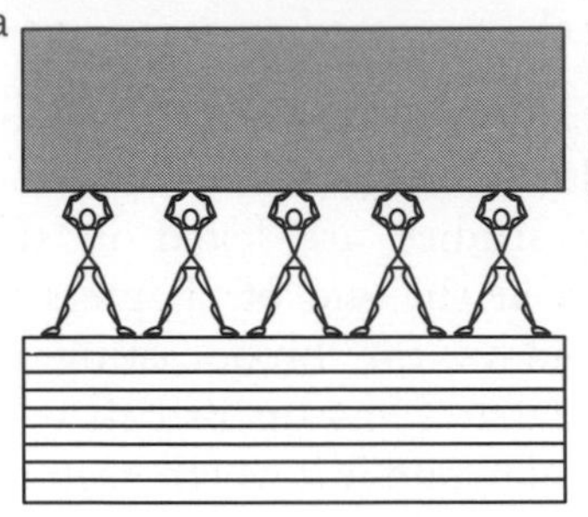

Bob Lockyer called this the '2/3:1/3' problem to film a line of dancers, the final image shows 1/3 floor. 1/3 cyclorama, 1/3 dancers.

b

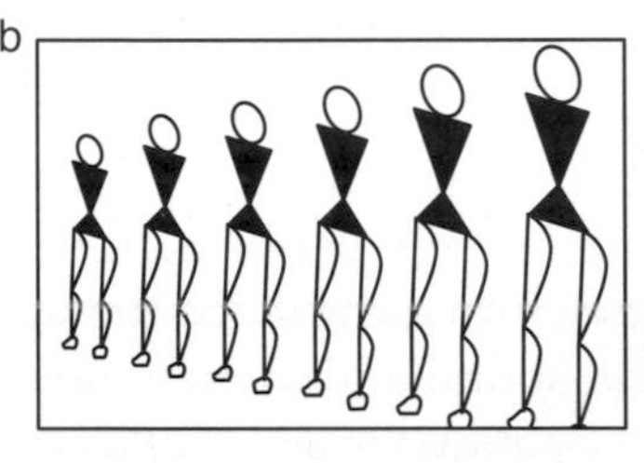

Looking down a line of dancers affects the look of choreography, and it is still not possible to fit them all in. This was used quite effectively in the filming of Robert North *Troy Games.*

c

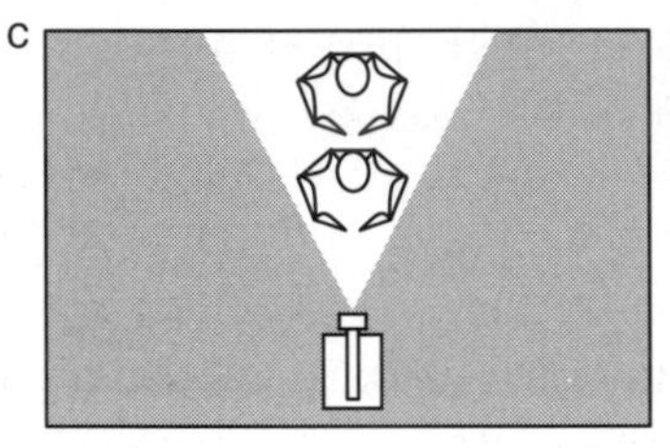

Here the field of a camera is a cone. The closer the dancers to the camera, the tighter the shot. This can make stage placings look quite different on film. This is used to good effect by Cunningham in *Points In Space*

ible. Long shots from static cameras are thus not an answer. Figure 7.6 shows the problem. (For a fuller explanation of this, see Bob Lockyer's article 'Dance and video: random thoughts', in *Dance Theatre Journal.*)

Possible solutions

Bob Lockyer went some way to solving this problem in attempting to stay true to the original stage work of Robert Cohan's *Forest* (filmed for television in 1980). At the start of the dance, the company enters in canon from stage right. Lockyer adapted this for the small screen by playing with the time element of the film. He *superimposed* one dancer doing the calling motif over the next and the next. This gave a filmed look which was close to the canon that the audience would have seen in the original stage work.

In his early research, Merce Cunningham discovered an important strategy in regard to this problem:

> The triangular floor (as seen by the camera's eye) has led Merce's exploiting depth as a way of choreographing. One of his achievements is that he has made dancing look very spacious in a very small area so that you don't necessarily feel that the camera is confining the dancers.
>
> (*Charles Atlas in* Dance Theatre Journal, *1983*)

In *Points in Space* (1987) for BBC2, Cunningham collaborated with director Eliot Caplin to create a videodance plus a documentary of the process of its making. The footage shows Cunningham watching rehearsals in New York through a camera viewfinder in preparation for the later filming which took place in London. There is a clear concern with making exits fit into the small screen scale, and some clever uses of foreground and background. It also shows the cameras moving amongst the dancers – Caplin calls this 'cameras dancing'. Interestingly, the final dance was later reworked for the stage – a complete turnaround from the usual convention of filming a stage work.

The problem of adapting stage works and long shots was also encountered by the Mumford-Alston collaboration on *Strong Language.* The form and structure of Alston's choreography did not work on film because it relied on the eye seeing *broad* shots of how movements played off one against the other.

The restructuring of the choreography for television opted for close-ups in order to build the interest of the viewer in relation to individual dancers and the small subtleties of their movement. Braun and Alston also used *split screen* so that a number of different images from the dance could be seen at once. This helped to fit the dance into the small screen without losing a sense of the original whole – even if this whole was now seen in a different way.

Long shots have their uses if a major-scale production, say of a classical ballet, is to be filmed for audiences who may not otherwise see it. However, they are limited in scope. In order for dance to have an impact on the small screen, *alternative ideas* for how best to put across the original kinetic feel and energy need to be generated.

Problem: the camera's eye versus the spectator's eye

> 'You're the choreographer', Glen Tetley said to me a few years ago ... 'You select the images the viewer sees.'
>
> (*Bob Lockyer in* Dance Theatre Journal, *1983*)

There is a key question to be asked here: should the director use the camera simply to present the dance to us, *or* should there be a creative freedom in the use of the camera which generates something entirely new? The first assumes that the camera is a mere substitute for the *audience's* eyes. The other is more about film using the dance as the subject matter to be *worked on* – just as a choreographer would choose certain *ideas* to work on. The choices of camera focus and angle and of editing styles are like choreography but in a different medium. There may be an approach which lies somewhere between the two.

The reality of being true to a stage work is not, however, quite so straightforward as it may first appear. At a basic level, each member of an audience will see and perceive a performance in their own individual way. So what hope is there of filming a 'perfect' view?

Furthermore, the camera can never see the same as the human eye. The *director's* view will always be the one finally seen, and this can never reproduce the whole of the live performance with all its dynamics and visual freedoms. Filming diminishes the three dimensions of space – as well as the raw energy, which is scaled down enormously.

Possible solutions

One solution preferred by some is to move the camera itself rather than to zoom in and out from static cameras. This solution is more suited to catching the energy and kinetic feel of dance, and it is often seen in work by Merce Cunningham in collaboration with directors like Charles Atlas and Eliot Caplin. It may not act as the perfect human eye, but it perhaps behaves more like one than do any alternative approaches. It still reduces the choices that the eyes of an audience in a theatre may have in what to watch – or what *not* to watch – but when combined with appropriate choices of effects, editing and cutting, it can give an enjoyable and fresh view of dance. For example, in the videodance *Outside In* (1994) featuring Candoco (with Margaret Williams as director and Victoria Marks as choreographer), the choice of changing locations, which works so well on film, is used to add interest for the viewer. The locations switch from green countryside to dark warehouse space. This is very much selecting what the audience sees, but it's a fair deal because it adds to the creative and imaginative impact of the final film. It also uses overhead shots in order to give greater insight into the differing qualities and ways of moving of the different performers. In this way, the director becomes almost like an additional choreographer, directing the viewer's eye in a very specific, organised way.

In adapting stage works to film, there may be more success to be found in looking for imaginative solutions which will *enhance* the original qualities rather than water them down. This may require subtle or drastic changes to the choreography in order for it to be better seen in a small-scale format. The art form of videodance is about creating new possibilities in how dance uses time, space and energy. It requires a different approach to the filming of dance, and could not operate in the way that a straightforward stage performance does. On the other hand, there may be some scope for imaginative adaptations of videodance to the theatre.

TASK FOUR

Using a dance which you have choreographed, think about how you might treat it in order to make a videodance. Remember, this is only a paper exercise, so let your imagination run away with you! Consider the possibilities of distorting a movement to enhance its inherent qualities and structures. What special effects and use of cameras would you choose? Which parts might be better shot in close-up, or in a long panning shot? Would you consider using any of the following: blurred shots; speeding up or slowing down; reversing the action; pauses; chopping up and rearranging movements into a different order from that in which they appeared in the original piece; overhead shots; upside-down shots; harsh cuts; moving cameras; the superimposing of one image over another; changing the accompaniment completely?

Problem: working with dancers

Dancers in rehearsal normally have to repeat many movements over and over again in order to improve the quality of execution, and so that the choreographer has a better idea of whether the dance is working or not. This repetitious and potentially injurious process is worsened by the addition of the demands of the camera operators and the film director, since there may be long gaps between shots when the dancers' muscles can cool down very quickly.

Solutions

There are various solutions to this problem, most of which require adequate preparation by the director in collaboration with the choreographer and the film team. In describing his approach to filming stage works, Bob Lockyer explains how he initially tries to remember his reactions on seeing the dance for the first time, before learning the dance and then, finally, writing it down. Clearly this is a time-consuming process, but a necessary one if dancers are to be spared endless repetitions and long waiting times. After such detailed preparations, Lockyer gives copies of the action plan to the camera operators and the vision mixer. Detailed lists of shots are made and given to the crew, so that after the dancers have done their usual warm-up, it's straight into the action. In this way, hopefully, excessive repetition may be avoided.

Problem: expense

The above detailed preparation can also help to keep down costs on what is already an expensive process. In *Dance Theatre Journal*, 1983, Bob Lockyer stated: 'Sadly, I can't seem to find, inside or outside the BBC, the money to make videodance.' Gladly, this situation seems to have improved, but budgets and funding remain a problem; and for a student, it must seem a problem of impossible proportions. Everyone seems to own some sort of camcorder these days, but producing a videodance is not always that simple. For the best results, more than one camera is needed – ideally, three at different angles and levels, and each of them with their own monitor so that shots can be seen clearly. On a low budget and with a single camera, there would have to be a great deal of imagination and skill in the treatment of the dance and its filming to make up for the lack of equipment.

The cutting and editing process is where much of the creativity and artistry of the art form lies, and access to editing suites may not be so easy to obtain, although recent technological developments in digital cameras and software are making production easier. Online access to video footage is also more available nowadays. Collaborating with students on media courses may be helpful here. Perhaps, making a joint assignment for a team of dancers, film crew and musicians might be exciting.

TASK FIVE

Information Technology and Working With Others

This is a lengthy task which will require scheduling over a whole term, as well as a close liaison between your teacher and people in other departments, if it is to be worth pursuing. The aim is to produce a four-to-five-minute-long videodance. It is important to discuss things together as a whole team – dancers, film crew and musicians – right from the start. Considerations about sound accompaniment, costumes and other physical settings should be looked at as early as possible in the project.

As a team, draw up a schedule to include rehearsal times, the shooting of the film, and the editing and final showing of the video. Using two or three outdoor locations (remember, you may need written permission for this) and a unifying theme, create small pieces of choreography for filming. As you work, allow the film crew to watch and to consider how they might video and edit the work in order to enhance the chosen theme. During the editing process, continue wherever possible to work as a team.

RECORDING DANCE – FINAL WORDS

Recording dance on film is an important part of creating an archive of dance for the future. Films and videos of dance for reconstruction can be most useful if the limitations and problems of such recordings are recognised. When supplemented with a notation score and dancer's memory, as full a record as is possible will result. If the aim of using a film/video record is to rework a new version of the original then it is a vital source of reference.

Videodance is an exciting art form with many possibilities. Try to watch out for new series and commissions on television. As a record of dance, if well directed, a videodance can add to our understanding of the original stage work by emphasising features such as the structure, dynamics and dancer's interpretation. As a stand-alone work it is a dance in its own right and may never have come from a live stage version. Thus it is *the* record of itself! In some cases the videodance can develop into a 'live' version. In turn this may have to be recorded for archive.

For the purposes of study a video library can be very helpful. After all, seeing the movement of the dance is a vital part of understanding it. Does your college library have a stock of dance videos and scores for you to study? If not perhaps a polite request to your teacher or librarian may help to start a collection.

TASK SIX

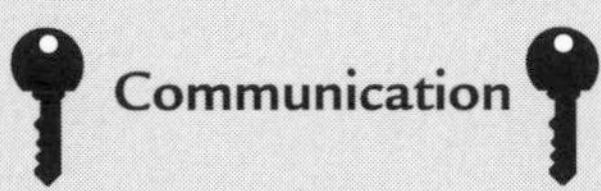

Select a video of a dance work by a choreographer whom you are studying. View it, or a five-minute extract of it, repeatedly and make notes as you watch to help you answer the questions below:

- Identify the full title, choreographer, date and company/dancers.
- Describe the content of the dance.
- Name the genre and any styles that are in use.
- Describe one main motif in terms of
  a) its constituent features and
  b) what the movement is expressing.
- Identify three choreographic devices and the form/structure.
- Explain what physical and interpretative skills the dancers need to perform this dance.
- Describe the feature of the physical setting and accompaniment.
- Give a brief evaluation of the success of the dance, considering any contextual factors which may be of influence.

Put your answers into a format that is suitable as a presentation to your group.

Present your findings to your group using a variety of types of presentation, including, for example, photos, demonstration, notation.

References and resources

BOOKS AND ARTICLES

Atlas, C., 'Filming Cunningham dance', *Dance Theatre Journal*, vol. 1, no. 1, 1983

Burnside, F., 'Television's summer of dance', *Dance Theatre Journal*, vol. 12, no. 2, 1995

Dancing Times, *Study Supplement 3 Reconstruction and Revival, Dancing Times*, LXXX 951, December 1989

Dunning, J., *Warning: Ephemeral but Private Property*, in *The New York Times*, July 27, 2000

de Marigny, C. and Rubidge, S. (conceived and devised), the 'Dance and television' issue, *Dance Theatre Journal*, vol. 6, no. 1, 1988

Hutchinson Guest A. UK Available from the Language of Dance Centre (see address below):

– *Your Move*, London: Gordon & Breach, 1995
– *Dancer's Glancer – a Quick Guide to Labanotation*, London: Gordon & Breach, 1992
– *A History of the Development of the Laban Notation System*, Cervera Press, 1995
– *Labanotation*, New York, 1977
Kipling Brown, A. and Parker, M., *Dance Notation for Beginners*, London: Dance Books, 1983 (a good guide to both Laban and Benesh Notation)
Lockyer, B., 'Dance on video – random thoughts', *Dance Theatre Journal*, vol. 1, no. 4, 1983
Mackrell, J., 'Dance to the music of time' in The *Guardian*, 29 April, 1996
Nagrin, D., in *Dance Theatre Journal*, 1988, vol. 6, no. 1
Partsch-Bergsohn, I., 'Laban: magic and science', *Dance Theatre Journal*, vol. 4, no. 3, 1986
Rubidge, S., 'Reconstruction and its problems', *Dance Theatre Journal*, vol. 12, no. 1, 1995
Wilford, J.N., 'In the Dawn of Society, Dance Was Centre Stage', in *The New York Times*, 27 February 2001

VIDEOS

www.britishcouncil.org.il The British Council have many videos of dance available for hire to institutions for an annual fee.

The videos listed below can be ordered online at: Dance Books www.dancebooks.co.uk

Other stockists include:

National Resource Centre for Dance
www.surrey.ac.uk/NRCD

www.arts-books.com

Videos listed alphabetically under surname of choreographer:

- Alvin Ailey: *For Bird with Love & Witness*; *Black Dance America*, includes work by Alvin Ailey among many.
- Merce Cunningham: *Changing Steps and Blue Studio: Five segments*. Two previews of video dance/second solo danced by Cunningham.
- Siobhan Davies: *Rushes*
- Mats Ek: *Sleeping Beauty* (2000); *Carmen*; *Giselle*.
- Martha Graham: *Five dances by Martha Graham*, includes *El Penitente*, *Diversion of Angels*, *Heriodiade*, *Steps in the Street*, *Maple Leaf Rag*.
- Kenneth MacMillan: *The Judas Tree* (1999), The Royal Ballet & Birmingham Royal Ballet; *Mayerling*, The Royal Ballet (1994); *Manon* The Australian Royal Ballet (produced by choreologist Monica Parker and Patricia Ruanne); *The Prince of Pagodas* – includes documentary extracts of MacMillan, *Gloria*, *Manon* & *Romeo and Juliet*; *Winter Dreams* (1993).
- Mark Murphy: *Where Angels Fear to Tread* (1996)
- Lloyd Newson, DV8: *Enter Achilles*; *Never Again*.
- *Paris Dances Diaghilev – Petrushka, Spectre de la rose, Faune, Les Noces*. Paris Opera Ballet, 1991.

Also see videos listed at the end of other chapters.

WEB SITES

www.bham.ac.uk/calaban - CALABAN (for p.c.s), available free.

www.benesh.org - The Benesh Institute, Benesh Notation Editor software.

www.balletabout.com - large list of relevant web sites, including sites to order MacBenesh software.

www.ballet.co.uk - dance companies.

www.dancefilmsassn.org - American dance films.

www.danceonvideo.com

www.ickl.org - International Council of Kinetography Laban/Labanotation.

www.laban.org - some interesting links here.

www.labanotation.institute - Labanwriter (for Applemacs) available here.

www.lodc.org - the Language of Dance Centre.

www.dancenotation.org - The Dance Notation Bureau.

www.preserve-inc.org - USA archive, but useful information on storing tapes, paper and photographic records.

www.rz.uni-frankfurt.de/~griesbec/LABAN - good full introduction. Some interesting links about applications of Labanotation.

EIGHT

Dance Today and Tomorrow

Photo: Chris Nash

In the UK and the Western world today, dance activity is rapidly expanding. New technologies, a concern for staying in touch with the past in order to *learn* from it and issues of dance provision are part of a pattern of growth. This chapter will focus on the following areas:

- computer technology;
- cross-cultural dance in society today;
- dance for all.

As a dance student, you may well be considering making dance a career, and it is important to be in touch with the ever-increasing possibilities that are available to you. The traditional options of stage school, West End musicals and performing are nowadays only one part of a much wider range of possibilities in dance careers. We see dance joining the other art forms as a grown-up. In this chapter, various options and considerations will be presented to you not only to help you pass the course which you are studying on at present, but also to support your decisions concerning where you might be heading afterwards.

Computer technology: new realities

The information superhighway is the communication medium of the future. Everywhere, this network spreads information as fast as you can think it up, from and to any part of the planet.

> The movement of information at approximately the speed of light has become by far the largest industry of the world.
>
> (*Marshall McLuhan in* Hot and Cool, *1968*)

Dance is closely involved with information and computer technologies. On the World Wide Web you can find all manner of information on the latest ideas in dance and cyberdance. On *The Electric Ballerina* site you can learn ballet. (All web site addresses are listed under Resources at the end of the chapter.) The DTZ: Dance Technology Zone site is packed with detail on research and instruction. There are also discussion groups and mailing lists where comment, ideas and information on workshops, conferences and performances are exchanged.

You can watch performances on various web sites. In 1997 *Bytes of Bryant Park* was a site-specific performance cybercast by Stephan Koplowitz in New York. The global online audience was invited to suggest movement based on a set of poses which could be downloaded. The poses could be pieced together with more detailed instructions, then posted to the dancers' web site. Script and poems could also be sent. The six-hour event connected the posted suggestions in improvisation with live video, aural commentary and interviews. After the show extracts of images and edited video were maintained on a site and are still available as a record of the work, or as a work in itself.

Computer technology can serve a variety of exciting purposes. You can choreograph on it, notate on it. With *virtual reality*, the flesh-and-blood human dance may even be a thing of the past! No need to put ourselves through all that agonising training and injury any more. Well, this may be an extreme view, but it is certainly a consideration. Preferences for the human presence may well still be the final choice over virtual reality.

The computer can be a tool but can also be the medium itself. Software packages such as *Life Forms* animate the human body and may make the physical presence of dancers no longer necessary. A free demonstration of *Life Forms* (developed by Thecla Schiphorst) can be obtained online. Merce Cunningham has been using it increasingly to choreograph with the aim to challenge the body's usual 'habits'. Here he describes his explorations with the software *Sequence Editor*:

> ... one can make up movements, put them in the memory, eventually have a phrase ... This can be examined from any angle ... certainly a boon for working with dance on camera ... On the computer the timing can be changed to see in slow motion how the body changes from one shape to another. Obviously it can produce shapes which are not available to humans, but as happened with the use of chance operations, followed by the use of camera on film and video, and now with the dance computer, I am aware once more of new possibilities with which to work.
>
> (*Merce Cunningham,* www.merce.org/technologylifeforms)

In this way he choreographed a commission for the Barbican, London (2000), *Biped*, which combined footage of virtual dancers on a front screen overlaid with digital footage of real dancers, whilst the dancers performed live behind the screen. It was described as:

> Like looking into a computer . . . The illusion of illusoriness is complete in their disembodied bodies, their fine-spun, precisely disconcerting dance, and yet they can also carry all sorts of metaphor – lost souls, massing sea birds, Giselle's Wilis, pixilated pixels.
>
> (*Ismene Brown in* The Electronic Telegraph, *October 2000*)

Using computers in this way Cunningham has produced innovative dance theatre, but it is the notion of *interactive* exchange which is the leading edge in this field.

> A basic definition of virtual reality is that it is the technology used to provide an intimate interaction between humans and computer imagery.
>
> (*Susan Kozel in* Dance Theatre Journal, *1994*)

The use of film as background is popular but putting dancers on stage with film footage does not involve the two 'interacting'. Connections are made in the minds of the viewers but not as a result of exchange in real time and space.

Using digital interactive technologies to devise and choreograph through computerised systems creates all manner of possiblities. The movement of dancers can trigger sound, light, projections, video footage. Perhaps the dancers' movement phrasing may control the sound so that the audience hear the dancers' musicality as well as see it. A performance by the company *Palindrome* allowed the audience to interact too. If they stood up they triggered the sound accompaniment. Sensory Systems or mini-video cameras attached to the dancer's body, or on the floor, can send signals to the lights, video and sound media.

In various experimental works, there seems to be a great potential for dance within this newest of human experiences. The 1994 conference at the ICA in London featured various works which used performers interacting in technological environments. The computer-generated information affects the performance space and the bodies performing in it. In the words of the critic Susan Kozel quoted above, the virtual reality as seen by the audience takes 'inspiration from physical experience to create new reality from art'. So, as the two dancers in *Chemical Wedding by Blast Theory* (1992), suspended above the heads of the audience, communicate by means of a video camera, new realities are presented. Or as Orlan, in *The Reincarnation of St. Orlan* (1994), transmits by video the painful transformations of her plastic surgery, the dilemma felt by dancers in training is expressed: dance is painful and yet at the same time uplifting. It attempts to control, and yet also always involves a *loss* of control. There is a moment where the inner self reaches out into the general space. In the words of the artists: 'in cyberspace we are choreographing experience . . . the interaction between people and computers as a sort of choreography' (Susan Kozel in *Dance Theatre Journal*, 1994).

The *Dance Umbrella* festival focused on dance and its interaction with computer technologies for the first time in 2000. One interactive installation which attracted attention was Thecla Schiphorst's *Body maps: artifacts of mortality, interfacing through and into the self*, originally made in 1996. The audience entered a dark room where a projection of a sleeping woman was seen over a white table. They were invited to interact with the virtual body. As with all dance it is subject to evaluation. One critic was apparently unimpressed by the range of responses that the image could express:

> Since the reaction of the woman does not include leaping up to slap the face of the male critic whom I saw place a hand on her virtual bottom, I lost belief after two minutes.
>
> (*Ismene Brown in* The Electronic Telegraph, *November 2000*)

Dance and dance training involve non-verbal knowledge and understandings. During training, rehearsal and performance dancers connect body to mind in order to improve technically and expressively. In virtual interactive performance the body and mind may be focused in a similar way. The computer technology is another non-verbal way of knowing. Many may consider disembodied dance as a threat to dance as an art form, but others see it as a way of discovering a deeper understanding of, and higher regard for, the body as it sits in the context of a post-modern society. Furthermore such interactive work assures a physical presence (however virtual) and may be regarded as essential to ensuring that technologies of the future serve human need and do not dictate social conditions.

> Multi-media computer research moves beyond the basic audio-visual framework by introducing two major elements: gesture and interactivity. When this train of scientific thought is combined with the frequently stated claim that researchers in computers and artificial intelligence look to the arts to provide impetus for new developments in virtual technologies, there is open invitation for dance to take the stage.
>
> (*Susan Kozel in* Dance Theatre Journal, *1995*)

What are your basic information technology skills like? It may be worth your while exploring and investigating a future in the Internet. The possibilities in *multi-media* work for performance and study are ever-increasing. Software offers the chance to combine text, graphics, sound, animation and video to create multi-media CD-ROMs. Clearly, the learning and performance potential here is enormous. A project by dancer and choreographer William Forsythe presents a CD-ROM containing categories of: Labanotation and composition; anatomical exercises; isometrics. Forsythe demonstrates about 100 short lessons, and shows some dancers from the Frankfurt Ballet rehearsing and performing his choreography for *Self Meant to Govern* (1995). The viewer can click back and forth, interacting with the screen, and so change the viewing angle, gain a close-up or distance shot, and of course switch between lessons. The research team which Forsythe worked with is called ZKM. They regard the project to be the creation of a 'digital dance school'.

COMPUTER TECHNOLOGY – CONCLUSION

These new computer technologies are only as much value to dance as we care to make them. There is much discussion around the issues related to dance and technology. Information on dance has always been available through writing, film and notation across the ages, and CD-ROM is a development of this. But if we are to take responsibility for putting dance on the global map of the future and making it count in people's lives, then we have to increase research and involvement. Computer technology is part of the future for dance.

Cross-cultural dance in society today: the 'global village'

The history of ballet goes back over centuries. In non-Western societies, many forms of traditional dance have similarly existed over centuries. At the beginning of the twentieth century, the revolution and rebellion of modern dance shook the world of dance. As global travel and communication have increased, and as populations have migrated, a melting-pot of dance and music, in fact of all the arts, has been the result.

> Cultural theorists now argue that national identities are not fixed but are in a constant state of flux.
>
> (*Sarah Rubidge in* Dance Theatre Journal, *1995*)

There is a new world order, and with it a new arrangement of cultural and political contexts. It is important to note that although the cross-cultural exchange process may be accelerated by new technologies and more and faster travel it is in fact nothing new:

> ... no story belongs to any one culture. What is interesting is to see the transformations that take place in various cultures. Take Romeo and Juliet for example. It originates as a kernel of a story in Arabia amongst the Moslems. It travels to Italy, becomes a novel, a searing romance, and then it becomes an English play, a classic.
>
> (*Jatinder Verma in* Dance Theatre Journal, *1992*)

Of course it also travelled again, this time across the Atlantic, to become one of the best-known musicals of all time, *West Side Story*. Even what may feel to be essentially English morris dance is traceable back to Moorish traditions from Africa via southern Spain.

In an article by Roger Copeland (*Dance Theatre Journal*, 1992), surprise was expressed by an African scholar, Robert Farris Thompson, when an African villager told him that the dance he was performing had been learnt from a Michael Jackson performance on MTV. Fluency and frequency of exchange has accelerated over the last 30 years. The global village was a concept thought up originally by Marshall McLuhan in 1968.

> Today the globe has shrunk in the wash with speeded-up information movement from all directions. We have, as it were, come to live in a global village ... on one hand a community of learning, and at the same time, with regard to the tightness of its inter-relationships, the globe has become a tiny village.
>
> (*Marshall McLuhan in* Hot and Cool, *1968*)

During the twentieth century the identity of British Dance was shaped by waves of immigrant influences: Russians in classical ballet; American enrichment of contemporary dance; and non-western cultures. Japanese *butoh* was first seen in Britain in the 1970s. Its intense exploration of the dark side of the soul now influences and inspires much new work. Butoh itself evolved in Japan in the 1950s. Back then its blend of Western contemporary dance with the Japanese classical traditions of noh and Kabuki was regarded as avant garde. In a perverse way it strived to reassert authentic national identity in Japan after the Second World War. Often such synthesis of two opposing genres can produce very stimulating work and push forward the boundaries of dance.

The Arts Council of England has been active in encouraging such cross-cultural work in dance. Choreographers like Shobana Jeyasingh - as already mentioned - experiment and explore the mixing of Western dance and traditional South Asian *Bharatha Natyam* dance.

Her early 1980 performances attempted to increase audience numbers for *Bharatha Natyam* but lacked new ways to present it. Only when she began to collaborate with Western composers, within strict Indian rhythmic structures, did her work start to evolve in new directions. Her style is a product of life in Britain in the late twentieth century. Her performing theatre work is extended by a programme of outreach and educational work as typified by *Home Patch* (2001), a project designed to develop access for young British Asians (especially woman) to her work. From the project a dance which explores ideas of identity and culture toured five UK cities.

In 1992 the director of The Place Theatre, London introduced a new season called *Vivarta.* This focused on choreographers working in India who were experimenting with their choreography so that it was not wholly in the classical traditions of Indian dance. A similar season featuring Chinese modern dance followed in 1995. Entitled *Re:Orient,* it included works by artists from China, Hong Kong, Taiwan, the UK and the USA. The following review of the *Spring Loaded 1994* season gives a flavour of what was on offer. It is describing the Nina Rajarani Company in *Kalpa Virksh*:

> In terms of visual effects, the piece offers an interesting fusion of cultures. While the movement is drawn from South Asian dance, all three dancers are white, and the costume, while broadly drawn on classical lines would not look out of place on the club scene ... makes effective and original treatment of British Asian culture.
>
> (*Uzma-Hameed in* Dance Theatre Journal, *1994*)

The fusion of two or more cultures in dance is not an easy task. There are bound to be some less successful attempts. Hameed, in the same article, points out that in another piece, *Golden Chains*, the claim to be 'progressive Indian dance' was not really justified. It lacked any depth of treatment in the narrative of the position of Asian women in society today:

> ... the plot lends itself more to a Hindi film style melodrama rather than to the deconstruction of stereotypes and the highlighting of cultural issues.
>
> (*Uzma-Hameed in* Dance Theatre Journal, *1994*)

Similarly, the performance by the Australian Bangarra Dance Theatre in the UK in 1994 threw up problems of fusing traditional and modern movement and ideas. Sarah Rubidge noted that the choreography of director Steven Page was a mismatch of the groundedness of Aboriginal movement with the modern dance style. Page himself was aware of the shortcomings of the attempted cross-cultural exchange, and remarked:

> Next piece. No split leaps, no pirouettes, no attitudes!
>
> (*Steven Page in* Dance Theatre Journal, *Rubidge, S. 1994*)

Rubidge suggests that he may have more success using a more 'released' style of post-modern dance. This would offer a more sympathetic context in which to place the traditional Aboriginal intensely concentrated face and body by using the natural body weight and generating energy from the centre of gravity – framing the traditional in a post-modern, anatomical-release style.

The post-modern values in society at large place dancers, and indeed all artists, in a situation where their traditional art forms and values are no longer solely enough to support their work. In the above-mentioned *Re:Orient* season, dance from oriental cultures was seen alongside the work of artists from the same cultural backgrounds but living in the West. The traditional style of Chinese dance was clearly evident – for example, in the use of props like fans, scarves and drums – but was mixed with other more Western influences. In the work of Taiwanese Ming-She Ku, release techniques and contact improvisation, which she had been introduced to during a stay in the USA, were both used.

From this point of view, there needs to be a long hard look at traditions which are openly resistant.

> ... the 'No Trespassing' disclaimer is unmasked as cowardice or imperialism of the most arrogant.
>
> (*Dwight Conquergood in* Performing as a Moral Act, *as quoted in* Dance Theatre Journal, *in Copeland, R. 1992*)

The alternative is to allow cross-fertilisation with ballet, modern African people's Asian and Pacific genres as part of a natural growth pattern. This process reflects the different cultural backgrounds of choreographers, directors and dancers alike. There seems little point in pursuing what may easily be misconstrued as a rather élitist direction if exclusion is the policy. On the other hand, it must be done thoughtfully and deliberately, and not in a manner as described in the following account:

> (To) gain artistic acknowledgement of their work ... some companies, in their frantic pursuit of acceptance, abandoned identification with their Black heritage and history, aspiring to be contemporary dancers who just happened to be black.
>
> (*David Bryan, in* Advancing Black Dancing, *as quoted by Peter Budejo*, Dance Theatre Journal, *1993*)

George Dzikunu's work in the UK from 1984 blends his Ghanaian performing arts experience with aspects of living in Britain. He founded Adzido Pan African Dance Ensemble and aims to promote traditional culture. Their programme *Chesa Chesa* (2000) depicts the clash of traditional African and Western worlds. Similarly work by companies such as Badejo, RJC and Union Dance Company generates work which examines, celebrates and blends cultural concepts and movement styles. These companies often have a strong community focus in their activities integrating provision of programmes for youth and community into their theatre and professional work.

In the ballet world, mention has already been made of modern versions of the classics. Royal Ballet-trained Jonathan Burrows is interested in finding new directions for classical ballet. Burrows describes his working in the show *Our* (1994), combining the use of low and high weight (which he associates with classical ballet) in the body. He states:

> In a sense those are the skills of the next generation of dancers ... I have no argu-

> ment with classical ballet . . . it has a three hundred year history. It's more like a martial art in that each subsequent dancing master has taken it and developed it, it's grown very humanly.
>
> (*Jonathan Burrows, in* Dance Theatre Journal, *Marigny C. de 1994*)

From his point of view, the repetitious nature of training undertaken by a classical dancer results in an ability to move with great freedom and openness. It is this that he sees as the classical style. Burrows sees himself as being on a creative continuum within this style, but without being restricted by the classical compositional structures.

> I would rather wrestle with the clichés of ballet than wrestle with the clichés and mannerisms of contemporary dance . . . it's horrible when an idea becomes a habit.
>
> (*Jonathan Burrows, in* Dance Theatre Journal, *Marigny C. de 1994*)

Burrows is concerned with *humanness* in dance, and this is of course a concern which many dance cultures have as a focus in one way or another. But as the heat of the cultural melting-pot intensifies one may ask how much longer can classical ballet as a genre continue before it transforms itself into something unrecognisable as 'ballet'? As it mixes more and more with modern, post-modern and non-western genres what will remain? Will the classics survive, and if so how should we 'read' them? Should ballet be redefined as a highly effective method of dance training? In 1987 critic Alastair Macaulay wrote about this question and ten years later returns to the subject:

> . . . wondering if the plant of classicism is dying?
>
> (*In* Dance Theatre Journal, *1997*)

In 1996 and 1997 the Royal Festival Hall Performing Arts Education organised a programme which included practical workshops and presentations exploring many aspects of classicism. One such was the issue of whether it is a fixed concept or one which evolves and renews itself in mutant forms that may be difficult to pinpoint.

Choreographer Mark Baldwin's recent *Ihi Frenzy* (2001) for the Royal New Zealand Ballet asks such a question. Weaving a mix of genres and styles its concern is that 'these metaphors in dance are reinvented for our modern times' (Mark Baldwin in programme note). The ballet, jazz and contemporary genres stand clearly, but nuances of genres of other cultures, namely Maori and Pacific as well as styles of other decades, are just as resonant.

Other European dance styles such as the expressionist legacies of Kurt Jooss, Mary Wigman and Hilde Holger are being reevaluated and realigned to play a more prominent role in the British Dance scene. In 1991 Hilde Holger reconstructed four of her early solos for dancer Liz Aggiss. One such, *Die Forelle* (1923), is an expression of deep inner feelings and is consciously informed by the work of Freud. In Aggiss's own work, as co-founder with Billy Cowie of the company *Divas,* the roots of European expressionism are retained and reworked for a new era.

In the dance world some old values are being preserved through consideration and reflection on the new; others are being transformed and reinvented.

'The ADZIDO Pan African Dance Ensemble'. Photo by HUGO Glendinning.

CROSS-CULTURAL DANCE – A CONCLUSION

The distinction between 'traditional' and 'modern' cultures is these days a tricky one. Some dance genres may try to cling onto their pure traditions, but the writing is on the wall. Traditions will undergo metamorphosis. Like the egg, larva and caterpillar, in the end they are all parts of the butterfly. Western and non-Western cultures are all undergoing change. You may be a tourist in West Africa watching a traditional dance, and it may be upsetting to notice that the dancers are wearing Ray Bans and Reeboks. Too bad! These performers, like you, live in the global village and are not museum exhibits. All traditions are undergoing an alchemical process in the melting-pot.

> It thus becomes apparent that the real East/West contrast isn't 'tradition *or* change' but rather 'continuity *and* change'. *All* traditions evolve, albeit not at the same pace.
>
> (*Roger Copeland in* Dance Theatre Journal, *1992*)

Evolution of dance genres and styles may occur in one, or as combinations, of the following: the movement itself; the type of dancers; the content; aspects of the physical/aural setting; the form; the contextual references.

It is vital, during such a complex exchange process, that the quality of the work be preserved. It is also vital that, whenever possible, the exchange be a *two-way* process which results in something new and not a mere copy or a fashionable pick 'n' mix .

When Denni Sayers reported on her 1992 visit to the Philippines she described (*Dance Theatre Journal*, 1992) how a peformance combined narrative form, contemporary movement style, local folk dance and a local reggae band. It expressed the struggle of the people in their poverty and oppression. The resistance of the people grew stronger as the dance progressed and finally broke into a triumphant local dance. The 2,000 strong local audience cheered in recognition. Sayers, reflecting on her visit, reminds us that:

> We as dancers and choreographers have so much to give, and we can learn from these extraordinary artists about the value of our craft in this constantly developing world.

TASK ONE

Information Technology and Communication

In groups of four or five, choose one of the statements/questions below and construct a 10-minute presentation which can be given to the rest of the group. Wherever possible, use examples of companies and performances that you have seen or know about from research. If possible, use publicity and other visual materials to illustrate your ideas.

1. Consider the role of African traditional dance or contemporary reworkings of African traditional dance in the UK.
2. How far can ballet address present concerns without losing the distinctive characteristics of its genre?
3. Ballet-trained choreographers make barefoot dances, and the influence of African and Indian dance is to be seen in post-modern dance. What is characteristic of post-modern dance today?
4. How might the dance of Indian dance artists develop in the UK today?

Dance for all

You may have had dance lessons at school before you started your A2 or AS Level, AVCE or GNVQ studies, and these may have been accompanied by lessons out of school time at a private dancing school. The fact that dance became part of the National Curriculum in 1992 is a fair measure of the progress it has made in the UK education system. This section will examine issues of how some of the gaps in provision of dance are being filled. You should feel free to take away and discuss these issues with dancers, non-dancers, parents, friends – in fact, anyone whose ear you can bend!

Unfortunately, dance is only optional at secondary level. The National Curriculum Council recommended this because it had been 'persuaded by agony stories from schools about boys having to do dance when they don't want to' (*Times Educational Supplement*, 1992). It seems that dance, to some educationalists, is only important for the younger age group, and then only for the girls! A strange sort of logic in the age of gender awareness, I hear you say. Of course, I would agree with you. One of the most disappointing aspects of my years of involvement with dance and education is the sexist treatment of it as an art form or as a subject on a curriculum. Such prejudices and opinions about the status of boys are quite unacceptable, and all students must be made aware of restricting traditional views of maleness and masculinity. How many boys are in your class? How much longer are females expected to endure living in a world which has its base in a chauvinistic value system? Where are the post-modern values that you have read so much about in this book? What are you doing to reinforce them in your day-to-day encounters? Remember, if you're not part of the solution, you are part of the problem. To give you some ammunition for your assault on the college football team, here are a few fascinating facts:

- The Physical Education Working Group that was appointed to name which activities were to be included in the National Curriculum did a great deal of thorough research, and decided that:

  > ... a broad and balanced programme of Physical Education, sensitively delivered, can help to extend boys' restricted perception of masculinity and masculine behaviour.
  >
  > (*P.E. Working group report National Curriculum Council*)

- 'Real men wear tights!' and 'Male dancers are happy to be hunky!' (in *The Sunday Express*, 2 February 1992).
- The wearing of tights is not compulsory, and reflecting on various forms of street dance and dance from other cultures – such as Banghra – it seems clear that dance *can* carry masculine value and status.
- Pre-industrial revolution, it was the role of *men* to lead the dancing in the community. Similarly, in ancient Greek and classical culture, a soldier was expected to be a good dancer also. Much of this is lost in the UK today. It seems that as people left the land to work in the towns, they left their culture of song, dance and story-telling behind. This happened alongside the growth in ballet of the importance of the ballerina and the lowering of the status of the male dancer. The outcome was the attachment of *effeminate* images to male dancers. This totally unjustified image remains ever strong today.

So, a tricky situation for the dance world to address.

> ... to what extent can man's achievements in dance be celebrated without at the same time reasserting male dominance and thus reinforcing the imbalance of power between men and women in our society?
>
> (*Ramsay Burt in* The Male Dancer: Bodies, Spectacles, Sexualities, *1995*)

If you do promote dance to male students, are you able to do so without using male-dominated values? If not, dance may become a mere spectacle of athletic prowess within such a value system, one which overlooks the other sensitive lyrical side of dance and human nature in case it implies that the dancer is homosexual. Often, the image of the male dancer is one of muscularity and body beautiful. These images only serve to reinforce the very male-dominated stereotypes which we are trying to avoid. In modern dance, 'men are men and women are women', like in any good Western film. In this way, the value system is the same as that for classical ballet. We only have to look at the works of Martha Graham and her followers to notice this. In many of her works, for example *Appalachian Spring* (1944), the norm for the male roles is one of strength, with high jumps and the like. It is interesting to note that in the early years of modern dance, the pioneers were women. Since then, as modern dance has become accepted and mainstream, dance-company directors and choreographers are men. Indeed, the women seem to be their own worst enemies in this matter. They have given away the power bases of whole companies from women as the founders to a complete succession of male directors.

The problem is not entirely solved in post-modern work either. The androgyny of The Cunningham Company conveniently ignores the gender issue. The high-powered hype and aggression in some contact improvisation reinforces a male-dominated social norm. What is necessary is to be aware of these values and to deconstruct them thoughtfully in order to produce reasoned alternative options.

Current work by such choreographers as Lea Anderson, Lloyd Newson, Matthew Bourne, the Europeans Pina Bausch and De Keersmaeker, and the American Mark Morris offer audiences such options. Just as Anderson is at pains not to show women being 'beaten up', she is also concerned with revealing the feminine side of men as acceptable. This is particularly noticeable in the Featherstonehaughs' *The Bends* (1994) which 'explores the role of men in isolation' (programme note, 1994). The dancers parody a number of fast-moving images, from tough commando Action Man-type soldiers through to the wearing of feather boas and the carrying-out of domestic chores.

In *Swan Lake* by Matthew Bourne (1995), the swans in Act Two are played by a corps de

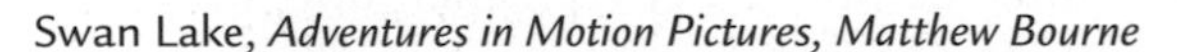

Swan Lake, *Adventures in Motion Pictures, Matthew Bourne*

ballet of men, beautiful dancers with soft curving lines as well as tensile strength. This strategy reinforces a more balanced view of maleness, and allows the narrative of the ballet to be told through the eyes of the Prince.

> When the torsos are bare and male, the arms are powerfully muscled and the tutus replaced by ruffled feather breeches, the effect is both peculiar and mysterious. ... These are dangerous feral creatures. ... After the second half I was snuffling into my handkerchief – which is more than I do at the Royal Ballet's or ENB's *Swan Lake* .. . Not bad for a small contemporary dance group with a daft name.
>
> (*Jan Parry in* Dance Now, *vol 4, no 4, winter 1995*)

> When people ask me what the themes of our work are I always resist, because I feel they are often trying to reduce it. Sexual politics, what's sexual politics? If you are talking about homosexuality what you mean is equality, you know, human equality. But the Royal Ballet is about sexual politics. I mean, when you see *Swan Lake* it's all sexual politics, they just don't call it that. It depends on how you view it. And to me too many critics want to categorise. ... In order to analyse it's often reduced, the issues are reduced, not expounded. And obviously being gay, the issue is oppression ... and conformity.
>
> (*Lloyd Newson, in* Dance Theatre Journal, *1993*)

The gender controversy has been raised in many films. *Turning Point* (1977) starred dancer Mikhail Baryshnikov as Yuri, a Russian defector to the USA. In the film a character comments, 'Yuri is going to make it more respectable for American boys to dance'. Twenty-three years later in *Billy Elliott* (set in 1984) the battle is still going on, although perhaps there has been some progress and it is possible that more males are dancing these days, but the social pressures and prejudices still exist. While some street dance, such as hip-hop, offer a niche of respect for male dance, the question is whether there is much transference of positive values between genres?

It is a matter not of forcing boys to do dance classes but of allowing them to relax and feel safe to enjoy movement as expression, for its own sake. It is an issue which all teachers and students need to grasp and feel able to speak up about. Otherwise, if it is swept under the carpet, how will things ever change? When will a balance ever be struck?

The work of such companies as Green Candle, Motionhouse and CandoCo has done much to provide opportunities to dance for all. A contact-improvisation and release workshop being taught to an *integrated group* (that is one consisting of dancers with and without disabilities) is well documented on the video *Different Dancers, Similar Motion* (1989). It shows work done on a residency over a fortnight in Oxford with integrated groups of adults and youth, and it demonstrates:

- how people can learn to overcome ignorance, anxieties, prejudices and inexperience through constructively led workshops;
- how some forms of movement, such as contact improvisation, are especially suitable for integrated workshops;
- how everyone can value everyone's role in the workshop;
- how people can learn to respect different rhythms, energies and styles of movement in one another.

(*From the sleeve notes for the video,* Different Dancers, Similar Motion, *1989*)

Such techniques as contact improvisation and release work have allowed far greater access to dance for those with learning difficulties, but there is a strong body of opinion that it should not end there: i.e. that dancers with disabilities should be encouraged, where appropriate, to attend other technique classes, say for ballet, in order to articulate arm and hand gestures. There may be many technique classes which could be adapted for the benefit of certain individuals, and training programmes could be made more flexible to accommodate such personalisations.

> It is not just steps up to the studio that prevent dancers with disabilities training; it is the lack of teachers who know what they're doing when you get there.
>
> (*David Toole in* CandoCo programme notes)

These values are becoming more and more a part of the whole dance picture, including the integration of dancers with disabilities into dance education. At Coventry University Performing Arts, a partnership has been struck up with the integrated dance company CandoCo to establish the first course which runs through further and higher education. It allows students both with and without disabilities to study together on a BA Hons Degree in Dance. The Laban Centre also reserves places on its Community Course for students with disabilities.

Celeste Dandeker was a dancer with London Contemporary Dance Theatre. Her career was ended when she broke her neck on stage. She now dances with CandoCo and uses a wheelchair, which may be seen as a drawback, to *advantage*:

> You have to remember that you've got a high-tech piece of equipment under you,

CandoCo Dance Company

> if you're in one of our chairs. It's very mobile, very light and can move incredibly fast.
>
> (*Celeste Dandeker in* Dance Theatre Journal, *1992*)

CandoCo's work is based on confronting the élitism of a dance world where only perfect bodies matter. In an article by Adam Benjamin, joint artistic director of CandoCo, the point is made that if disabled and non-disabled people are encouraged to study dance together, there is a chance to develop much more the possibilities of employment and research, as well as other opportunities generally, for the disabled dancer. He reflects on problems that will have to be solved, and on lessons that should be learnt from dance history:

> ... the lessons we learn therefore will be more than academic; they will have an impact not only on dance as an art form, but on the way we perceive, treat and respect each other as human beings. Surely this in the end is the test of a vital, effective and truly contemporary art form.
>
> (*Adam Benjamin in* Dance Theatre Journal, *1995*)

Another issue of interest to many is that of age and dance. No longer is it considered necessary to be a bright young thing to qualify as a dancer. Fergus Early's *Tales From The Citadel* (1996) for his Green Candle dance company was devised and performed by older dancers including Jane Dudley who was a soloist with Martha Graham, 1936–46. Early founded Green Candle in 1987 basing it on his belief that '... everyone has a birthright to communicate, express themselves and enjoy themselves through dance.'

Similarly *From Here To Maturity Dance Company* developed from a mature dancer's day which was part of the South Bank's 1999 Blitz Festival. Their performance of *Legs To*

Tales From The Citadel, *Green Candle, 1996. Jane Dudley seated centre*

Stand On included dancers such as Lucy Burge (danced with Ballet Rambert 1970–85) and their director Ann Dickie who returned to the stage after a double hip replacement. All the dancers were between 40 and 54 years old. In previous times the dance world would have regarded such dancers as retired, but now we recognise the wealth of physical intellect that they hold as interesting and important.

In Lloyd Newson's *Bound To Please*, Diana Payne-Myers, at 70 years of age, performed naked. Newson remarks:

> ... for me was infinitely more beautiful than seeing a gorgeous tall Swiss blond do a perfect arabesque – because it is the context and meaning that makes something beautiful and touching. Beauty is the breadth of human experience – the struggle can also be beautiful. And so much of dance is to deny the struggle.
>
> (*Lloyd Newson in interview with Jo Butterworth, 1998*)

When we see and make dance we need to bear in mind such developments. Perhaps for too long dance has lived in a Ken and Barbie world. No longer is the only value how many pirouettes you can do. Like the other arts dance can examine the real world in all its light and shade. Dancers and choreographers must be encouraged to use their minds as well as their bodies.

Integral to this is the value that we place on the knowledge and experience that mature dancers possess. When Russian classically trained dancer Mikhail Baryshnikov defected to the USA in 1971 he didn't change only his nationality. In 1989 he founded a dance company, The Whiteoak Dance Project, and he defected to the post-modern genre. In 2000 he presented PASTForward, a retrospective of 1960s post-modern dance. He performed a dance by Steve Paxton (*Flat*, 1964) which was minimal in style comprising little more than walking, dressing and undressing. As such it challenged audiences in 2000 as much as it did 40 years earlier.

The issues are many and complex, and highlight those covered in the chapters of this book. PASTForward allowed audiences to see a piece of dance history, little of which had been recorded, which would have been lost for the future. The 1960s was a time of anti-dance politics, of which Steve Reich (composer) once said: 'One would go to a dance performance where nobody danced, followed by a party where every one danced.' Baryshnikov found this style deeply interesting. He exchanged his previous training, where technique and projection were everything, for the simplest movements possible, performed with an inward, intimate style. However, what he carries implanted in his 53-year-old muscles is a visceral depth of knowledge and dance experience that prompts critics to note:

> ... although the musculature of his small, squarish frame is less glossy than it once was, his body moves with a sinewy intelligence that can be as mesmerising as his youthful pyrotechnics were.
>
> (*Judith Mackrell in* 'Some people think it's not dance. But they're learning', *The Guardian, August 2001*)

It is this deepest physical integrity of a dancer in performance which offers dance today a future of great promise and excitement.

Conclusion

Perhaps after your studies you may choose to pursue a career in something completely different from dance, keeping it as a life-enhancing interest. Remembering the pleasure, challenges and value it gave you, you could still be part of the growing supporters of dance for the future. The dance world needs dancing dentists, accountants, health workers and, most of all, politicians! Peter Brinson, the famous dance educator, commented that the dance world:

> ... doesn't pay half enough attention to the powers and the politics which have sustained it, or cast it down, throughout history.
>
> (*Peter Brinson in* Dance as Education: Towards a National Dance Culture, *1991*)

The story of dance is still being written and choreographed, and you as a student of dance are a part of it, walking backwards into the future. Your own contribution to making dance a part of a truly human world is as important, unique and vital as anyone's.

References and resources

BOOKS AND ARTICLES

Beal, R. and Berryman Miller, S. (eds), *Dance for Older Adults* USA: NDA/AAHPERD, 1988

Brinson, P., *Dance as Education: Towards a National Dance Culture*, London: Falmer Press, 1991

Foster S.L. (ed), *Choreographing History*, How the body is presented as political, aesthetic and physical objects. Indiana Univ. Press, 1995

Green Candle Dance Company, *Growing Bolder*, a start-up guide to creating dance with older people, 1997

McLuhan, M., *Hot and Cool*, Harmondsworth: Penguin, 1968

Roberts, H (ed.), 'Black dance in the UK' Guildford: National Resource Centre for Dance, 2000.

Publications from Arts Council of England:

Clarke, G. and Gibson, R., *Independent Dance Sector, Review and Report*, 1998

Jarrett-Macaulay, D., *Review of South Asian dance in England*, 1997

McIntosh, H., Yates, L. and McDonald, C., *Time for a Change: a framework for the development of African People's dance forms*, 2000

From the *Dance Theatre Journal*:

Benjamin, A., 'Unfound movement', vol. 12, no. 1, 1995

Bryan, D., and Badejo, P., *What is Black Dance in Britain?*, vol. 10, no. 4, 1993

Alexandra Carter's Review of *The Male Dancer*, by Ramsay Burt, vol. 12, no. 2, 1995

Copeland, R., *The Black Swan and the Dervishes – Cross-Cultural Approaches*, vol. 9, no. 4, 1992

Dandeker, C., vol. 10, no. 1, 1992

de Marigny, C., *Johnathan Burrows*, vol. 11, no. 2, 1994

Hameed, U., *Spring Loaded*, vol. 11, no. 2, 1994

Kozel, S., *Virtual Reality*, vol. 11, no. 2, 1994

Kozel, S., *Spacemaking: experience of a virtual body*, vol. 11, no. 3, 1995

Kozel, S., *Reshaping Space: focusing time*, vol. 12, no. 2, 1995

Macaulay, A., *Notes on Classicism*, vol. 5, no. 2, 1987

Macaulay, A., *Further Notes on Classicism*, vol. 13, no. 3, 1997

Lloyd Newson on MSM, vol. 10, no. 4, 1993

Rubidge, S., *Aborigine Dreams*, vol. 11, no. 2, 1994

Rubidge, S., *Cultural identity and the new aesthetic*, vol. 12, no. 3, 1995

Rubidge, S., and Verma, J., *Cross Cultural Theatre*, vol 10, no. 1, 1992

Sayers, D., *Dance in the Philippines*, vol. 9, no. 4, 1992

Semple, M., *African Dance Adzido*, vol. 10, no. 4, 1992

Siddall, J., 'Fair play: the debate about dance and the National Curriculum', vol. 9, no. 4, 1992

VIDEOS

From NRCD www.surrey.ac.uk/NRCD

Adzido Pan African Dance Ensemble *Coming Home* (*Dzikunu*, 1988)

From www.greencandledance.com

Tales from the Citadel, Fergus Early, 1996

The Road Home, Fergus Early, 1992

From The Video Place, email thevideoplace@theplace.dircon.co.uk

Spring Re-loaded Seasons.

WEB SITE ADDRESSES

General information

www.artscouncil.org.uk/futurealert/

Foundation of Community Dance – www.communitydance.org.uk

National Dance Teachers Association – www.ndta.org.uk

www.dancer.com/dance-links

www.theplace.org.uk

www.balletcompanies.com

www.ascendance.web.co.uk

www.dancenorthwest.org.uk

www.url.co.nz/arts/dance

Royal Festival Hall – www.rfh.org.uk

The South Bank – www.sbc.org.uk

Companies

www.adzido.co.uk

For Badejo Dance Company – www.sussex dance.co.uk

For company profiles e.g. CandoCo, Jeyasingh, RJC: www.britishcouncil.org/arts/theatredance/companies

Newspapers

www.sunday-times.co.uk

Digital artists/interactive sites

www.art.net/~dtz – Thecla Schiphorst

www.bigroom.co.uk

www.credo-interactive.com – Life-Forms

www.danceonline.com/video

www.frankfurt-ballett.de/billycd. – CDRom Improvisation, William Forsythe

www.nuttysites.com – dancing cats, penguins, dogs, fish

www.ourworld.compuserve.com/palindrome – interactive technologies for performance

www.randomdance.org – Wayne McGregor

www.riverbed.com – Paul Kaiser and Shelley Eshkar

www.sartorimedia.com/hands-on – interactive dance making

www.webbedfeats.org

www.webdances.com – Richard Lord

The Electric Ballerina: www.novia.net/~jlw/electric

GLOSSARY

Abduction movement away from the midline of the body.

Abstraction process of reducing something to its most basic form.

Acetabulum cup-shaped cavity of the pelvic bone, in which the head of the femur bone sits.

Adduction movement towards the midline of the body.

Accelerando gradual increase of tempo or speed.

Accent stress on a beat or movement.

Actions the six dance skills of travel, turn, jump, stillness, gesture and fall.

Aerobic exercise which uses oxygen and develops cardiovascular (of the heart) endurance.

Agonist the muscle or muscle group that is contracting.

Alignment proper posture as near to a straight line as possible from head to toe when standing.

Anacrusis an up-beat before the main accent at the start of a phrase; equivalent in movement is a preparatory motion.

Antagonistic muscle the muscle or muscle group in opposition to the agonist (contracting) muscle.

Anterior sited in the front part.

Articulation the meeting point of bones forming a joint.

Assemblé a jump when one leg lifts as one foot brushes off floor, take-off from supporting leg. Land on both feet in fifth position.

Asymmetric uneven in space, time or dynamics.

Atrophy tissue wasting away.

Augmentation increase in the time a movement or sound takes up.

Ballet a highly stylised technique of dance which originated in Europe in the seventeenth century.

Ballistic stretch achieved by bouncing (not generally recommended).

Bar a vertical line that divides one bar of music from another.

Battement the free leg gestures forwards, back or sideways with a downward accent. Petit battement is small, leg only just off floor. Grand battement is large, leg raises to medium level.

Beat the underlying regular pulse of movement or music.

Binary a two part form in composition, AB.

Body image the picture in one's mind of one's own body.

Brush a leg lifts with foot brushing along floor with an upward accent.

Bunion Inflammation of the bursa over the first metatarso-phalangeal joint.

Bursa small sac of synovial fluid which reduces friction where muscles or tendons glide over the bone.

Bursitis Inflammation of a bursa.

Cadence the closing section of a phrase.

Calcaneus heel bone.

Canon an overlap in the dancers' movements.

Cartilage in joints, hyaline cartilage protects the ends of bones from wear and absorbs shock.

Centre of gravity the densest part of the body, sited just below the navel.

Centring bringing together the physical centre with that of the mind.

Cervical spine seven vertebrae of the neck.

Chiropractic therapy to treat illness/injury by manipulating the spine.

Choreography art of arranging movement into a finished performance.

Climax the main highpoint of a dance.

Chronic a long term, recurring injury that may not respond to treatment.

Coccyx the bottom of the spine, the tail-bone.

Collapse a released fall which gives into gravity through the centre and does not usually rebound.

Complementary movements which are similar but not the same.

Composition organising and arranging sounds, words, movement, images into a unified whole.

Concentric muscle contraction which involves fibres shortening.

Consonant harmonious balance, opposite of dissonant.

Contemporary dance see *modern dance*.

Content the central idea of the dance.

Contact improvisation spontaneous movement to support, bounce off and onto etc. a partner or group.

Contrapuntal forms two or more themes interweave independently.

Contrast movement opposite to the main ones of a dance.

Contusion a bruise caused by external force in which the skin does not break.

Counts the number of beats within the measure.

Crescendo gradual increase in speed, dynamics or sound.

Criticism a judgement of a dance based on appreciation of choreographic and technical principles.

Curvature of the spine distortion of proper alignment of spine, usually in a sideways direction.

Curves of the spine natural forward and backward bends which spread and support the weight of the various sections of the body.

Cyclorama a stretched curtain or wall at the back of the stage.

Development altering the action, space, time and quality of motifs so that when they are repeated, they remain interesting.

Diminuendo gradual reduction in force or volume.

Disc cartilage inbetween the vertebrae.

Dissonance clashing harmonies which feel

strange or disturbing. Opposite to consonant.

Dorsiflexion the foot pulls upwards.

Downstage the space towards the front of the stage.

Dynamics variety of force, accent and quality of movement.

Eccentric contraction muscle contraction which involves the fibres lengthening.

Effort actions when weight, time and space are combined, there are eight possible ways of moving. As identified by Rudolf Laban.

Elevation jumping or rising.

Endurance the ability to keep moving over time (stamina).

Enchainment a linked series of movement.

Energy potential to move.

Eversion the sole of the foot rotates outwards, away from the midline.

Extension lengthening of body part/s outwards. Important factor in a dancer's training. Opposite to flexion.

Fall a lowering to the floor following loss of balance.

Femur the thigh bone.

Flexibility the range of movement possible in the joints. Important to increase this in dance training.

Flexion movement when a joint bends, opposite to extension.

Floor pattern an imagined path on the floor left as a dancer travels. Part of spatial patterning/design in dance composition.

Flow free or bound in movement; flexible or direct through space; successive or simultaneous through the body. (As named by Rudolf Laban.)

Focus the dancer's sight line used to increase communication with the audience.

Force intensity of weight, ranging from firm to light.

Form the structure of a planned dance composition which organises the themes and motifs.

Fresnel a device used on a light to change the size of area lit.

Fugue (in music and dance) the theme is varied and played versus itself.

Gels transparent plastic in different colours, placed in front of lights.

Gesture movements which do not transfer or bear weight.

Gradual stretch stretching through held stillness. Opposite of ballistic stretching.

Ground Bass the basic theme is repeated as background for other themes.

Group awareness to dance in relation to others by taking cues from each other.

Hallux Rigidis degenerative disease of the bone of the metatarso-phalangeal joint of the big toe.

Hallux Valgus big toe deviates laterally.

Hammer toe big toe deformed so that it points upwards, while second and third phalanges flex downwards.

Hamstring muscles at the back of the thigh, extend the thigh and flex the knee.

Highlights the moments of greater visual note in a dance.

Holistic health approach to health that considers every aspect of the whole person.

Hyperextension movement of a joint beyond a normal extension.

Improvisation unplanned exploration in movement.

Inversion the sole of the foot inwards and lifts up.

Inflammation as a result of injury or infection, tissue will appear hot. There may also be redness, swelling and pain.

Isolation movement restricted to a single joint or muscle group, frequently used in Jazz Dance.

Isometric muscle contraction when muscle length does not change, but tone increases.

Isotonic a muscle contraction when muscle shortens.

Jeté a leap, take-off one foot land on the other.

Joint a place where two bones meet. There are four types which allow for varying amounts of movement.

Jumper's Knee pain in the knee caused by excess strain on the patellar ligament.

Kinesiology study of movement.

Kinesthetic sense sensing through nerves to muscles of body positions, movement and tension.

Lateral on the outer side of the body.

Legato musical term to describe a flowing, smooth style.

Ligament Band of tough tissue which connects bones and stabilises joints.

Lumbar the small of the back. Five vertebrae.

March Fracture stress fracture of the metatarsal bone.

Mark rehearsing movement without going full-out.

Mental rehearsal going through movement in the mind without actual movement.

Measures groups of beats separated by bars into intervals.

Medial on the inner side of the body.

Meniscus half-moon-shaped cartilage of the knee.

Metabolism all the physical and chemical processes which maintain the human organism.

Meter notes how many beats are in a measure.

Mixed meter rhythm made up of underlying beats in different meters.

Modern dance a dance genre which emphasises the importance of choreographers' choice of theme, intent and style. Originated in the twentieth century.

Modulate musical term to moderate tempo.

Motif the central movement theme of a dance which is repeated, developed and varied.

Muscle groups of fibres which contract and extend to produce a movement.

Nervous system the brain, spinal cord and nerves that send messages to the muscles to produce movement.

New Dance a style of dance in Britain which has evolved as a reaction against more traditional styles.

Opposition a natural movement of an opposite body part to maintain balance.

Orthopedist doctor specialising in the skeleton.

Osteoporosis bone atrophy.

Pace the overall speed of sections of a dance.

Parallel when standing the thighs, knees and toes facing directly forwards.

Patella kneecap.

Percussive a quality movement which has sharp starts and stops.

Phrase a sentence of movement of varying lengths.

Physiotherapy use of physical elements such as heat, water, massage or machine to treat injury.

Placement balanced alignment of level hips, legs placed in line in the hips, shoulders relaxed, spine extended, abdominal area lifted.

Plantar flex ankles extends so that toes point.

Plié a bend of the knees keeping the body aligned. When grand or deep, heels peel off, or demi.

Podiatrist treats foot disorders.

Port de Bras various arm gestures in combinations as they move through the five positions.

Positions the five positions of the feet in ballet, invented in seventeenth-century dance.

Posterior the back of a limb or torso.

Post-modern dance started in New York in the 1960s, to experiment with dance.

Preparation movement which allows the body time to prepare for a specific turn, step, jump or fall.

Projection communication by the dancer to the audience of the content of the dance, by throwing out energy.

Pronation foot rolling inwards on the arch, combines abduction and eversion.

Proprioceptors receptors in the muscles, joints tendons and inner ears which monitor the body position in relation to muscle tension and position.

Proscenium the frame of the stage through which dance is seen.

Quadriceps muscle group at front of thigh. Flexes thigh and extends knee.

Quality determined by the varied use of weight and dynamics e.g. percussive, swings, vibrate.

Release letting go of tension. In Graham technique it usually follows a contraction. In New Dance it is used to relax the body and mind so as to encourage ease of movement and creativity.

Relevé raising onto half-toe.

Reciprocal stretching stretching which uses the stretch reflex. Contracting one muscle releases the opposite one which is then more effectively stretched.

Rhythm a structure of movement patterns in time.

Rondo a dance form of three or more themes which alternate with return to the main theme.

Rotation movement that turns around the long axis of a bone.

Sagittal a plane which gives rise to advancing/retreating movements.

Scoliosis lateral curvature of the spine.

Screwing the knee caused by incorrect technique in plié, when turn-out is obtained by rotating the tibia, instead of from the hip.

Section a large separate part of a dance composition.

Shin splints Painful strain of muscles, common in lower leg.

Sickling rolling in or out of foot and ankle while on demi-pointe.

Skeleton the frame of bones that supports the body.

Spondylolysis a displacement of the vertebrae.

Spotting during turning the eyes fix on a spot and the head is quickly brought round at the last possible moment to refocus on the spot again. Avoids dizziness.

Sprain injury to ligaments.

Sonata structure in music which uses three or four contrasting rhythms and moods that relate in tone and style.

Staccato abrupt sharp movement or music.

Strain tear of muscle/tendon.

Strength muscle power to be increased through dance training.

Stretch range of movement to be increased by lengthening muscles through dance training.

Style distinctive manner of choreographing or performing.

Supination foot rolls to its outer border, combines adduction and inversion.

Suspension a floating, breathy, light quality of movement.

Sustained a constant, continuous smooth movement.

Swing pendulum-like movement with an easy natural feel.

Symmetry balanced or even in time, space or dynamics.

Syncopation stress on the beat which is not in the usual place.

Synovial type of joint which allows for largest range of movement.

Talus ankle bone.

Technique skill in dance movement.

Tempo the speed of the movement or music.

Tendon tough chords which end muscles and connect them to the bones.

Tendinitis inflammation of a tendon.

Tension Nervousness which may tighten muscles.

Ternary a three part form, such as ABA.

Thoracic chest area of spine: 12 vertebrae curves backwards.

Tour de force highly skilled spectacular movement.

Transition links between movement themes, motifs, phrases or sections.

Triplets a three-step pattern.

Turn-out outward rotation of the legs from the hips.

Ultrasound Use of mechanical vibration to treat injury.

Unguis Incarnatus ingrown toenail.

Unison dancers moving at the same time.

Unity a sense of an harmonious whole in the dance form.

Upstage the space towards the back of the stage.

Variation a motif or theme is modified without losing its character.

Verbetrae single bones that make up the spine.

Vibratory a quality of movement which is jittery, fast stops and starts.

Visualise holding a picture in the mind.

Warm-up muscle preparation for exercise to avoid injury.

Wings sides of the stage.

Xylophone musical instrument of flat heavy wooden bars struck with a hammer.

Yoga Hindu system of relaxation and mediation.

Zapateado dance with rhythmic stamping of the feet.

INDEX

Note: Page numbers in **boldface** indicate diagrams or tables. Those in *italic* indicate photographic illustrations.